Arthur Holborow

Evolution and Scripture

Or the Relation Between the Teaching of Scripture and the Conclusions of

Astronomy, Geology and Biology

Arthur Holborow

Evolution and Scripture
Or the Relation Between the Teaching of Scripture and the Conclusions of Astronomy, Geology and Biology

ISBN/EAN: 9783337063726

Printed in Europe, USA, Canada, Australia, Japan

Cover: Foto ©Lupo / pixelio.de

More available books at **www.hansebooks.com**

EVOLUTION AND SCRIPTURE

OR

THE RELATION BETWEEN THE TEACHING OF SCRIPTURE AND THE CONCLUSIONS OF ASTRONOMY, GEOLOGY, AND BIOLOGY

WITH AN INQUIRY INTO THE NATURE OF THE SCRIPTURES AND INSPIRATION

BY

ARTHUR HOLBOROW

"*The words that I speak unto you, they are spirit.*"
JOHN vi. 63

LONDON
KEGAN PAUL, TRENCH, TRÜBNER & CO., Ltd.
PATERNOSTER HOUSE, CHARING CROSS ROAD
1892

OPINIONS OF THE PRESS.

THE SUSSEX DAILY NEWS.
"The book shows profound research into the most stupendous problems with which the mind could be confronted."

THE CRITICAL REVIEW.
"An interesting book."

THE LIVERPOOL MERCURY.
"This is a volume of calm and scholarly thought, pleasantly written, and making, from the latest facts of science, a groundwork for an insight into the biblical records of creation, which gives the writer a clear horizon and a wide outlook. . . . . He draws some fine and useful distinctions between the evolution theory of Darwin and that of Wallace, and shows generally an independence of men and a confidence in truth that make his book exceptionally gratifying."

THE CHRISTIAN WORLD.
"A thoughtful contribution to the subject, marked by varied knowledge, and instinct throughout with reverence and faith."

THE SCOTSMAN.
"Compared with the attempts that used to be made to reconcile Genesis and Science, this work marks a distinct advance."

THE CHRISTIAN MIRROR.
"We commend the work to the attention of all Christian ministers and Divinity students, and indeed all who take an interest in the modern theory of Evolution."

THE MANCHESTER EXAMINER.
"To some readers the book will be full of interest."

THE BRITISH WEEKLY.
"It contains a great deal that is original, and many suggestions which will be helpful to the student."

THE RELIGIOUS REVIEW OF REVIEWS.
"The book deserves the careful study and attention of all who are interested in the mental combat of science and theology."

PREFACE.

This work has more to do with the Book of Genesis than with any other Scripture; but as it has, notwithstanding, much to do with the Bible as a whole, the title *Evolution and Scripture* has been chosen.

The first half of the work is occupied chiefly with the nature of the Scriptures and their inspiration, the remainder with Gen. i.-xi. Evolution is dealt with chiefly in the first and eighth chapters.

To do justice to the subject is obviously difficult. Much has been written on Science and Scripture, and of late years the question of *Inspiration* has also received much attention. Still it is the author's belief that more remains to be said; and that a work of this description, dealing with the whole subject as here sketched out, and more particularly with the complex question of Evolution, will be helpful to many.

The work is not intended for those who can read their Bibles in simple faith, unaffected by difficulties; nor yet for those who see some difficulties, but have arrived at a solution of them which they deem satisfactory. To these, the Bible is the Work of God, and anything that the author can say will not make it more; whilst it is possible that the discussion may have the undesired effect of making it less. For it is easier to 'raise the giant' than to slay him, and the frank discussion of numerous difficulties may suggest problems new to the reader, and may leave him unsatisfied by the solutions given. However excellent a cure may be, we would not make our friends ill in order to prove its efficacy.

Moreover, many of us have in our childhood acquired beliefs which, though closely associated in our minds with some of the doctrines of Scripture—so closely indeed that they are regarded by many as essential parts of Scripture—are none the less erroneous. These errors must be eliminated, and there is obvious danger lest when uprooting the tares, we uproot also the wheat. The process of elimination should at least be gradual, and natural to the peculiarities of each person; there is danger lest a compressed discussion, such as this, bring about too abrupt a change. Many of the questions raised require careful study, and it would doubtless be better that this study should be given to Scriptural truths than to the difficulties suggested by the conclusions of modern science. For these reasons the author would warn those readers who have no serious difficulties, that *this work is not intended for them.*

There are many believers who have modified their views about Inspiration; others, educated in modern science and theology, have never held the older views. To such the mode of treatment adopted here may seem unusual; it need not, however, be unfruitful.

But this work is addressed rather to those who find it difficult to reconcile some of the conclusions of modern science with their Bible, and especially to those who have been impressed with the reasonableness of evolutionary ideas. To such readers this book is commended, in the belief that it will throw light on these matters, and with the confidence that what it presents is, in substance at least, *the Truth.*

CONTENTS.

CHAPTER I.
                                                            PAGE

INTRODUCTION 1

CHAPTER II.
THE WORD OF GOD AND THE SCOPE OF SCRIPTURE . . 32

CHAPTER III.
THE WRITERS OF SCRIPTURE AND THE DEVELOPMENT OF THE KNOWLEDGE OF GOD 51

CHAPTER IV.
SEVERAL PHASES OF THE DEVELOPMENT OF THE KNOWLEDGE OF GOD: THE BOOK OF ENOCH . . . 86

CHAPTER V.
INSPIRATION AND THE GENERAL STRUCTURE OF THE BIBLE 139

CHAPTER VI.
THE CHALDEAN ACCOUNT OF GENESIS . . . 163

CHAPTER VII.

The Creation 192

CHAPTER VIII.

Human Evolution and the Fall . . . 231

CHAPTER IX.

The Flood 299

EVOLUTION AND SCRIPTURE.

CHAPTER I.

INTRODUCTION.

MAN has received from God two revelations—the Word of God and His Works, the Bible and the Book of Nature. Both of these we read.

Of these two books the Bible has the higher place. It contains truths of a higher order than those which can be gathered from a perusal of the Book of Nature. At the same time the Book of Nature ought not to be, and cannot be entirely, disregarded. For, (1) the Bible itself appeals to Nature more than once; notably in Rom. i. 20, "For the invisible things of him since the creation of the world are clearly seen, being perceived through the things that are made, even his everlasting power and divinity." (2) Our own mental and bodily structure is itself part of Nature, and constitutes the only means whereby the written Word can be read. Without our own pre-existing thoughts and experience, Scripture would be to us nothing more than a page in some unknown language. We could not read a word of it. And how far our thoughts are literally composed of our experience of Nature outside of ourselves, becomes ever more and more apparent the more the subject is studied. Whence it appears that, whereas the Bible occupies the higher position of these two books, Nature occupies—or at least some parts of it do—the first position, in being nearer to ourselves, verily a part of ourselves, and the only means of access to the written Word.

I do not mean to say that the evil part of human nature forms the terms wherein Scripture truths must be conceived. For, although in man evil nature co-exists with the nature that is the work of God's hands, the two are distinct. Moreover, a new light is revealed with the study of the Word of God, and new terms of thought are formed; but these are only possible by means of our previous knowledge, upon which the new thoughts are grafted. When we use the term 'Nature,' the nature that is the work of God's hands is generally understood, especially as it is not so often applied to man himself as to the phenomena around him. In this sense the term is used in the foregoing remarks, as it will be generally, if not always, throughout this work. In using the term above, however, I have included man's mental structure and knowledge, and these (always excluding his evil nature) are as much a portion of the Work of God's hands as any other reality.

Human knowledge then, being essential to any knowledge of the truths of Scripture, as well as being a most important part of man himself, is entitled to all respect. And Science, as everybody knows, is simply an extension of human knowledge. It has brought many blessings to mankind; its light is a gift from God. It cannot therefore be lightly esteemed.

Now, as others have remarked, if Nature is the work of God's hands, and if the Bible is the Word of God, it is impossible that the two should disagree; and Science, if it be indeed Science, must be in accord with both. Science may not, indeed, arrive at the spiritual truths contained in Scripture, but it cannot possibly reveal anything really at variance with those truths.

INTRODUCTION. 3

But is this dogmatic assertion confirmed by a *cursory* perusal of the first few chapters of Genesis? Certainly not. It requires but a rudimentary knowledge of astronomy or geology to bring difficulties before the reader's mind; and the more he examines the text, with a view, it may be, to clear them up, the greater do these difficulties become. Many of those who read the Bible have no idea of the number, extent, and serious nature of these difficulties. And it is well that they are ignorant of them; for the true and full explanation does not readily occur to the reader. Consequently, if he is not satisfied with some of the current explanations, he seems forced to the conclusion—at any rate many have arrived at the conclusion—that the Bible is man's word, not God's. And of all conclusions this is one of the most fatal at which he could possibly arrive; for he has thereby removed from beneath his feet the only sure foundation existing in this whole world.

Volumes have been written to prove, and to disprove, the agreement of the early chapters of Genesis with known scientific truth. In this place it must suffice to notice some of the most important questions at issue.

The first is both astronomical and geological, namely, the creation of heaven and earth and the contents of the latter in six days. The meaning attached to the passage by those who are not scientifically educated is, that the whole work was done in six consecutive ordinary twenty-four-hour days. But every student of geology knows that vast periods of time were occupied in the work. To meet this difficulty it was formerly argued that Gen. i. 1 does not record part of the six days' work, but an act prior to, and possibly vast ages prior to, the commencement of the six days. In reply to this Exodus xx. 11 was quoted, "For in six days the Lord made heaven and earth, the sea, and all that in them is, and rested the seventh day; wherefore the Lord blessed the sabbath day, and hallowed it." The rejoinder was that the word in Exodus is not 'created' as in Gen. i. 1, but 'made'; that the Hebrew word is not in other places in Genesis (where it occurs 154 times) once rendered 'created,' but is used in the sense of 'did, appointed, constituted, set for a particular purpose or use;' and that therefore Gen. i. 1 relates to the primordial creation of matter, and Exodus xx. 11 to the subsequent six days' work of Gen. i. 2—31. To this it was replied that the Hebrew word, however translated, *is* used elsewhere, as in Gen. i. 25, 26 ; vi. 6, in the sense of 'create.' Which party was right on this point I will not undertake to say; but will pass to the explanation most generally accepted, which is supposed to clear up the foregoing difficulty and also the following one.

Geological science has established the fact that, not six days only, but thousands, even millions, of years were occupied in the separating of land and water, and the creation of plants and animals. The explanation now very generally adopted is that the days of Gen. i. are not meant as twenty-four-hour days, but as vast periods of time. To this, however, it is replied that ordinary days are clearly indicated in the text; that a twenty-four-hour day is unquestionably meant in verse 14, and it is unreasonable to attribute a different meaning to the word in the other places, especially as it would then be used in two different senses in the two adjacent verses 13 and 14. It is also objected that in Gen. ii. 2, 3, and Exodus xx. 11, the seventh day is virtually stated to have been an ordinary day; for how should the Sabbath be an ordinary day and the seventh day a long period? that the word 'day' has here again to be taken in two different senses in the same short sentence. It is urged that the description of a week, the mention of evening and morning, the appointment of the Sabbath because God rested on the seventh day, and the whole context, all clearly relate to ordinary days.

The expounders of these passages are also charged with applying new meanings to the words of Scripture in order to make them agree with Science.

Then another difficulty arises. From astronomy and geology it is known that the work of Creation was not all done in the chronological order which Gen. i. appears to state. The heavenly bodies were not created some time after the earth (see Gen. i. 14—19), but in most cases long before it. Throughout the whole period of organic creation, sea and land have been continually exchanging places; and the present distribution of land and water was accomplished long after the lower forms of life had appeared on the earth; in fact after the greater number of vegetable and animal forms had been created. Gen. i. 9 appears, at first sight, to state that this separation of land and water was effected once for all on the third day, before any living forms were created, animal or vegetable. Here, however, it requires but a moment's thought to see that the separation referred to may just as well be the *original* separation of land and water as the present distribution of the two. It is known, too, that plants, inhabitants of the water, of the air, and of the land, were not created precisely in the order given, and in mutually exclusive periods of time. For instance, some of the water animals appeared in the beginning, and others towards the end, of the whole period of creation of things on the earth. Many parts of the work of creation went on at the same time. Yet nothing is more certain, from the remains of extinct animals buried in rocks of different ages, than the broad fact that the lower forms of life appeared first and the higher ones last. Here at any rate there is a general agreement between the record in Genesis and the conclusions of science.

This upward progress of life is described by Dr. Draper (*History of the Conflict between Religion and Science*, London, 1887, p. 191), as follows:—

". . . there has been an advancing physiological progression of organic forms, both vegetable and animal; . . . those which inhabit the surface in our times are but an insignificant fraction of the prodigious multitude that have inhabited it heretofore; for each species now living there are thousands that have become extinct. Though special formations are so strikingly characterized by some predominating type of life as to justify such expressions as the age of mollusks, the age of reptiles, the age of mammals, the introduction of the new-comers did not take place abruptly, as by sudden creation. They gradually emerged in an antecedent age, reached their culmination in the one which they characterize, and then gradually died out in a succeeding. There is no such thing as a sudden creation, a sudden strange appearance—but there is a slow metamorphosis, a slow development from a pre-existing form."

Such is the Theory of Evolution. The alternative supposition is that species almost innumerable were created, destroyed, and superior species created in their places; this process being repeated a very great number of times at intervals of thousands or millions of years.

At this point the believer in Scripture has generally declined to follow further the conclusions of students of science, the divergence from his creed being too great. He has adhered to the hypothesis of successive creations and rejected that of the Evolutionists.

Some years ago the teachings of geologists were regarded as opposed to Scripture. Kalisch gives an instance of resistance to their theories in his work on Genesis. He says:—

"It was, and—incredible to say—is still (1853) asserted, that the fossils have never been animated structures, but were formed in the rocks through the planetary influences,—that the mammoth, which at the conclusion of the last century was found in the ice of the polar regions in such remarkable preservation that dogs and bears fed upon its flesh, had never been a living creature, but was created under the ice, and then preserved, instead of being transmuted into stone,—that all organisms found in the depth of the earth are models, created in the first day, to typify the living plants and animals to be produced in the subsequent part of the creative week; but, inasmuch as many forms, which lie buried *in* the earth, do not exist *on* the earth, these latter were rejected, as inappropriate or imperfect. . . . See *A Brief and Complete Refutation of the Antiscriptural Theory of Geologists*, by 'a Clergyman of the Church of England.'"

A better informed writer, a learned Professor, has asserted that demoniacal powers interfered in the course of creation, probably by corrupting or misleading the animals; that they "stirred up the dark fiery principle of the creature, and made unnatural mixtures and mongrel formations, mutual murder, disease and death, common among the races of God-created animals;" that in consequence of this, whole generations, called into existence by God, were swept away on account of their unfitness; that "the shaping of the mountains began on the Third Day, without having been brought to a close when plants and animals began to appear. The earth became again and again the grave of the organic beings, which she had long borne upon her surface." He supposes the last creation of animals and plants to have taken place on the Sixth Day, after man's creation; referring to which he says, "The nature, which was taken possession of by the spirits of evil, is destroyed, and . . . a plant-world and an animal-world have now come into being (as the last links of the plant-and-animal-creation which was *begun* with the third and sixth days), such as corresponds to him, who is called to be lord and conqueror of evil, viz. Man" . . .[1]

---

[1] Quoted from Delitzsch by Bishop Colenso, *The Pentateuch*, p. 334: abridged.

One object of this last theory is to reconcile the two accounts of the Creation in Gen. i. and ii. with each other; for, as the attentive reader of his Bible will have noticed, Gen. i. places the creation of plants and animals before that of man, whereas Gen. ii. places that of man first.

The above are some of the greatest difficulties attaching to the Cosmogony of Gen. i. The reader will see they are serious, and that the explanations above given are unsatisfactory or incomplete. On the other hand, one is struck with the fact that the general divisions of the work of creation are drawn by a masterly hand. It is a short grand outline of the work. Such an account could not possibly have been produced by one ignorant of the essential facts.

The covering of the earth with water, and certain other things related in the Story of the Flood, present much greater difficulties, and there the language does not admit of doubt as to the writer's meaning. All these matters will be more fully treated of in a later portion of this work.

Let us now refer briefly to the history of this important question before our own time. The Earth was formerly thought to be flat and vastly larger than the celestial bodies, which were regarded as small objects fixed in the sky. Gen. i. 6—18 was supposed to maintain this view of the structure of the Universe; both Catholics and Protestants so read it in the Middle Ages. When people began to reason from the Sun's motions and other facts that it must pass every night under the Earth, theories were invented to account for such phenomena upon grounds compatible with the teaching of Scripture as they understood it. One of these theories asserted that, in the northern parts of the flat Earth there is an immense mountain behind which the Sun passes every night. When Copernicus was convincing the world that the Sun was the great centre of the Solar System (as we now call it), and the Earth merely one of a number of much smaller bodies which revolve round it, the Catholic Church condemned his work on the ground that it was *entirely contrary to the Holy Scriptures*. In those days, however, stronger measures were taken than in the present day, for the suppression of error. Galileo, who helped to establish the Copernican theory by his telescopic discoveries, was summoned before the Inquisition, accused of having taught a doctrine utterly contrary to the Scriptures, and imprisoned. Scientific truth had something to contend with in those days; but, *being truth*, it overcame every obstacle.

We have little idea of what seemed to be surrendered to Science in that contest, from a religious point of view. If the reader will turn to the foot of page 301, and read the outline there given of the old notions about the structure of the Universe, he will see that, to the people of the time, the theory of Copernicus involved much. For, to them, the region situated over the Earth was transformed by it from being *God's dwelling-place*, into *a mere empty space*. We are children of a subsequent education, having quite new ideas as to the heaven where God dwells. The Copernican theory has not destroyed belief in the *existence* of such a heaven, but it has utterly changed men's views as to its situation and character. And this is the nature of every one of the victories of Science over Christian beliefs. In the questions before referred to, the *fact* of God's having created all is not touched, but only the *manner* of His doing so. The *shell* is taken away (and ofttimes it is not a bad riddance), but the *kernel* remains untouched. The conflict with Evolution (though not with *automatic* Evolution) is one of the same character—it touches only the *means*, not the *fact* of God's action in the matter.

But, leaving theological considerations, in the meantime let us see briefly what Science says (1) as to Evolution as a process, (2) as to self-acting or spontaneous Evolution, which is held by some writers.

(1) It is a wide subject, but the issue can be stated in few words.

BIOLOGICAL.

I. COMPARATIVE ANATOMY contributes strong evidence in favour of the theory. Within each great group the members exhibit great similarities of structure, they are built on the same type; this fact suggests community of descent. Man himself in his bodily structure resembles the anthropoid apes, from which " in all parts of his organization he differs less than these do from the lower members of the same group." [2]

II. EMBRYOLOGY affords more convincing evidence: witness the famous induction of von Baer, of which Mr. Herbert Spencer gives the following exposition [3]:—

"The germ out of which a human being is evolved, differs in no visible respect from the germ out of which every animal and plant is evolved. The first conspicuous structural change undergone by this human germ, is one characterizing the germs of animals only—differentiates them from the germs of plants. The next distinction established, is a distinction exhibited by all *Vertebrata;* but never exhibited by *Annulosa, Mollusca,* or *Cœlenterata*. Instead of continuing to resemble, as it now does, the rudiments of all fishes, reptiles, birds, and mammals; this rudiment of a man, assumes a structure that is seen only in the rudiments of mammals. Later, the embryo undergoes changes which exclude it from the group of implacental mammals; and prove that it belongs to the group of placental mammals. Later still, it grows unlike the embryos of those placental mammals distinguished as ungulate or hoofed; and continues to resemble only the unguiculate or clawed. By and by, it ceases to be like any

---

[2] Quoted by Mr. Darwin from Professor Huxley (*Descent of Man*, p. 150).

[3] *Principles of Biology*, 1884, vol. 1, p. 142.

INTRODUCTION. 11

fœtuses but those of the quadrumana; and eventually the fœtuses of only the higher quadrumana are simulated. Lastly, at birth, the infant, belonging to whichever human race it may do, is structurally very much like the infants of all other human races; and only afterwards acquires those various minor peculiarities of form that distinguish the variety of man to which it belongs."

III. PALEONTOLOGY. The manner of the appearance of the different species in geological times has been already noticed.[4] There is also the fact of the former existence of animal forms intermediate between now-existing ones, as between the reptile and the bird. The conclusion naturally follows that the higher forms of life, both animal and plant, are the modified descendants of lower forms; and—still more important—that man himself forms no exception to this. In geological formations which, although the latest in the whole series, are yet generally admitted to be tens of thousands of years old, have been found the bones and flint implements of man. In some cases they were intermixed with the bones of the mammoth and other extinct animals of the Glacial Epoch. In certain other cases the significant fact is the order of superposition of the implements discovered. The lowest down are manifestly the oldest; and the lowest down are rough or chipped flint, then come polished flint, then bone or horn, then bronze. From this is inferred the primitive rude state of the first men, and their gradual progress in knowledge and habits of life.

IV. In DOMESTIC ANIMALS we have the clearest evidence of the plasticity of animal forms. So unlike are many varieties of the dog (for instance) which are of common descent, that these would be unhesitatingly regarded as distinct species if found in the wild state. So with the pigeon, the history of which is still better known.

[4] See the quotation from Dr. Draper's work on p. 6.

Human.

V. ETHNOLOGY furnishes evidence that the physical characteristics of the different races of men cannot be reconciled with the theory of their descent from a perfect man. The same applies to their mental qualities, habits, manners and customs, and civilizations—the latter having been separate growths, effected under different conditions of life as these races have developed from primitive men of a lower mental condition, and traceable largely to the climates and to the physical and other features of their respective habitats. There has been degeneration in some cases; but, even with the lower races, the course has been not down, but up.

VI. THE SCIENCE OF LANGUAGE testifies that languages (speaking generally) have in like manner separately developed from small beginnings, the art of speech itself having been one of man's greatest achievements, though accomplished when his intellect was young.

VII. PSYCHOLOGY, SOCIOLOGY, and COMPARATIVE MYTHOLOGY contribute their respective testimonies to the truth of the theory of Evolution.

Inorganic.

VIII. Evolution (or development) is exhibited throughout the INORGANIC WORLD, as revealed by astronomy, geology, etc.

Religious.

IX. THE BIBLE illustrates the evolution of the true Religion, from the original Israelitish polytheism (Josh. xxiv. 2) up to the full knowledge of the true God, as revealed in the New Testament.

Indeed the fact of Evolution is now accepted by nearly all students of science, by biologists and anthropologists, philologists and psychologists alike. And we all are not so opposed to its principle as we perhaps think. For all living things come into being now by a process of evolution, and creation by miracle is a phenomenon of which we have no knowledge; yet we recognize God as the maker of all.

Some of the foregoing facts can be accounted for upon other theories than Evolution, whilst others are denied by some writers. An unbiassed judgment, however, must admit that, though the writers' motives may be good, these arguments generally savour of special pleading.

(2) So much in favour of Evolution as a process. But what must be said about *the Cause?* Is there evidence that Evolution is self-acting and self-originated? There is indeed considerable evidence of the natural and necessary working out of the laws of nature in certain parts of the process; but there is, in the results, incontestible evidence of Design. From universal experience we have all arrived at at least this scientific generalization, that the forces of nature if undirected are liable to soon destroy what they have produced. This theory of automatic evolution is based ultimately upon *chance*, strangely blind as its supporters are to the fact. And—without here going into details—if we apply to the theory the Rules of Logic for the calculation of chances, the fraction representing the evidence in its favour will have 1 for its numerator, and for its denominator the algebraic symbol for infinity, or something very like it. In other words the chances are almost infinity to one against such a theory; its foundations are utterly swept away.[5] Whereas, therefore, we are compelled to admit that the evidence of Science in favour of Evolution as a process is overwhelming, the evidence against its undirected,

---

[5] In order to avoid interrupting the argument, I reserve further remarks on this matter for the supplement to this chapter.

self-acting, and self-originated character, is far more overwhelming. So much as to the words of Science.

But what does the Word of God say? If there are any fundamental principles in it, this is one, that organic beings, and especially Man, are not the outcome of accident, but were designedly created by God. Scripture and Science are agreed, therefore, as to the *kernel*. As to the shell, it will be shown in this work that the antithesis supposed to exist between the Word of God and Evolution (as a process) is not real but apparent only. Here we can only stay to remark that the *principle* of growth and development is taught in many places in the Bible.

Of those interested in these matters, the Christian is in the best position to judge the general question of Design (though not to decide if *every* biological phenomenon is the result of special design, for many of these are unknown to him). But the free-thinking man of science is in the best position to judge the other question, that of Evolution as a process. For the former studies much less those branches of science which (rightly or wrongly) he believes to oppose the Scriptures; nor, until the truth is forced upon him from without, does he believe it. He abstains from reading the works that treat of such subjects; and wisely, so long as he cannot reconcile their conclusions with Scripture. He has enough to contend with in his spiritual course, without raising unnecessary obstacles to his faith.

Let us now return and briefly summarize this long contest between Science and the Traditionary Interpretation of Scripture. At first men sought to explain astronomical phenomena in accordance with the old views about the structure of the physical universe, which they believed to be maintained in Genesis i. When, about 400 years ago, students of Astronomy began to show that those views were wrong, they were regarded by the Church as infidels, and their

INTRODUCTION. 15

theories were condemned as false. In like manner, when, about half a century ago, students of Geology began to substantiate their views, these also were regarded as false by those who believed in Scripture. So, lately, with the theory of Evolution.

But the views of those astronomers, whilst containing some errors, were in the main correct. Their errors were eliminated, but their views prevailed, and are now accepted undoubtingly by all. The Principles of Geology, also undergoing the sifting process, in like manner stood their ground, and are now universally accepted.

And what is the state of affairs in regard to the theory of Evolution? It is being accepted among the best-informed, and, through them among the less-well-informed, as surely as Astronomy and Geology have been before it. Not only so; but, just as Astronomy and Geology underwent the sifting process, so is the Evolution theory being cleared of the great error before indicated. For many now who believe in it see that the Darwinian theory is not reconcilable with some of the facts. Many evolutionists are departing from the strict Darwinian formula—of natural selection operating on fortuitous variations—and approximating to a conception of necessary growth; as the result of which all organic forms would be in a sense designed, for all would be outcrops of what is implicit in the beginning. A more important fact is that evolutionists now generally make the all-important distinction between the fact of evolution and its method.[6] Nor is this all, for there are

---

[6] J. Le Conte, for instance, says (*Evolution and its Relation to Religious Thought*, p. 253), " Let it not be concluded . . . that the *law of evolution* is still in the region of uncertainty. It cannot be too strongly insisted on that the fact of evolution as a universal law must be kept distinct from the causes, the factors, the conditions, the processes, of evolution. The former is certain, the latter are still imperfectly understood."

many learned men who believe in the divine origin of the Bible and also believe in Evolution.

Writers, too, who on religious grounds still oppose the theory of Evolution, seem to do so with less confidence—and, one is glad to add, with less bitterness—than those who have opposed it in the past.

This concurrence of facts of so many kinds can only be accounted for in one way—we had better take a lesson from the former victories of Science and accept the fact—the Theory of Evolution is triumphing because IT IS TRUE.

Here and henceforward the term 'Evolution' is used in this work to designate the process only, expressly rejecting the conception of automatic mechanism, which is often implied in the use of the term.

Upon examining in the light of Science the opening chapters of Genesis, in order to separate the real from the apparent, the *all-important* spiritual truth from the *unimportant* terms in which it is expressed; it becomes evident that we cannot maintain the historical character of the whole of the narrative of the Garden, nor that of certain other portions of the first eleven chapters of Genesis. Dr. Kinns, who cannot believe in any ignorance on the part of the writers of Scripture—unless perhaps, in one case[7]—remarks in regard to the Antiquity of Man :—

". . . . . some striking facts have come out in reference to the time of man's first appearance, which seem to place the date much farther back than has been generally received. This, however, will not affect the authenticity of Holy Writ, for there are no dates mentioned in the Bible. It is only the commentators and the compilers of chronological systems who

---

[7] Where (referring to the universality of the Deluge) he says (*Moses and Geology*, p. 398), "There can, I think, be no doubt but that Moses obtained his information from some tablets written by Noah, who only spoke of what he saw, and his range of vision was limited by the horizon."

have put forward the 6000 years; but so completely has it taken hold of the human mind, that a little while ago it would have been thought by many persons the direst heresy to mention a longer period. Human remains have been found in strata which would seem to make man contemporary with the Mammoth and other wild beasts which have long since passed away. . . . . . There are others who think differently from both Hugh Miller and Lyell, and say that a primitive race of men might have existed long before Adam, but that they were destroyed by some sudden glacial condition of the districts inhabited by them, or by some great convulsion similar to the Noachian Deluge, and that the Adamic creation took place afterwards . . . . . I am inclined to think that the first chapter of Genesis gives the general account of man's creation, and the second the special creation of Adam as the ancestor of our Lord, and that he was endowed with a high amount of knowledge and refinement . . . . . I certainly cannot believe that Adam was an untutored savage; and if ethnologists insist upon asserting that the rude implements found with human bones are evidences of his uncivilized condition, then I must go back to my former proposition, that the record of the first chapter of Genesis relates to these primeval men, and the second to the ancestor of our Saviour and ourselves. And with regard to those contemporaries of the Mammoth, let me say that ignorance of the arts would not at all imply that they had savage and brutal minds. . . . ."[8]

We have been familiar with these stories in Gen. i. to xi. from our childhood, and both their spiritual truths and their historical details have become sacred in our eyes. It does not readily occur to us, and we are perhaps unwilling to believe, that the former of these may have been wisely hidden in the latter, in order to meet our mental condition and that of our predecessors. Yet in some of these scriptures I doubt not that it is so. This subject will be more fully discussed in a later page. In another place, too, we shall see other reasons for judging of the historical character of Gen. i. to xi. in a somewhat different light from the later portions of Scripture history. Here let us only pause and ask ourselves critically the question, Is it our con-

[8] *Moses and Geology,* p. 352—355.

viction that these first chapters of the Bible *contain* no assertions that are not historically true or consistent with Science? or is the conviction really that they *can contain* none such? Is it not that, having both been taught and proved for ourselves that the Bible is the Work of God, we know the Word of God *cannot err?* That is the impregnable position, not the other. That is the conviction which Dr. Kinns has expressed when he says [9] ". . . . the time will come when the advance of Science will remove every difficulty, and make scepticism synonymous with ignorance. For the Word of God *must* prevail." The *spirit* has shed its power over the *letter*, whilst the letter has been the vehicle of the spirit, so that we unconsciously attribute to the letter the virtue that belongs to the spirit alone.

Bearing this in mind—when from these early chapters of Genesis Science has swept away portions of the letter, and when consequently we may be inclined to let the spirit of those portions go with them, only maintaining with the more tenacity such other portions of the letter as we think may yet defy Science—we shall do well to pause and consider whether or not we are cleaving to something that is worthless, and letting the valuable part go. This I think we do, if we assert that the Deluge was not meant to be represented as universal, or that 'the man' of Gen. ii., iii. does not represent the first of mankind. Leaving further remarks hereon to a later page, I have only now to add, that I am therefore not anxious to maintain the historical accuracy of these ancient stories. "The words that I speak [10] unto you, they are spirit." This doubtless applies to Scripture generally, as well as to the special words referred to in John vi. 63.

Most of the works that have been produced in the past

---

[9] *Moses and Geology*, p. 16.   [10] Or "have spoken," R.A.V.

for the purpose of defending Scripture may be referred to two classes :—(1) those which resist science ; (2) those which, accepting its conclusions, endeavour to reconcile the language of Scripture with them. Those of the first class do much harm.

Both merited and unmerited obloquy have been cast upon men of science. The first attaches to those who were brought up in the belief in the divine authority of Scripture, but have rejected that authority and sought to lead others in their step. The second attaches to those who have been educated in those sciences which are too often thought to negative the divine authority of Scripture, and have had little or no respect for the latter instilled into them in their youth. The mistake of such scientific men lies in the too hasty inference that that which, in certain places, seems to contain scientific error, cannot be the organ of Divine Truth. The mistake of the orthodox party is that, in refusing the false theological conclusions of such men of science, they also prematurely conclude that their science is false too. Upon the questions at issue it may be said that Astronomy, Geology, and Evolution represent the physical side, and that Scripture represents the psychical side. The prevalent misunderstanding is in great part due to the fact that both sides overlook the distinction between scientific conclusions and spiritual truths. The former are based on the data of our sense-experience, and are reached by the use of our powers of induction. The latter are attained by the ' understanding of the heart,' by the acceptance of God's revelation of Himself. Scientific conclusions are expressed in the sciences—such as Astronomy, Geology, and Biology, and the theory of Evolution is one of their most important generalizations. Spiritual truths are expressed in the language of religion, and it is as an expression of these that the Scripture account must be appreciated.

The writings in defence of the traditional reading of Scripture answer the purpose of satisfying the reader when the following five conditions are fulfilled : (1) the explanation of one text not noticed to be at variance with some other text, or (2) not seen to be at variance with the explanation given of some other text; (3) the verbal contents of two texts not noticed to disagree (as in the case of the order of creation in Gen. i., ii.) ; (4) the reconciliation of a text with one fact of science not noticed to be nullified by some other fact of science ; (5) only a few of these difficulties recognized at the same time. These conditions are often fulfilled, perhaps in most cases in which Christian men who are not scientifically educated, have had their attention called to the existence of such difficulties. And thus, by missing enlightenment on an insignificant fact, they escape the most fatal error of the day—that of questioning, or still worse, disbelieving, the divine origin of the Bible. Thus such writings do much good.

But unfortunately they also do much harm, especially when they resist science. For what does the better-informed man, the man of science, think of them when they state what he knows to be wrong ? Naturally he regards them as the offspring of ignorance, and—more than anything else does—they tend to confirm him in the belief that Scripture is the work of man. For if, as has been stubbornly maintained, these ignorant beliefs are necessary doctrines of Scripture, then indeed it seals its own doom. Also, when he is told that the words of Scripture do not mean what they have always been supposed to mean, he is entitled to an answer to the question, Why then are such words used ? But this is far from all. Science spreads from its special students to other people ; in this case too often accompanied by the belief that it negatives Scripture. Thus the fatal error spreads over civilized society.

INTRODUCTION.

There are several classes in the present day who are differently affected by the foregoing facts. There are those who are convinced, from their superior knowledge of all the sciences concerned, that the traditionary reading of Gen. ii. to xi. cannot possibly be maintained. There are others who, from their knowledge of one or more of those sciences, perceive great difficulty in maintaining it. There are a still larger class who, not possessing sufficient knowledge of their own to notice these difficulties, yet hear of them through the better-informed.

Most important, however, are the young, who are taught, and will be taught, much more about those conclusions which negative the traditionary belief than their fathers knew; who have, moreover, a belief in Scripture much less undoubting than that which their fathers enjoyed. So that, as knowledge spreads amongst the present generation, and still more as these pass away and their children take their places, belief in the Bible must become less and less, if it is maintained that the traditionary reading of Gen. ii. to xi. is of the essence of Scripture.

I may here quote an extract from *The Unseen Universe*, relating to the increasing disbelief in resurrection (p. 23 5th edition):—

" . . . the disbelievers in such doctrines form a minority of the race, but at the same time it must be acknowledged that the strength of this minority has of late years greatly increased, so much so that at the present moment it numbers in its ranks not a few of the most intelligent, the most earnest, and the most virtuous of men. . . . Now these men can have had nothing to gain, but rather much to lose, in arriving at this result. It has been reached by them with reluctance, with misgivings, not without a certain kind of persecution, nor without the loss of friends and the stirring up of strife; still they have fearlessly looked things in the face, and have followed whithersoever they imagined they were led by facts, even to the brink of an abyss."

Dr. Draper takes a very serious view of the matter on other than religious grounds. In his preface to the *History of the Conflict between Religion and Science*, he writes:—

" Whoever has had an opportunity of becoming acquainted with the mental condition of the intelligent classes in Europe and America, must have perceived that there is a great and rapidly-increasing departure from the public religious faith, and that, while among the more frank this divergence is not concealed, there is a far more extensive and far more dangerous secession, private and unacknowledged. So widespread and so powerful is this secession, that it can neither be treated with contempt nor with punishment. It cannot be extinguished by derision, by vituperation, or by force. The time is rapidly approaching when it will give rise to serious political results. . . . The tranquillity of society depends so much on the stability of its religious convictions. . . ."

This departure from the faith is partly due to the fact that increase of knowledge has made it manifest that the early chapters of the Bible cannot be accepted (everywhere at least) in their literal reading ; whilst the letter has been so much insisted on by exegetes, that it has been commonly regarded as an essential part of Scripture. Dr. Draper also writes :—

" . . . we have to admit a primitive animalized state (of man), and a slow, a gradual development. But this forlorn, this savage condition of humanity is in strong contrast to the paradisiacal happiness of the Garden of Eden, and, what is far more serious, it is inconsistent with the theory of the Fall." . . .

"Many good and well-meaning men have attempted to reconcile the statements of Genesis with the discoveries of Science, but it is in vain. The divergence has increased so much, that it has become an absolute opposition. One of the antagonists must give way." . . .

" What then ? shall we give up these books ? (the Penta-

INTRODUCTION.   23

teuch). Does not the admission that the narrative of the fall in Eden is legendary carry with it the surrender of that most solemn and sacred of Christian doctrines, the atonement?"[11]

This writer professes to take, as far as possible, an impartial view of the matter. One can but regard his opinions as honest.

Yet there are those of us who know, *by the surest of convictions*, that the Bible is indeed the Book of the Living God. It is a marvellous fact of our experience that through its pages we have entered into knowledge of His Person. By experience we have proved that the Word, and the Word alone, is a safe and infallible rock to rest on—a sure guide through life. And there is even many a humble cottager who could laugh at the doubts of the man of science; so real, so certain, is his knowledge of God, acquired through this book, the Bible.

It is scarcely hoped that this work will, of itself, convince any that the Bible is God's Book. The Word itself must do that. And if the Scriptures are duly searched it will do so, as effectually as it acquired its supremacy over civilized society in the past. But it is hoped that the work will present to the general reader a satisfactory explanation of the difficulties before referred to, especially those attending the question of Evolution; and that thus to some readers it will be the means of preventing the entrance being closed to the sacred truths of the Bible.

Such then is the object of this work:—(1) To show that there is no real antagonism between the Word of God and Evolution; (2) To show why there is much in the *language* of Gen. i.—xi. that is inconsistent with Science; and (3)

---

[11] *History of the Conflict between Religion and Science*, pages 199, 219, 224.

in the most important cases, to separate the divine truth from its verbal covering—the kernel from the shell.[12]

It is evident that the true and full explanation does not readily occur to the reader of these Scriptures. Yet, when the matter is duly examined, that explanation is most simple, most natural, most satisfactory; revealing not less, but more, of the wisdom of their Divine Author; and especially is this the case with the *first three chapters of Genesis*. But to the reader who does not believe in Evolution, and to whom the traditionary reading of Gen. i. to xi. presents no difficulty, the case may be otherwise. For much that he perhaps regards as fundamental truth will have to be rejected as nothing more than 'shell,' and therefore what is here presented may be neither satisfactory nor acceptable. The work is not meant *for him*. The student of Nature, however—the one who is deeply impressed with these important questions—is earnestly invited to accompany the writer through this investigation. Especially he is requested to study for himself the various questions which will be touched upon, and others which may occur to him by the way. His trouble will not be thrown away: the subject is all-important.

[12] The three things will not be dealt with in the order given here.

SUPPLEMENT TO CHAPTER I.

As some readers may not have bestowed much thought upon all the bearings of the important question of Evolution, it may be well to supplement what has been said by an illustration and some further remarks.

Let us suppose some far-distant age when the present race of men shall have passed from off the earth. In the tract of land we now call England there are a few scattered remains of its former industries, not sufficient to reveal their nature or the ways of civilized man. We ourselves come upon the scene as intelligent beings but otherwise unlike man, and all that we find here is strange to us. Traversing the land we come upon the ruins of some engineering works. In one part of the ruined building there are a few vestiges of lathes, drilling and planing-machines, etc. Of these we can make nothing; but in another compartment we see in wonderful preservation a complete, high-class, modern steam-engine. We are not the first visitors: others have examined the engine before, and seen how admirably it used to work. So great a source of wonder is it that there is now a resident guide, who exhibits it and explains its mechanism to visitors. We ask him how he accounts for the existence of this engine. He has a ready answer, " Some great one amongst the wonderful former inhabitants of the land conceived the plan, called upon the engine to appear, and forthwith it arose, complete as it now stands."

A few years afterwards we visit the place again. In the meantime excavations have been made. One who has been an active agent in these, and has spent much labour in endeavours to understand the meaning of what has been discovered, is now our cicerone. He has been able so far to restore some of the other machinery about the place, that he now understands how the lathes used to work, how the power was transmitted from wheel to wheel throughout the manufactory, how the whole was driven by an engine like the one in question, with boiler to supply the steam. There is even a half-planed casting in one of the old planing-machines, with the tool-marks on it—clear evidence of how it used to work. We ask him how *he* accounts for the existence of this engine. In reply he directs our attention to the things just named, and particularly to the half-planed casting; then takes us to the cylinder of the engine, removes the cover, and triumphantly points out some tool-marks there, closely like the others. "This part," he says, "was planed in that planing-machine, like the piece which you saw there; this piston-rod was turned in one of those lathes; this surface was chipped by chisel, that smoothed by file." But we are at a loss to see his meaning; for he has never hinted at human agency and intelligence as the prime cause of all. The restored machines are standing there, still as death; the old chisels and files lie motionless upon the bench; the engine stands here, the old machines are over yonder. We venture to suggest this last difficulty. He points triumphantly to the crane.

But we are still in doubt about his meaning, till he has explained at length that the force which is in the steam can set the lathes in motion, can work the crane and so transfer the parts across to these machines and back again. He tells how the iron was first melted in the cupola and ran into moulds, where it cooled and hardened into the shapes of the various castings in the engine. He does not say much about the files, how they did their work; nor how the moulds were made, and the shaft forged—all that is not well understood yet. Neither does he tell us *how the lathes and other machines happened to be there*, each one so well suited for its appointed work. But the strangest part is that it should seem quite natural to him that all the parts of this complex engine should have been so made by these blind material agencies, as to exactly fit each other, forming such an admirable and useful whole. "Was this by chance?" we ask. "Oh no; every motion is produced by some other motion or force; everything has its definite cause; there is no such thing as chance."

In order to convince us he goes up to the old boring-machine and points out that if the cylinder of the engine were lying in a certain position thereon, with the boring-tool in its place and the machine once set in motion, the tool would be *obliged* to bore out just such a smooth straight hole as the one we see in it. He shows us, too, that some of the lathes would turn a long bar just as *necessarily*, and as accurately, when once set in motion. Similarly with the planing-machine. Here then is positive proof that it only required certain conditions and the results *must* follow, whilst we have the evidence that there have been the conditions and the results. "Doubtless," he adds, "it was a case of necessity throughout the whole process, as it was here."

We have heard two theories. The first we cannot well

accept, for we can see that the engine is composed of parts, and each part we know to be composed of numerous molecules; and we cannot well believe that all of these jumped by magic into their proper places. And then there are those tool-marks to be accounted for. But the second theory is worse. Those necessary sequences tend to blind one to the fact, but it depends on accident in the end; and that the engine was not made by accident is *most* certain. And what machines can have worked those files and chisels?

We pay a third visit, finding still further discoveries have been made. A human body has been dug up, so well preserved that its marvellous internal mechanism has revealed itself to careful students—all except its mind, of whose very existence nothing is known. Such a thing as mind connected with matter is beyond our discoverers' conception. Here then, in this automaton, is an agency which may have done those parts of the work of which our cicerone has before failed to give an account, and which involved so many minor changes, so much irregularity of motion. To him the chain of evidence is now complete. But we cannot understand how these automata happened to perform *in the proper order* all those myriads of minor changes which were necessary to the moulding, and to the fitting especially: how they came to put each bar or casting into the lathe and take it out again *just at the right moment*. We turn our glance upon the cylinder, the crank, the condenser, the valve gear, noticing the wonderful fit of each part to each other part, the mutual action of the parts, the marvellous control exerted by the governor upon the working of the whole. The theory will not do.

But we come for a fourth and last time. The secret is out now. For books have been found and deciphered, works on psychology amongst others; and the drawing-office with its contents have also come to light. All can see plainly now how the whole was planned by one who never put his own hands to the actual work of manufacture; how, through the light of their intelligence, his living human servants formed the moulds, carried the ladles, or worked the cranes that lifted them, and so transferred the molten iron and brass from cupola to mould; how they controlled the machinery, putting each part in and taking it out when done; how they worked the files to and fro upon the castings, chipped the iron with hammer and chisel, fitting each piece, great and small; and finally joined the whole together as it now is.

It is seldom that the artificial well illustrates the natural, and here the parallel by no means holds throughout, whilst sundry inconsistencies in the story will not have escaped the reader's notice. The mechanism of the steam-engine is but a poor substitute for the marvellous structure of the human body; not to mention all else there is in Nature to be accounted for. At the same time the above necessary sequences do not well illustrate those in organic creation, upon which the Automatic-Evolutionists build so much. The forces are all external, instead of being chiefly internal. But in the history of the lathe we may trace a general parallel with the growth of the machinery of Nature, from the earth as a homogeneous gaseous mass to the infinity of complicated natural phenomena it presents to-day; or we may compare it to the development from the first germ to the plant and animal forms now existing. In tracing the history of the lathe, we begin at the rude paleolithic stone celt, the first known implement of man. By its means is produced in time the polished celt, then bronze, and later, iron, instruments. By this stage we have the more complex apparatus, a rude forge, then perhaps a roughly-constructed wooden lathe, then a rude iron one, finally the admirable machine of to-day. The fact to be noted is, how each one of these has come into existence solely through the ingenuity of man, and how each one could only be made by means of its simpler predecessor. Similarly in Nature. We do not attribute the implements to accident; those which precede history are attributed to human manufacture as much as the others, where this is traceable. Is it not the most natural (i.e. the most scientific) conclusion, that the Creator constructed first the simple and then thereby the complex in the machinery of Nature? It is one of man's highest achievements to make a machine which will do his work better than his unaided hands could do, requiring only supervision, sometimes not even that. Such things would be to a discoverer in later times the greatest testimony to the ingenuity of their constructors; yet like agencies in Nature are to some the proof that they have made themselves, or necessarily developed from their simpler predecessors, and this because some necessary links in the chain can be discerned! Especially we admire such automatic action as the well-governed engine presents—a grand result of man's invention and constructive skill. Yet necessary sequence, or automatic action, where these do appear in Nature—as in the development of the embryo, or in 'natural selection'—are not a proof of Creative Skill, but of the absence of a Creator altogether!!

Although Creative Design is persistently ignored throughout the Darwinian system, yet Mr. Darwin himself clearly saw the difficulty of accounting for things generally without it. He says (*Descent of Man*, 1888, p. 613):—

SUPPLEMENT TO CHAPTER I. 29

"The birth both of the species and of the individual are equally parts of that grand sequence of events, which our minds refuse to accept as the result of blind chance. The understanding revolts at such a conclusion, whether or not we are able to believe that every slight variation of structure,— the union of each pair in marriage,—the dissemination of each seed,—and other such events, have all been ordained for some special purpose."

On the other hand, Mr. Darwin assumed that if there was Design at all, then *every* biological phenomenon, great and small, must have been specially ordained (see the end of *Variations of Animals and Plants under Domestication*); and he concluded that this difficulty was insoluble.

Yet the matter seems to me very simple. If I take a plant, and, in order to improve its appearance, or for other reason, cut off some of its branches and leaves, my act may result in the death, or changed conditions of life, of many insects who are deriving their means of subsistence from those leaves. These changes may in their turn affect other creatures in the animal-world. Yet, whether I know of these matters or not, they do not occur through my *willing* that they should do so. My volition relates only to the appearance of the plant: these other things are merely *contingent results of that volition*. Again, if I use a machine for cutting out things to a required shape, which it is only capable of doing with precision when running at a high speed; it may very probably cut some such things imperfectly, when attaining to its proper speed. Or it may be necessary to trim the material before it will be fit to go into the machine; the trimmings being merely so much waste, or perhaps used for other purposes.

Now if the Creator made use of such an agency as 'natural selection' in the work of creation, we can clearly see that some such contingent results would naturally follow, unless special provision were made to prevent it. There would be thousands of such cases.

If then we go so far as to assert that the Creator does use any such agencies for carrying out His purposes, there is no occasion to wonder that there are things in the organic world which are not the outcome of special design. The wonder would be if there were none such. We must not forget, however, that such results have been turned to wonderful account in many known ways, and doubtless in infinitely more ways that are unknown.

Physical fatalism is in like manner opposed by what we find in Nature. Does the persistence of force tie the hands of man? With the example before our eyes of those stores of energy which man has at his command, it is nonsense to assert that there can be no such stores at the command of the Creator, ready to be utilized where and how He will.

But how ? What connection can there be between Unseen and Seen such that the first can thus control the second ? A parallel is close at hand. If we take a voluntary motion of a human limb and trace it to its cause, we find it in the first place due to the movement of a tendon; this to the contraction of muscles adjacent to that tendon; this to the action of the nerves upon those muscles, caused in its turn by a molecular current from the brain. All these things belong to the visible world, and investigation of the Visible can take us no farther. We must go to the region of the Unseen for further information. There by the light of Mind we find that a volition to move the limb was the secret cause of its motion. However closely related mental activity and molecular motion in the brain may be, whatever be the precise relation between Mind and Matter, what we are most sure of is, that we will to move the limb and that in normal conditions it does move. This action of Mind upon Matter, of Unseen upon Seen, may be but little like what occurs in the Divine control of natural agencies, but may yet suffice to indicate something of its nature.

There is no more rational method of interpreting natural phenomena than this application of well-known processes to explain the nature of processes that are unknown, or partly known.

It matters little to us here whether the process of Creation was designed and arranged once for all in the beginning, and then set in motion like a wound-up clock, after the manner of some thinkers; or whether the whole process was subjected to incessant supervision, planned out in general at the beginning, worked out in detail as it went on. For in either case there is the Design of the Creator, and that is all that concerns us here. The first hypothesis is, however, somewhat like the theory of creation by miracle—it is unnatural.

As before seen, Embryology affords most convincing evidence in favour of Evolution, the individual embryo assuming in succession those forms which its ancestors assumed in the evolution of the race. Here the characteristics of the mature organism are in some way determined by the fertilized germ; in normal conditions there is a continuous unfolding and development of these from first to last. But this affords no evidence that in the evolution of the race, the forms of later and higher organisms were *in any way* inherent in the earlier and lower ones. There is this wide difference between the two cases—*now* the system of reproduction with its mechanism is complete; *then* it had to be made.

Supplement to Chapter I.

It is much more rational to suppose that the process of creation was of a similar nature to that of the manufacture of the steam-engine before described—that natural agencies did the work, or much of the work, under the control and direction of the Creator. And in those cases where we find these natural agencies possess a mechanical or automatic character—as in the development of the embryo, in natural selection, in numbers of physical processes—it is natural to conclude that such agencies were constructed by the Creator to do their appointed work.

It seems to me that men of science are much too slow in making such practical applications to explain what they find in Nature. It is characteristic of only a part of Nature, and that its lower part, that event demonstrably follows cause in a purely mechanical way; in its higher parts we find that Mind, which often regulates the course of things, is a factor that must be taken into account; man, his will and ways, occupying the foreground. To obtain a rational explanation of Nature, the *whole* of Nature should be applied; and this brings us at once to predicate *a personal, intelligent, and active Creator.*

Moreover, if the divine control of natural agencies be an action of Mind upon Matter, it is obvious that investigation of natural phenomena can never directly reveal that control: outwardly every event must appear to be caused by an antecedent visible one, there must be the appearance of necessary sequence everywhere, Evolution must appear to be a mechanical process such as the 'natural evolution' theory assumes; whilst he who builds his philosophy on these appearances only, must arrive at erroneous conclusions, missing the ultimate cause which alone explains the whole.

In conclusion, special creation by miracle may be theoretically possible, but it is not scientifically verifiable. Evolution without Design is neither theoretically conceivable nor scientifically verifiable. Creation by natural means, the process being an evolution, is both conceivable and verifiable.

CHAPTER II.

THE WORD OF GOD AND THE SCOPE OF SCRIPTURE.

"Every word of Scripture is the Word of God." What are the contents of this apparently simple proposition? It pre-supposes a superior Being, God, who speaks; an inferior being, man, to whom He speaks; and a written language known to both, wherein the Divine message is expressed. As a general expression of the facts this outline is correct enough; but it is far from being an accurate expression of all the facts. A correct understanding of this matter is of vital importance to the present inquiry. No superficial knowledge will help us; we must carefully analyze what we mean when we call the Scriptures the Word of God.

The Scriptures, as we have them, are not expressed in the English language of to-day, but in that which was spoken by our forefathers between 200 and 300 years ago. They were not originally delivered to mankind in that language, nor in any language of that Northern European group to which the English language belongs; nor yet in any modern language. They were delivered[1] to mankind originally in two ancient languages—the New Testament in a language (Greek) of the same (Indo-European) race that we English people belong to; the Old Testament in Hebrew, the language of the very distinct Semitic race. And respecting

[1] This expression must not be taken too literally. What qualification it requires will be seen in the next chapter.

the Old Testament, it is further to be noted that its latter part was originally delivered in the language of the Hebrews when they were a more or less developed nation, whereas its first part was delivered in the language of that nation when in its youth, and consequently in a somewhat crude state of society and literature.

All these facts apparently count for nothing when it is remembered that the Scriptures have been translated into the English language of 200-300 years ago, and that that language is much the same as the English of to-day. But the true meaning of these facts will become manifest from the following considerations.

All language is *nothing more* than a system of conventional signs used for the communication of ideas and feelings. *There is no inherent meaning in words, all the meaning which they possess being lent to them by the mind.* The mental states are the all-important realities, *not* the linguistic signs by which they are conveyed.

If the reader has not given thought to this subject, he may be inclined to doubt this statement. If he is one of those who believe that there can be no thought except by means of language, he may be reminded that even on that supposition, Mind is still the principal and language the instrument, the latter deriving all its meaning, all its virtue, from the mental states to which it is so powerful a help. Professor Whitney, referring to the Chinese language, makes the following remark :—[2]

" It illustrates in a manner which the student of language cannot too carefully heed, the truth that language is only an instrumentality, and the mind the force that uses it; that the mind which in all its employment of speech implies a great deal more than it expresses, is able to do a high quality of work with only the scantiest hints of expression,

[2] *Life and Growth of Language,* 2nd Edition, p. 239.

catching from the connection and from position the shades of meaning and the modes of relation which it needs."

It does not come within the scope of this work to elucidate this matter, which belongs to the sciences of Language and of Mind. A few facts, however, may be given.

The notion that meaning is inherent in words arises partly from the way in which we learnt from our spelling books, and still learn from our dictionaries. We were taught that a certain word means so and so. But we overlook the facts, that it only possesses that meaning because, and as long as, *the community choose to use it in that sense;* and that they use it in that sense because their predecessors at some past time *attached that meaning to the word when they wanted to communicate a certain idea.* Language does not arise ready-made. It comes into existence only as it is needed for the expression of thought; and this is true of it from its very beginning. The beginning of speech was largely, if not entirely, onomatopoetic; the beginning of writing, hieroglyphic—the first representing the sound, the second the appearance, of the thing signified. In both these cases we find the language-making closely associated with the perception of similarity.

When our forefathers wished to express in language the thought that some person or deed bore a resemblance to God, they said that he, or it, was 'God-like'; and usage has transformed the word into 'godly.' Bearing in mind how this suffix *ly* has been formed, the following extract from Prof. Whitney will illustrate the matter further :— [3]

"Often, as everyone knows, there is an accumulation of formative elements in the same word. In *truthfully*, for example, we have the adverbial suffix *ly* added to the primitive *truthful;* in which, again, the adjective suffix *ful* has performed

---

[3] *Language and the Study of Language,* 1884, pp. 64, 65.

the same office toward the remoter primitive *truth*. By the use of a formative element of another kind, a prefix, we might have made the yet more intricate compound *untruthfully*. Nay, further, *truth* itself contains a suffix, and is a derivative from the adjective *true*, as appears from its analogy with *wealth* from *well*, *width* from *wide*, *strength* from *strong*, and many other like words; and even *true*, did we trace its history to the beginning, we should find ending in a formative element, and deriving its origin from a verbal root meaning 'to be firm, strong, reliable.' . . . The term *inapplicabilities* contains two prefixes, the negative *in* and the proposition *ad*, which means 'to,' and three suffixes, *able*, forming adjectives, *ty*, forming abstract nouns from adjectives, and *s*, the plural ending, all clustered about the verbal root *plic*, which we have already seen itself forming a suffix, in *double*, *triple*, and so forth, and which conveys the idea of 'bending' or 'folding.' By successive extensions and modifications of meaning, by transferral from one category to another through means of their appropriate signs, we have developed this simple idea into a form which can only be represented by the long paraphrase 'numerous conditions of being not able to bend (or fit) to something.''

And he adds this striking remark:—

"With but few exceptions—which, moreover, are only apparent ones—all the words of our language admit of such analysis as this, which discovers in them at least two elements, whereof the one conveys the central or fundamental idea, and the other indicates a restriction, application, or relation of that idea."

These facts illustrate how words come into existence only as the mind requires their help, and how they get their meaning from the mind. When, however, they have been long in use, they often lose all traces of their origin, retaining their meaning by the consent of the community through force of habit. Thus not only single words, but sequences of words, possess a purely conventional meaning. It is at this stage that the meaning seems to be inherent in the words. We have just seen, however, that it originated in Mind and remains associated with the words by the consent of Mind. It is also a mental property; it has no existence apart from the Mind; the words (and sequences of words) are only signs which call up the mental states—a process which may be likened to the firing of a gun by striking the cap. The mental states are the realities, which the signs merely serve to excite. Thus Mind is the principal; Language only the instrument.[4]

It may be added that the literal meaning (as we call it) often forms the basis on which are built, or out of which are developed, further meanings and shades of meaning. In some of these cases the literal meaning does an office very like that of the verbal sign itself. For as this literal meaning was first attached by the mind to the verbal sign, so to this literal meaning are attached by the mind further meanings and shades of meaning. In such cases the verbal signs, (in reading) call up the literal meaning, and then the literal meaning calls up the vital meaning which is conveyed by the passage. But this process is not always gone through; and when it is, it is done too quickly, perhaps, to be noticed.

It follows from this important fact that there is no such thing as a common language unless there is likeness between the minds which use such language for expressing their ideas and feelings.

If we seek an instance of such community of ideas, we shall probably find the nearest approach to it in the case of brothers or sisters who have always lived together, have been educated alike, and have never even moved in different spheres. They have inherited the family likeness of mind, and have not been subjected to different conditions of life, so as to have differences wrought in their minds. They have had the same teaching, been occupied with the same things, have therefore much the same thoughts,

---

[4] It may be said that no well-informed person supposes that meaning is inherent in words. But (even supposing this work was intended only for well-informed persons) many do so practically. There is often an unconscious assumption that language arises ready-made, containing within itself the meaning which in reality the mind lends to it as it uses it.

and use much the same words to express those thoughts. They, more than most people, may be said to have throughout, common ideas and a common range of words whereby they communicate those ideas. Even here, however, sundry individual differences of character and of mental range intervene, and even these brothers or sisters cannot strictly be said to speak a common language.

There is only one true instance of such a community of ideas, namely that which may be said to exist between one's own mind and the several mental states which compose that mind. Every one has a range of mental states common to himself alone; he habitually uses certain groups of words for the expression of those mental states, and in terms of those same mental states he reads (or it may be said translates to himself) all words which come to him from other minds, whether spoken or written. He passes through a great number of these mental states, they are his whole experience, the sum of his mind, of his knowledge, of his inner self; he cannot think of anything except in the terms which these furnish (though they are ever being modified by external influences), and he cannot consequently attach any meaning to spoken words or written signs until they have been rendered into these mental states. But he is not conscious of going through this translating process when he is spoken to or when he reads. For, during all his life, the spoken sounds or written signs have been so frequently associated with the corresponding ideas, that his mental structure has become moulded into conformity with them; and the co-adjustment has become so complete that the sounds and signs call up immediately the corresponding ideas, and the ideas call up immediately the corresponding sounds and signs, automatically. The process is a rapid and unconscious one.

Since then no two minds [5] are quite alike, and all spoken

[5] The reader should be advised that the term 'Mind' is used here,

or written language acquires meaning only when it has been rendered into the hearer's or reader's ideas, it follows that every one gives it a more or less different rendering from that of others, and therefore *a truly common language cannot exist.* It further follows that the true difference between the languages used by different individuals is in proportion to the difference between their minds. And the differences between the minds existing on the earth are enormous, as everybody knows. We may notice a few of them.

People of the same class or station in life, but of different occupations, or some living in town and others in the country, differ more than the brothers or sisters before mentioned. But with people of different classes, even though they may dwell in the same place, the difference is far wider. The difference between the mental states of the master and those of the servant are manifestly great ; and correspondingly great are the differences between the meanings which they attach to the same words. The difference between dialects in different parts of a country where the same language is spoken, is an expression of other differences between the inhabitants of those respective parts. The next difference we have to note is that existing between people speaking languages which have a family resemblance. After this the gap widens fast, when we consider people of different races, people inhabiting countries with different climates, physical and other differences of many kinds, all of which stamp their effect on the inhabitants. Lastly we have to note the vast difference between people in a highly-developed and cultivated state of society and people in a crude social state.[c]

and generally throughout this work, in the psychological sense, as equivalent to the whole ego, sensational, intellectual, and emotional, not to the intellect only.

[c] I have seen somewhere an old proverb (I think Latin) to the effect that "If two languages say the same thing, it is not the same thing."

All these facts should therefore be borne in mind when it is stated that the Scriptures have been translated into our own language. We must remember that the translation of any passage can be perfect only in as far as the English mind resembles that of the Hebrew of the period when that passage was written. It will be approximately correct where these minds do not differ much. It will be no translation at all where, if anywhere, they differ totally. The translation will obviously be least accurate in the early parts of the Old Testament, where the mental difference is greatest.

When a person reads the Bible in the present day, he naturally, but unconsciously, goes through the rendering process referred to above, interpreting the written symbols in terms of his own ideas, expecting to find the same conformity between the language of Scripture and his own ideas as exists between the language of his own composing and those ideas. With some qualifications, perhaps, he thus expects to find all the truths of Scripture conveyed in those forms of thought and those sequences of words which, as before explained, we may call his own peculiar language; just as if God had, for his own sole and peculiar benefit, written the words of Scripture that same day! Seldom or never does it occur to him that Scripture is intended to reach the widely-different minds of people of all those classes which dwell upon the earth—minds very different in calibre, in education, in nature, and even in structure. Scripture truth could not therefore be expressed everywhere, though it may be in some parts, in those particular forms of thought which constitute the reader's own peculiar language. It needs be expressed in such ways as can be rendered into the widely-different ideas of all mankind; from those of the critical, accurately-thinking, cultivated man, to those of the extreme rustic, or even of the savage, who can gain a glimmering of meaning only from something in the form of a story or parable.

Even therefore supposing that the truths of Scripture had come direct from the Mind of God and had been penned by His own hand to-day, and supposing further that those truths were not of a nature different from that of ordinary knowledge; its language would necessarily differ much from the peculiar language of the reader. Both of these suppositions are, however, far from according with the facts. Let us consider the last of them first. In doing so we shall clear up a difficulty which may have occurred to the reader, or which certainly would occur to him when we are considering the wider differences necessarily existing between each man's peculiar language and the language of some parts of Scripture. The question is this—If there be differences so wide, how do we understand it so well? Briefly, the answer is, that every divinely-taught reader of Scripture has, during his acquisition of its divine truths, had his mind moulded into conformity with those truths, and his thoughts accustomed and adapted to the Scripture language.

I have said that the nature of Scripture truths differs from that of ordinary knowledge. The fact is that those truths are indissolubly associated with the divine Person, and a real reading of those truths involves contact with that Person. *God Himself is the true Word*, as Scripture itself teaches [7] (John i. 1; Heb. iv. 12, 13; 1 John i. 1-3); and, just as other literature is but the instrument whereby the writer communicates with the reader, so the words of Scripture are but the channel of communication between God and the reader of Scripture. The believer has a por-

---

[7] It may appear to the reader an inconsistency to appeal to the Bible as teaching that the real Word of God is something different from the Scripture language. Reflection, however, will show that the inconsistency is apparent only, the appeal not being to the language, but to its underlying truth.

THE WORD OF GOD. 41

tion of God's spirit dwelling within him, closely associated with his own spirit (Rom. viii. 9, 16; 1 John iv. 15). He may, or may not, have been conscious of its first entrance there; but since that time it has been quietly working, moulding his mind more and more into conformity with God; so that from that time forward and increasingly, God dwells within him.

The first entrance of that Spirit took place by means of Scripture truth, which by the light of God he was then enabled to apprehend; and, as at that time so afterwards, Scripture has been the channel of communication, though not the only one, between God and him. *This intercourse between his mind and God's mind constitutes the only true reading of the Word of God.*

Scripture is a vast store of written symbols whereby God's mind is thus revealed to his mind. He sees those symbols, and they call up in him mental states, which are produced, modified, deepened, by the indwelling Spirit of God; by whose light (together with the light of his pre-existing knowledge) he is enabled to perceive what underlies those symbols, and so to come into closer contact with, and know more and more of, the Person of God.

In that Mind of God there are infinite depth and variety, both intellectual and emotional. In order that these may be effectually communicated to the believer's mind, many kinds of literary composition are adopted in the Bible. Some of its truths are so simple, so manifestly expressed in the ordinary meanings of words, that a child can understand them. Others are apprehended only after the spiritual training just referred to. Others can reach the mind only by means of a parable; others, as those in Revelation, by means of pure symbols.

Need we be surprised, then, if we have to find that, as New Testament parables and symbols serve only to impart spiritual truths, so the ancient stories of the Garden and the Flood are adopted, partly or wholly, to convey truths which, whether historical or not, are couched within those narratives; these truths being the vitally important part, and the details of the stories unimportant? The believer, however, who is accustomed to regard the parables as symbolic and these narratives as history, will perhaps answer, "*Of course* the former are symbolic and the latter purely historical." There is, however, no "of course" about it, except that he has always been accustomed to regard them so, and therefore *to him* it appears that they must be so. At the same time there are differences between the two cases, and these we shall consider later on. Attention is only called to the matter here in order to show the congruity of such a reading of those particular Scriptures with the principles which we here find to hold for Scripture as a whole.

It is natural to us all to regard the meaning as inherent in the words, overlooking that all their meaning is lent to them by the mind which uses them—attached to them by the writer, detached from them by the reader. Therefore the divinely-taught reader of the Bible does not often notice the facts on which we have been dwelling. He knows, indeed, that formerly *he saw no such meaning in the passages of Scripture as he now sees;* and that, as he has learnt more of God, more and more truths have been made known to him through those same passages. But, in many cases at least, he does not see that the education of his own mind has wrought the change; and that, through the improved condition of *his own mind*, he has been reading more and more of *God's mind*—the Spirit of God attaching to, and he detaching from, *the same words*, more and more spiritual truths which God by them has spoken to his soul. But so it is, and necessarily. For if, as we have seen, the mind in all its employment of language implies much more than it

THE WORD OF GOD. 43

expresses, even in regard to every-day subjects; how much more must it be so with those spiritual truths which are above, and of a nature different from, ordinary knowledge. How much more, when God speaks by Bible words, must He light up those words with the divine meaning which He conveys through them to the reader.

It is not meant that the student of Scripture ought to be occupied with these facts. It is to the present inquiry that they possess such importance. They should not, however, lower the Bible in the reader's eyes; they only give it a somewhat different position. It is God's Book; it is of God's construction; it is admirably adapted through its many kinds of literary productions to reach the minds of all classes; it is that whereby God speaks; that to which He has given His name; that with which He is so closely associated that we may say He dwells in it. For we may compare the written word and the Living Word, which is God, to the body and mind of man. As the body lives and acts reasonably because of the mind which dwells in it, so the written word is animated by the Living Word; and as the mind manifests itself through the body, so God manifests Himself through the written word. The two are vitally united: yet only so when God speaks by it to man, for the Bible may lie for ages lifeless, if unread.

The above wonderful truth explains a fact on which the sceptical mind will do well to reflect. Without coercion the Bible has taken its place before civilized society as the Word of God, and has maintained that position. The more it is studied, and the better one becomes acquainted with its nature and its truths, the more does one find that it is indeed God's Book[8]; its depths do not become ex-

[8] In many cases in this work I have made a verbal distinction corresponding to the all-important real distinction between the Word of God and the Book of God. Where this is not done I believe the reader will see the meaning without difficulty.

hausted, but show themselves ever deeper. If believing readers have not such knowledge on some matters as highly-educated men of science, on the other hand they are not fools. If there had not been something in the Book which is not of man, would they not have *practically* found it out, and neglected it because it yielded nothing? The secret is that in its pages they find a *living* substratum, a Being of exhaustless depth.

The sceptics build up their philosophy on what they call 'facts of experience'; what I suggest is that they should recognize with more respect this outstanding fact of experience—the Christian consciousness. They should surely be slow to depreciate Christians for being in thought and action true to *their* experience. They should be equally slow to assume that the experience of others may not be larger than their own.

The foregoing remarks may perhaps seem to imply that the truths of Scripture are inaccessible to most people, or at any rate difficult of access; that readers are so placed as to be very liable to misunderstand it; that even its plainest statements which are known to everybody, are perhaps misunderstood. It is not meant, however, that that preparation of the believer's mind which we saw to be necessary for the comprehension of its deepest truths, is the only preparation that takes place. Indeed not one of its truths—nor truths of any kind—could be grasped without previous preparation of the mind. But, as we shall see more fully in the following chapters, not only the believer's mind, but the minds of all civilized men, have been for a long time undergoing preparation. The education we have had as children in the doctrines of Scripture, and even the acquisition of ordinary knowledge, constitute such a preparation. The Christian conception of God, for instance, which we should not have had if we had not learnt it, is a funda-

THE WORD OF GOD. 45

mental piece of preparation. We have all our days been taught many of the leading truths of Scripture, and much of the New Testament is expressed in language so familiar to all, so like the common language of every day, and therefore so nearly like each one's peculiar language, as to present no difficulties of this kind. And it is in the New Testament that those truths are enunciated which everyone should know. Those truths, therefore, are expressed in (what we call) the literal meanings of the words. This general preparation, this co-adjustment of the civilized man and the language in which the Gospel is expressed, forms the gateway, open to all, heading the road to deeper truths within. The explanation here given, to be enlarged on later in this work, does not therefore create any difficulties of this kind. The important fact is that while these portions of Scripture are so adapted that they can be readily appreciated by modern readers, other portions of the Book are less perfectly adjusted. As far as we have yet examined the matter, the factors which have produced this divergence may not have appeared very important. We shall arrive at more important ones.

But what has become of the apparently simple and important proposition which stands at the head of this chapter? As very commonly understood, it asserts that what God has to say to man is inherent in the words of the Bible; it also implies that this is all expressed in those forms of thought which its readers are so accustomed to as to regard them as the literal meanings of the words. For obviously, if the meaning does not lie in this so-called literal sense, it could not be inherent in any other way; for that is the only sense which words could, by themselves, determine. It would follow therefore that in the words of Scripture there could be but one meaning (though in many cases we know that more than one truth is conveyed by the same words). Therefore all truths must be expressed alike, (i.e. literally), and all the important meaning would be at once shorn away from the parable and the symbol. This conclusion overlooks that there are individual differences in respect of those mental states which are the foundation of thought, so that the so-called literal meaning differs in many cases in the minds of different readers. It overlooks that divine truths are different in nature from ordinary knowledge, and are of many kinds; and that the Bible is designed to carry those truths in different ways to minds of many classes. It forgets that Scripture was not written to-day for the reader's own particular use, but has only reached him through the minds of other nations, some of them with modes of thought very different from his own. So that this apparently simple proposition, " Every word of Scripture is the word of God," when analyzed, resolves itself into, or necessarily implies, several distinct propositions, many, if not all of which, are false; although it is meant to express an important truth. Had the sentence run thus: " Every part of Scripture is of God's construction, designed to communicate His mind to man," it would have been both true and important. But so completely does it mix up together the contents of these *two* propositions, that, when analyzed, it falls all to pieces.

Indeed we might have arrived at a similar result, though not so completely, if we had tested this proposition by a few cases. When we read in one place that "the earth abideth for ever," and in another place that "heaven and earth shall pass away"; in one place "fear not," and in another place "let us therefore fear"; it is evident that, if the meaning is inherent in the words alone, we here have contradictions. And when, admitting as we must, that these groups of words have different meanings in the two cases, we pass on to inquire how they have this; we at once see that they cannot have two intrinsic different meanings, (possessing nothing of their own to distinguish these); and therefore they must derive them from *the mind* which employs them to express different things. When we read in Rev. xiii. 1, " And I stood upon the sand of the sea, and saw a beast rise up out of the sea," we know that the ordinary meaning of these words has nothing to do with the divine meaning which is attached to them.[9] Again, when we remember how much of Scripture is devoted to giving information about the nature of God and about the nature and condition of man, we see that the language *there* derives its meaning from what it describes, namely the mind of God and that of man. So that when the reader comes to search for the supposed inherent literal meaning of the words quoted above, he has at once to turn *from the words to the mind* in order to find it. The case just given shows us, tao, that the Word is not altogether as something that has come down to man from another region; for its very essence there lies in the spiritual condition of man himself; and, as God is its author, it shows how closely God and man are in this sense together—how Scripture comes from a God who is present in this scene, to whose eyes all things are naked and open, who is in truth a discerner of the thoughts and intents of the heart. " The word is nigh thee, in thy mouth, and in thy heart."

Look at the matter which way we will, we see that the two all-important factors are the Mind of God and that of man, and that the words of the Bible are nothing but symbols, deriving all their virtue and signification from these minds and their mutual intercourse.

From this it follows that that will be the best arrange-

[9] Here the literal meaning is first called up in the mind, and then in its turn calls up the divine meaning, as noticed on page 36.

ment of these signs, which will be most successful in calling up in man's mind, the states necessary for his reception of the communication from God. Clearly too, the best arrangement of these signs, or in other words the best kind of literary production, will depend upon the nature and condition of man's mind; so that for reaching all minds, different kinds of literary productions should be used—as they are. For minds much prepared, the common language of every day (regarded as using words in their literal meanings) is very effective. This is so much the case amongst us, that most of the Bible's greatest truths are thus presented; and doubtless were thus presented for the same reason to the early Christians in the Greek language which they spoke. But for reaching minds little prepared, or almost totally unprepared, something different is necessary—something which may still be effectual with well-prepared minds, but may offend them in other ways.

Let us here clear the ground of one other mistake, which is natural to us all—that of supposing the Bible was ever intended to teach Science. To the thoughtless it may seem that this wonderful Book of God should contain the sum of all knowledge. This was a prevalent misunderstanding in the early Church, long surviving in the antagonism of the Church to secular knowledge. Further on we shall find strong reasons why the language of Scripture should sometimes *not* accord with the language of Science. Here let us only note these important facts—that man can acquire scientific knowledge by his own efforts, and that the Bible's mission is to teach truths of a higher order, which man cannot gather for himself. In short, as already explained, the Bible is a revelation of spiritual truth.

We might here proceed to examine the unscientific passages in Gen. i.-xi. in the light of the foregoing conclusions—the six-day division of Creation, for instance. We

THE WORD OF GOD.

know that the *Word of God* in this passage is not that the work was done in six ordinary days; for it was not. Neither can it be that the days mean long periods, for the passage has never given that impression to anybody.[10] But there is this truth—God has chosen to divide the work into six parts which He has likened to the days of a week, with the seventh devoted to rest. Also in Exod. xx. 11, we find this view of the work connected with the institution of the Sabbath for the Hebrew; and it seems to be, partly at least, for the latter purpose that the periods of Creation are so very like ordinary days in Gen. i. Here then are two things, the one connected with the Sabbath having special application for the Hebrew; the other—this divine view and division of the work—being a truth for all people in all ages. Are not these the *Word of God*, communicated by the *verbal signs*[11] of the passage; not scientific statements, but words of religious significance, with a message to the Hebrews specially, but also to all men?

Again, in Gen. ii. 7 Jehovah-Elohim (or the Lord God) is represented as having "formed man of the dust of the ground, and breathed into his nostrils the breath of life." Here we see at once the important truths, that God made man, and that He made him of the earth earthy; and there is also the implication that He gave him a certain kind of relationship with Himself. These are the *Word of God*, which the language is well adapted to convey; whilst it is ill adapted to convey a correct idea of the manner in which man was made, this being a subject for scientific inquiry, unimportant to Scripture.

There are, however, a great many other facts which we

---

[10] But they may cover long periods notwithstanding, as we shall see in chap. vii.
[11] By the intermediation in this case of the literal meaning as noticed on page 36.

need to understand before we shall be duly prepared to examine these chapters and compare them with the conclusions of science. We need a correct understanding of the circumstances under which Scripture was delivered to man, and of the means adopted by God for its production. These, therefore, will form the subject of the next two or three chapters.

Summary.

Let us now sum up the conclusions of this short chapter. They are of vital importance to the present inquiry.

I. Scripture was not specially prepared for any one class of readers (such as ourselves), but was intended for man generally, and has therefore to meet the needs of minds of all orders in all ages.

II. The meaning is not, and cannot be, inherent in the words. The real Word of God is quite distinct from the language of the Bible. The Word of God is that portion of His mind which He desires to communicate to man. The two all-important factors are thus the mind of God and that of man, the Bible being nothing more than a store of verbal signs adapted for the communication of the former to the latter.

III. Its truths are of a nature different from ordinary knowledge, and they are of various kinds. Since, therefore, its object is to teach truths of this higher order, and of various kinds, to minds of all classes, *its excellence must essentially consist in its suitability for this purpose.*

IV. It is no part of its object to teach science.

CHAPTER III.

THE WRITERS OF SCRIPTURE AND THE DEVELOPMENT OF THE KNOWLEDGE OF GOD.

It was tacitly assumed in the last chapter that the course adopted by God for giving man a knowledge of spiritual truths is not a course of miracle but a natural course. Indeed the whole argument of the present work accords with, and depends upon, the fact that God works naturally, and not by miracle, in all departments of which man has any knowledge, and that such is the normal course of His actions. This matter therefore calls for a few remarks in this place.

Everybody knows that there is continuous and orderly sequence throughout the world of things which we see around us in the present day. But only the student of Nature knows how universally this is true, and how thoroughly it can be verified. He also is the one who knows that this orderly course of Nature can be traced out, as in the present, so in the past, back almost to the foundation of worlds. But he is not generally the one who knows—and those who do know are not so much given as he would be to *notice* the fact—that this truth applies in the present day, not only to the work of God in Nature, but also to His spiritual work in the hearts of men. We have had occasion to notice this process in the case of the believer who, by the improvement in his own spiritual state, is fitted for, and enabled to receive, deeper and deeper spiritual truths as he studies Scripture. No one looks for miracles here any more than in the world around.

These two departments, in which the natural course is found to hold universally, fill the whole realm of man's experience, the whole region of which he can gain any knowledge by observation.

But in regard to Scripture history, it is not uncommon to predicate the miraculous rather than the natural, to a very great extent. This is quite unwarranted by the Word of God. Moreover, this assumption of miracle is likewise extended to the case of the writers of Scripture, under the name of 'Inspiration.' But it by no means follows, because miracles are recorded in Scripture history, that its general course was miraculous rather than natural. Nor does it by any means follow, because the necessary measures were taken for delivering the Word of God to man through the agency of human writers, that those writers were miraculously endowed with knowledge in advance of their times. Both of these are mistaken conclusions. They may speak well for the believer's reverence for the Bible, but they are false conclusions none the less, and fruitful of much error.

It is necessary to distinguish clearly between an arbitrary interference with the course of nature, an event to outward appearance in opposition to its laws, which is never known now; and a definite or special manifestation of God's action which is yet seen to be accomplished by natural means, such as *is* experienced by Christians in the present day. To the former class only I apply the term 'miracle' in this work. Raising the dead, causing iron to swim, I should call miracles. The sudden endowing of an Englishman who did not know a word of French, with a full knowledge of that language, I should call a miracle. But if God should prevent a person by some particular event, or chain of events, from embarking on a ship doomed to be lost, I should not call it a miracle. The spiritual work of God in man's heart, although opposed to the evil part of human nature, of 'the spirit' and not of 'the natural man,' I do not call miraculous, for the process is natural, orderly, gradual, although in a sense supernatural.

This use of the terms 'natural' and 'miraculous' may be objectionable to those who believe that God takes no active part in the present course of things—that event follows cause everywhere in a purely mechanical way. To them nothing is natural that is not mechanical from beginning to end; wherever there is interference with this course, there is an end to natural sequence. Unlike these, I have no doubt that God does take an active part, chiefly in the affairs of men, but also in Nature outside of man—not by opposing the course of nature, but by controlling it, when such is His will. As man does not stop a steam-engine (to return to a former illustration) by laying hold of the connecting-rod, but by shutting off the steam, so it is natural to suppose that God would direct the course of nature by regulating at the source, rather than where the current is at the full. As we saw before that to interpret Nature rightly the whole of Nature should be taken into account, so using the term 'natural' in this wider and truer sense, we see here that a course of things may still be natural though subjected to such Divine control. Even such a process of controlling may be called natural, as it would be accomplished in an orderly and not unnatural way.

But that is not all. For although an influx of the Spirit is a supernatural occurrence, yet growth in grace and other spiritual processes are natural, whilst at the same time supernatural. This subject—the naturalness of the Supernatural—has been so well treated by Professor Drummond in his excellent work *Natural Law in the Spiritual World*, as to need no further remarks in this place. But a clear understanding of my use of these terms 'natural' and 'miraculous' is necessary, to prevent misapprehension of what follows.

The more we examine the facts, the more it appears that the general course of Scripture history was a natural one; and that when we read of miracle, it is either for a special sign or to meet some special necessity. This question is not of so much importance to the present inquiry as the other referred to above, that of *Inspiration*. But the two are in a measure connected, and a few remarks upon it will not be out of place. We have to deal with stern facts in this matter; and it is therefore necessary to base our conclusions upon facts, and to clear our minds of such theories as will not bear the light of investigation. These have done more harm than enough.

In the first place we do not find that the chosen people was a supernaturally-produced nation, nor yet that its life history was of a different character *outwardly* from that of other early nations. At first there are pastoral families under patriarchal authority. When their numbers have increased they are governed by heroes who have delivered them from their enemies and then exercise judicial authority. Later on there is a government by kings. The nation knows successes and reverses. It suffers from internal discord, resulting in the division of the Kingdom into two parts. After many other vicissitudes it declines, as other nations have done and are still doing.[1]

But all through its history God was amongst its people, working an *internal* spiritual work, analogous to that which He carries on to-day in His people. They were, however, an earthly people, and therefore, according to their obedience

---

[1] Of course this is not meant to imply that the Jews will not again become a nation. Scripture seems to teach that they will.

or disobedience, they were made to prosper or to suffer in temporal things. But, with few exceptions at most, there was no reversing of the ordinary course of a nation's history.

Notwithstanding, the Scripture record, which enables us to see behind the scenes, and traces out the secret spring of their successes and reverses, makes them figure differently from other nations. The active part which God takes in their history is a characteristic feature possessed by no other nation.

In their history we find presented an imposing system of priesthood and sacrifices, with sacred buildings—Tabernacle and Temple—which call up in the reader's mind pictures of visible manifestations of the divine Presence such as one hears of nowhere else. Then there are the recorded miracles, which convey a like impression. All history has the effect of investing events with a glamour which is absent in life itself : how much more has the history of God's people this effect. From these facts, and another to be named presently, it is no wonder that Hebrew history should seem to us as a time when God was present among men in a manner very different from what ever occurred elsewhere. Upon examination, however, much of this proves to be appearance only ; whilst the *unobtrusive spiritual work* in their midst, with God's active part in their destinies, remain as the real and vitally important thing.

As to the sacred buildings, priesthood, and sacrifices, we know from Acts vii. 48, Heb. ix., x., that all these things did not possess the virtue that was attributed to them : they were merely figures of the realities manifested at a later date—figures which served to convey certain truths to Hebrew minds, and thus to prepare them for the realities when these should be revealed.

The language of the historical books of the Old Testament is, perhaps, the chief thing that gives the above wrong impression. We conclude that there must have been direct intercourse with God, such as never occurred since, when we read many of its passages.

The following extract from the inscription of Mesha, king of Moab, discovered in 1869, throws some light on this matter. Not only does the inscription corroborate a portion of Old Testament history, but it even reads, as Professor Sayce has remarked,[2] like a chapter from one of the historical books of the Old Testament.

"And Chemosh said to me, 'Go take Nebo against Israel.' And I went in the night, and I fought against it from the break of dawn till noon, and I took it and slew in all seven thousand men. . . . And the king of Israel fortified Jahaz and occupied it when he made war against me; and Chemosh drove him out before me. . . . And Chemosh said to me, 'Go down, make war against Horonaim and take it.' And I assaulted it, and I took it, and Chemosh restored it."[3] . . .

One other line of the inscription may be added, "And I took from it the vessels of Jahveh (the Hebrew name translated "the Lord" in the A.V.), and offered them before Chemosh."

Now this inscription brings home to us, as nothing else would do, the fact that there is much in the wording of the historical books of the Old Testament which is solely due to the language and custom of the times. We make a great mistake when we treat these parts of the Old Testament as we treat passages in the New Testament. Perhaps it was this free use of the name Jehovah (or Jahveh) amongst the Israelites that is condemned in Exod. xx. 7 and Deut. v. 11, "Thou shalt not take the name of Jehovah thy God in vain." Whilst, however, we find that much of the apparent direct intercourse with God in Israelitish history is

---

[2] *Fresh Light from the Ancient Monuments*, p. 76.
[3] *Fresh Light from the Ancient Monuments*, 1890, p. 75.

only apparent, being due to the language and custom of the times, the reality of the unseen presence of God remains. The spiritual work in their hearts was going on, slowly but surely. And according to their ways were they made to prosper or to suffer.

When we consider the miracles of which we read in the Bible, we find most of them grouped together at two periods in the nation's history. The first group comprises those in Egypt and the Desert; the second group those performed by Christ and His disciples. In Exod. vii. 3—5, we read that those in Egypt were for special signs and for the deliverance of Israel from Egyptian power; those in the Desert clearly relate to the stern necessities of Israel when passing through it. Also in John ii. 11 and other places we read that some at least of Christ's miracles were performed for a testimony to His divine mission. The others of the second group probably answered both purposes, that of testimony and that of meeting the need of those who were afflicted. If we trace out the other miracles recorded in the Bible, we likewise find some of them performed for signs (as that of Gideon's fleece in Judges vi. 36—40, and the one related in Isa. xxxviii. 7, 8); and I think it may be safely said about all the rest, that some special necessity calls them forth.

Further, it is to be remarked that, apart from these two special groups, there are not a great number recorded, considering the long period of nearly 2000 years of Jewish history.

It appears then that there was no wholesale, continuous, prodigal, or uncalled-for manifestation of miracle throughout Hebrew history.

On the other hand, when we trace out the manner in which God took that active part in the nation's history, we find traces of natural means everywhere. One of the most striking features of that history, and common to its whole course, is the repeated chastisement inflicted on the Israelites for their transgressions. But how are they chastised? In the most natural way. Things are so ordered that their enemies overcome them. When they are a very small nation it is their near neighbours that afflict them. Afterwards, when they are more powerful, it is their more distant neighbours, the great Powers of those days. Occasionally it is Pestilence (2 Sam. xxiv. 15; Jer. xliv. 13), or civil war (1 Kings xi. 11).

Times out of number we read of this triumph of their enemies as a punishment for their sins; as when (after the sin of Achan) in Josh. vii. they are overcome by the men of Ai; by the king of Mesopotamia (Judges iii. 8); by the king of Moab (Judges iii. 12); by Jabin, king of Canaan (Judges iv. 1, 2); by the Philistines and Ammonites (Judges x. 7); by the Philistines (Judges xiii. 1). And so on time after time, until finally the ten tribes are carried away by the king of Assyria (2 Kings xvii. 18, 23); and the remaining two tribes by Nebuchadnezzar, king of Babylon (2 Kings xxiv. 1, 3; xxv.). Likewise in New Testament times they are finally carried away and their capital destroyed by the Romans.

When we inquire into the manner of their deliverance from their enemies, we find, with few exceptions, that the course is still a natural one. Men are raised up to lead them; as Othniel (Judges iii. 9), Ehud (Judges iii. 15), Barak (Judges iv. 15), Gideon (Judges vi. 12, etc.), Jephthah (Judges xi. 1), Saul, David, and others. Or the heart of Cyrus is moved to let Judah return (Ezra. i), or Esther comes into favour with Ahasuerus and procures their deliverance. Or they are relieved from famine and the Syrians by a panic among the latter (2 Kings vii. 6).

We may notice instances of other kinds where nature

takes its course :—how Jacob's speckled cattle are increased (Gen. xxxi. 12); flesh is provided for Israel by quails brought by a wind from the sea (Num. xi. 31); the cursed children are destroyed by bears (2 Kings ii. 24) ; and when Christ Himself appears on the earth, He is born and brought up by a woman in a manner as far as possible a natural one.

Perhaps as the reader has reviewed the above cases, others of the opposite kind have been thought of which have not been mentioned here. Whilst, however, he has thought of the miracles noticed above, or of others, *have there in like manner occurred to him other instances of God's acting without miracle ?* I venture to say, No. This fact is very significant. It shows that the mind is quick to notice anything unusual, and correspondingly slow to notice that which is usual. And hence, throughout all Scripture history, the reader is so impressed with those miracles which are recorded, and so unimpressed by their absence where there are none recorded, that he unconsciously arrives at the notion of abundance of miracle in that history. This is a most fruitful cause of the mistake of predicating miracle so freely of Hebrew history.

I might multiply instances of the use of natural means similar to those noticed above, and give numbers of others which are only seen when one traces out the spiritual work of God in the nation. But the latter will become more apparent as we go on, and then only will their full significance be seen.

Perhaps the Enemy's suggestions " Cast thyself down," " Command that these stones be made bread," and the Lord's answers, are not without significance for this question of prodigality of miracle.

I think enough has now been said to show that—as in all other fields of God's action which are open to man's investigation, so in this particular field of Scripture history—the course of nature is the course adopted, miracle, where it occurs, being the special exception.

What else could we expect? If nature is God's appointed course, and therefore a good course, why should it be departed from in Scripture history any more than elsewhere? Clearly the only things that should call forth a departure from it, are the two that we have noticed, namely, special necessity, or a special proof of God's action.

No sooner, moreover, would the miracle become common, than it would cease to be regarded as miracle, and so would lose all its significance.

What, however, concerns us here is not so much the history of the Hebrews, as the spiritual work of God in the hearts of men, which is connected with the delivery of the Word of God to mankind; and which covers the whole period from the beginning of Hebrew history to the present time; but which for the most part corresponds with the period embraced by the Scripture record. Now the object of that work was, undoubtedly, to give man a Bible which should meet his needs just as he is; and this involves a mutual adaptation of the written word to man and of man's state to the written word, as we noticed in the last chapter. Therefore *the special need in this matter is a natural process*, not a miraculous one. Miracle here would require miracle throughout, in order to make the process work. Instead of being a help to the course of nature it would be a *positive hindrance*.

We find therefore every reason to predicate a natural process throughout this spiritual work which was connected with, and necessary for, the delivery of the Word of God to man; and we find nothing in Scripture to show that such a process was not the one adopted.[4]

[4] The question of the Inspiration of the writers will be better

Recalling then two of the conclusions arrived at in the last chapter—(1) that the all-important factors are the mind of God and the mind of man, Scripture being only a store of verbal signs, designed for the communication of the former to the latter; (2) that therefore its excellence must essentially consist in its suitability for this purpose ; or, in other words, in its adjustment to man's mental condition—let us now proceed to trace out the course of the production of Scripture. We will note both what we should expect to find, and what we do find.

When two things have to work together, no matter what their nature may be, they must fit into each other in their working parts. Something of this is seen when a person enters a room full of strangers; or if he goes to a strange place where he must at once find his way about; or if he suddenly make any great change in his surroundings; or if, in taking up a fresh subject, a host of new facts are suddenly forced on his mind all together ; or even if he lay his head sideways on the ground and look at a familiar landscape. All these are but instances of a partial change in his environment. Yet in every one of them he is at first more or less perplexed ; and the *only possible way* out of the difficulty is to familiarize himself *one by one* with his new surroundings. Those with which he familiarizes himself at first then form stepping stones to the next, these to the next, and so throughout ; until he " knows his way about," and has become familiar with, or in other words fitted or adjusted to, them all, and they in their turn fitted or adjusted to him. If, instead of a partial change like these, he should undergo a *total* change in his environment, he could not take the first step towards adjustment ; he could not con-

treated of further on, when it will be seen that it presents nothing in opposition to the above conclusion. Facts having an important bearing on this question will come out as we proceed.

tinue to live. Life generally, as Mr. Herbert Spencer shows in his *Principles of Biology*, is " the continuous adjustment of internal relations to external relations "—a correspondence or intercourse between the organism and its environment. This correspondence can only be brought about, as illustrated above, by a process of evolution.

Now this shows that a complete Scripture could not be delivered to man in one piece. We might, perhaps, conceive of such a book, composed in the language of another world, being handed to him complete (though even that supposition would not bear analyzing); but then he could not possibly understand a word of it. There must be a small beginning of the process out of which the whole is developed step by step, each modification forming a basis for further development. There must be throughout a mutual process of adaptation; both Scripture and man's mind being moulded by each other little by little to suit each other. *The two must grow up together.*

Not only so, but if the mind of God and that of man are to correspond with each other, there need be also a mutual adjustment, and even a kind of growing up together, between these two. This reads, perhaps, like a strange assertion; but the following truths will explain its significance. The love and mercy of God are verily called into activity by the condition of man. So in the case of the Christian; not only is God moved by his prayers, but there is an even closer vital intercourse between the two. In all these cases adjustments are involved on the part of both minds. Mistaken reverence may seem obliged to predicate a rigid God, but the very Soul of Religion is—what the heart of man requires—a Living One.

But it may appear that Scripture is sometimes received in one piece by man; as when one who has hardly read any of it during all his previous life, is converted, and takes to

THE WRITERS OF SCRIPTURE, ETC. 63

reading it all at once ; or when a heathen receives it through a translation into his own language.

In the first of these two cases the fact is liable to be overlooked, that such a one has been instructed more or less in the leading truths of Scripture by his parents or teachers, or even unavoidably by living in a community where such truths are commonly believed. But where did this community get them from ? A moment's thought, and we trace their origin backwards from people to people to the Apostles who first propagated them ; i.e. to the Hebrew nation to which the Apostles belonged. Both the written word and the means of understanding its leading truths are thus traced back to the Jews, these truths having been passed from mind to mind from the Apostles down to ourselves.

As regards the second case mentioned above, that of the heathen, we must remember that he has been taught some at least of these same truths by the missionary who gives him the translation, or perhaps by other converts. He does not receive the word all at once, but little by little. Possibly, however, he may glean the way of salvation from the Bible itself without such help ; which fact will be explained presently.

Again we have to note that no one who receives the knowledge of the way of salvation becomes acquainted with *all* the truths of Scripture ; and that the amount of each one's acquaintance with these is just in proportion to the amount of his previous adjustment to them and to the language of the Bible.

In neither of these cases then is the Word of God received all at once.

There is in the present day no adjustment of the language of the Bible. All the adjustment that takes place now is on one side ; and hence—as before remarked, and more fully to be seen later on—the incompleteness of the adaptation of Scripture language to readers of the present day. Here we see again that Scripture, being specially adjusted to the *Hebrew* people who first received it, cannot therefore be perfectly suited to the mind of each of its multiform readers in the whole world.

But there is another point. Two things cannot grow up together in mutual adjustment without being first placed in contact. So it must be with God and man, before there can be that correspondence between them which is involved in a real reading of the Word by man. "The Word is nigh thee, in thy mouth, and in thy heart." We have here, however, two kinds of correspondence. There is that closest correspondence of hearts which requires the indwelling Spirit of God, and there is that fainter correspondence of the intellect alone. A measure of the latter is involved in that general knowledge of Scripture truths which is possessed by all civilized nations; and which constitutes, as we have seen, the means whereby the closer correspondence is formed —a channel of communication between God and man along which the deeper life can flow.

Man is placed then in a position sufficiently near to God for this first contact, the knowledge of general divine truths, to be formed in him; after which follows in the Christian's case the closer growth to God which is involved in true communion. With the civilized man this outer contact is, as we have seen, already formed. But how about the savage? If there are, as some travellers have said, a few of the lowest who have *no* conception of any god, this outer contact is in their case totally unformed. Clearly no translation of Scripture into the language of such a savage could enable him to acquire a knowledge of God; for he has no ideas, and therefore *no language*, of the kind involved in such translation. He must be taught as a child is taught, little by little, *and very little by very little*, before any progress can be made.

This shows that in the hypothetical case of a heathen's learning by his own unaided efforts from Scripture, there *must* have been *some* previous preparation.

In what does it consist? The missionary best can tell—he who has to work upon, modify, and develop, as best he can, such crude ideas of a superior being, such gods of his own imagining, as the savage may possess. *These crude ideas of a god are then the first preparation of man for the knowledge of God.* They are in many cases not only very low, but positively sensual and wicked. The idolatry of the higher nations of antiquity was such; their gods immoral like themselves. But Comparative Mythology reveals the fact that in the beginning it was not so. Primitive man supposed the sun, moon, and stars to be living beings superior to himself. The storm, the thunder, the day, and all physical phenomena, were interpreted in like manner by his simple mind. It was only as man himself grew in sin more and more that his worship became so corrupt and defiled. The belief in and reverence for higher powers were pure in themselves, though we cannot say that there was a time when *no* evil co-existed with them.

Putting all these facts together, we arrive at the conclusion that these primitive ideas of gods were the work of God's own hand, or at least that their growth was overruled by Him so as to produce the notions which, in some form or other, were absolutely necessary before any knowledge of God could possibly be acquired by man. They form the very basis for that first contact (a knowledge of general truths about God) which must be possessed before there can be vital correspondence between God and man—before the minds of the two can be united and grow together. Some such notions of the Deity are possessed by almost all, if not all, inhabitants of the earth.

We are now in a position to take an outline view of the course which God took in the manifestation of Himself to mankind. He bestowed upon all peoples a measure of preparation—that fundamental possession with which none can dispense—some crude notions of the Deity. From the most advanced of the nations of antiquity, He selected one, the Hebrew, and taught that people a full knowledge of Himself. Finally He directed them to communicate that knowledge to the others, whom He had already so far prepared that they could receive it.

We find, however, that the blessings of this knowledge of God, both in its special and in its general character, have been hitherto received by the higher races alone, the exceptions being relatively unimportant. When we come to the Scripture story of the Flood, we shall see reason to believe it has some bearing on this fact, amongst others. It appears that these blessings, though open to all, were specially intended for these higher races. No doubt they are the best qualified to receive and appreciate them. Moreover, those only who are acquainted with the state of morality in the great nations of antiquity can form a correct idea as to how much these races needed them. They had a deeper need for this Great Light than the savage had. It was necessary to the very existence of a moral and stable state of society.

We need not here trace out further the initial work of God among all nations, or that diffusion of the knowledge of God from the Hebrews to other nations. What we have now to consider is the delivery of the Bible to the Hebrew nation. We have to trace out that process of growing together in mutual adjustment of the mind of that people and the mind of God, together with the production of Scripture in their midst, whereby this correspondence of minds was wrought out. As we might expect, we shall find it a process of evolution.

The first thing we notice is that the Bible was not all delivered to the Hebrews at one time, but little by little, during a period of from one to two thousand years. Together with this we find that that period covered nearly the whole of the nation's history, during which great changes took place. In the beginning of that history they are a small people, a pastoral people. After awhile they are much increased in numbers, and have become an agricultural people. Whereas in the first place they are subject only to patriarchal authority, when they have become an agricultural and settled people they are governed by heroes who have delivered them from their enemies, and then exercise judicial authority over them. These Judges, moreover, do not succeed each other regularly, but arise at intervals. After this they are ruled by kings. Then the kingdom is divided, and each part has its own king. Then they are carried away captive to a foreign land. After their return from captivity they pass through a long series of vicissitudes, as recorded, more or less correctly, in the Apocrypha. Finally, they are made tributary to the Romans and governed by a Procurator.

I wish I could portray for my own and the reader's benefit the mind of an average Hebrew at each stage above noticed in the nation's history. Then we should see at a glance what differences there needed to be in the Books of the Bible, as successively delivered to them, if these writings were to be effectual in reaching their intellects and their hearts. What great changes there must have been in their modes of life, in their customs, in their intellectual capacity; and hence in their *forms of thought and the language which accorded thereto*. If, moreover, it was necessary that each portion of Scripture should meet the needs of its recipients, it is evident that no class of literature could do this so effectually as the class to which they were accustomed. We must remember, however, not only that there were no printed books in existence in the earlier part of their history, but also that there were then very few manuscripts; so that in those days reading must have been confined to the few learned. At that time extreme simplicity of thought must inevitably have prevailed amongst the people.

In the next place we see that no agent would be so suitable for the writing of the Scriptures, in the language of the people, so as to meet their needs, as one chosen from amongst themselves. This, accordingly, we find to have been the course adopted by God for the production of the Bible.

It will appear, however, from the above facts, that each book of the Bible should exactly portray the mind of the people, or of the better educated among them, at the time it was written. But this is not altogether the case, as we shall see.

Here then we are introduced to a third factor in the delivery of God's Word to man. Hitherto (with one or two unavoidable exceptions) the subject has been treated as if the Bible had been penned by God's own hand. Now *we have to note the action of an intermediate agent—the human writer.*

This agent is of great importance to the present inquiry respecting the unscientific character of the language of the opening chapters of the Bible. To a later page must be deferred the investigation of the question what Scriptural grounds there are for predicating miraculous inspiration of the writers of Scripture. Here let us notice what we should expect to find, if God was educating a nation in the knowledge of Himself, and at the same time producing His written word.

We have seen that each original writer is one of the people for whose benefit he wrote. Like everyone else he is a creature of his time. His manner of life, his customs, his knowledge, both of natural and of spiritual things, his modes of thought, his language, are all those of his fellow-countrymen; with only this difference, that one of the more advanced, not one of the common people, would be chosen by God for the work. If, as we before concluded, the excellence of Scripture must essentially consist in its adaptation to man's mental state, then the features just noticed would form the *highest qualification* the writer could have, of course combined with a knowledge of the spiritual truth which he had to communicate. And in most cases no one would possess and teach this spiritual truth so well as he who had learnt it thoroughly for himself; whilst he would learn it most thoroughly who did so experimentally, i.e. by a grafting of it upon, and in part development out of, previously-possessed knowledge in a natural way.

In the ordinary course of things, all knowledge, whether natural or spiritual, is acquired by a slight advance upon previously-possessed knowledge, on which it is grafted, out of which it partly grows, without which it has no basis, no means of its being apprehended. Therefore, in the case of such a writer, not only would scientific knowledge beyond that of his time be a psychological impossibility, but the *greatest hindrance* would be caused to his readers in their apprehension of the spiritual truth expressed in his writings, if he mixed up science with his proper subject. No mill-wright in making a pair of cog-wheels which are to work together would think of putting one or two of the cogs ten times larger than, or differently shaped from, the others; for he knows this would smash both of them to pieces. Yet it is very commonly supposed that a parallel course must have been taken in the composition of the Bible!

But we have also to note that the delivery of spiritual truth to the Hebrews was very gradual. The Law, the Psalms, the Prophets, the Gospels, the Epistles, illustrate this. Moreover, as we shall see more fully in the next chapter, combined with this gradual delivery of those truths *to* the nation, there was a gradual evolution of spiritual knowledge *in* the nation. Each increase of spiritual knowledge in the people naturally produced a man fit to receive from God spiritual truth in advance of that which his contemporaries had, and then fit to communicate such further truth to the people. *Thus the delivery of Scripture to the Hebrews proceeded pari passu with their advance in the knowledge of God.*

This progressive character of revelation, which is in accord with the principle of evolution, is not altogether new to theologians. It seems to have received increased attention lately, being parallel to the attention which students of science are on all sides directing to evolution. Thus Dr. Stoughton writes in his Introduction to *The Progress of Divine Revelation*, pages 3 to 5:—

"Revelation may be conceived of as communicated at once, or nearly so, in systematic and complete form; but such has not been the method actually adopted. 'God, who at sundry times, and in divers manners,' *bit by bit,* 'spake in time past unto the fathers by the prophets, hath in these last days spoken unto us by His Son.' The record of the Divine communication extends over the space of far more than 4000 years. The last revelation is nearly 2000 years old. The first is much more than twice that age. Between, there comes advance now rapid, now slow, now a mighty leap, now a gentle step, now a wide rent in the clouds, and an opening into the Heaven of Heavens; now the breaking out of a new star, perhaps, in the midst of a long-watched constellation. The history of this progress, as a characteristic fact, is over and over again recognized and illustrated in the Book itself. 'The law was given by Moses, but grace and truth came by Jesus Christ.' . . . 'These things have I spoken unto you in proverbs (or parables) : but the time cometh, when I shall no more speak unto you in proverbs, but I shall show you plainly of the Father.' . . . Nor can there be any question as to the wisdom of such an arrangement. If revelation could have been conveyed at once, it could not have been apprehended at once. Much time was requisite to learn the momentous lessons; and, partly at least on that account, much time was taken up in sending them. In all God's works *adaptation* is seen. Especially is it manifest in this instance. The method of Paul was the method of every Divine teacher. 'I have fed you with milk, and not with meat: for hitherto ye were not *able to bear it*.' The Master laid down the principle with regard to his own teaching. . . . Things must sort; and lessons must sort with the capacity and previous attainments of the learner."

It is only the evolutionist who can see the full extent of this progress of divine revelation, from its first small beginning when the human mind became capable of receiving, up to the fullest divine light which was bestowed on the greatest Apostles, and even beyond that to full light in the world to come.

It is of the utmost importance to this inquiry to understand these circumstances under which Scripture was produced, little by little, and what was the first work which each portion of it had to do. How each portion must not only meet the needs of the people as they were, but must also do its work amongst them so effectually as to produce a writer qualified to produce the next portion. This progress of the people in knowledge and true religion was therefore of *quite as much importance* as the writing of the Bible, and was *indispensable to the progress of that work*. For this reason it will be well for us to trace out the evolution of the knowledge of God.

But first let us briefly observe what this necessary adaptation naturally involves. If our Bible is a verbatim copy of the original writings which were current amongst the Hebrews, we should expect much defective knowledge to be manifested in its earlier parts, not only scientific but also religious. We should also expect the divine truths contained in those earlier parts to be couched in literature of a crude description. We know, however, that although not written specially for ourselves or any other class except its original recipients, the Bible was intended for the use of all classes. How has this difficulty been met?

How should we expect it to have been met? By miraculous inspiration of the writer? It is well to see what that means, and how far it would have been effective.

Let us take a somewhat parallel case. Here are a class of children, the youngest of whom knows that two and two make four, an average child can add up a column of pounds, shillings, and pence. The most advanced child is set to teach the others by the master, who is well acquainted with the formula :—

$$\tfrac{1}{4}\pi = 4\tan^{-1}\tfrac{1}{5} - \tan^{-1}\tfrac{1}{239}$$

and whose name is associated with the work of the said pupil teacher. For this reason the examples which the pupil teacher gives the class to do are expected by some to exhibit a knowledge equal to that of the master, and he must therefore incorporate this formula with them. Is the pupil teacher to be suddenly endowed (1) with a full knowledge of arithmetic, (2) with a full knowledge of algebra, (3) with a full knowledge of plane trigonometry? or is he to be made to understand the above formula without first having *any such basis laid* for his knowledge of

THE WRITERS OF SCRIPTURE, ETC. 73

it? In either case one would pity his pupils. Long indeed will it be before they know trigonometry, or even make further progress in arithmetic.

Yet a miracle as great, or greater, would have been necessary to enable a heathen Hebrew of the earliest times (see Josh. xxiv. 2) to write a passage of one of the apostle Paul's epistles, or even to write a small portion of Gen. ii. in language consistent with the facts of Evolution.[5] When this knowledge had been given to the writer, it would have been necessary to create language for its expression—a small matter perhaps. Then we have to consider how this unexceptionable phraseology would re-appear in subsequent editions of the Book. Under such circumstances the inspired writer could not have communicated such knowledge to his successor unless he also were miraculously inspired, and so throughout. The written characters might, however, be perpetuated; but they would have *no meaning* after their writer's decease. On either supposition the miracle would have had to be repeated for the enlightenment of our translators of 1611 and all others, if it was a passage containing advanced scientific truth. Perhaps, however, the case would have been better met by miraculously inspiring the whole Hebrew nation, instead of giving them some 1500 years of progressive education in spiritual truth; whereas the world has taken three or four thousand years to learn its science. But if such things were, there would be little need for any Bible at all.

It does not concern us here to inquire whether God *could* do such things as these or not. Let it be understood the position is put thus in order to show what the miracle-

---

[5] Even in this day Evolution is by many supposed to imply that man is (essentially) a developed monkey. What effect then would its principles have had upon simple people whom it was desired to teach that God was their Creator!

theory leads to when it is examined. It is a harmless theory to believe in; but it is the greatest mistake to present it for the acceptance of those who see very plainly that the miracle-course was not adopted, whilst they do not see *why* it was not adopted. Such theories are like the views formerly held respecting the nature of geological processes; whereas the true history of revelation is like that of the earth, as first clearly read to us by Lyell—a history, not of cataclysms, sudden interpolations, and revolutions, but of uniform progress and continuous development.

Let us now ask, What *natural* course would have met the case? It occurs to us that, as spiritual knowledge progressed among the Hebrews, the original writings might have been superseded or revised through the agency of later writers. We must not forget, however, that it was necessary *some* writings should occupy continuously the position of being sacred in the people's eyes. Sudden change would not do at all, and therefore sudden superseding of older writings by others would not meet the case. People would not exchange the old writings for the new in that way. It appears then that transformations or revisions of the original writings, retaining the essential part of their substance and leaving the remainder to perish, would be the best course to meet all the necessities of the case.

Be this judgment right or wrong, there is much evidence that some such course was taken in the production of some parts of the Bible. We read here and there in the Old Testament of certain 'books' which do not appear in the Bible. In Josh. x. 13 and 2 Sam i. 18, we find a reference to the 'Book of Jasher,' as the source from which the writer has taken certain facts. In 1 Chron. xxix. 29, there is a reference to the 'Book of Nathan, the prophet,' and the 'Book of Gad, the seer.' Also in Num. xxi. 14, there seems to be a reference to a 'Book of the wars of Jehovah' once existing.

It seems very likely then that in the early times, when morality and spiritual knowledge were very defective, the course adopted by God in the production of Scripture consisted in the selection of the essential parts of older writings, and in revisions of older writings by the agency of writers of more enlightened times; and that this latter process was carried as far as it could be without destroying their structure altogether; whilst those manifestations of the writer's imperfect knowledge which remained after this process, were nullified by the truths of later Scriptures.

The subjection of the Old Testament to such an analysis as it has received from German and other writers, is not a study calculated to reveal what God has to say by it. At the same time it is neither possible nor needful to resist some of the conclusions of those writers. For instance, analysis of the language of the Pentateuch must produce some true evidence as to the period of its composition in its present form, and also as to authorship. It is quite impossible to maintain the theory that it was all written by Moses,[6] as was formerly supposed. I see no need to

[6] Upon this question Bishop Colenso writes (*Colenso on the Pentateuch*, p. 94):—"The books of the Pentateuch are never ascribed to Moses in the inscriptions of Hebrew manuscripts, or in printed copies of the Hebrew Bible. Nor are they even styled the 'Books of Moses' in the Greek Septuagint or Latin Vulgate, but only in our modern translations, after the example of many eminent Fathers of the Church, who, with the exception of Jerome, and, perhaps, Origen, were, one and all of them, very little acquainted with the Hebrew language, and still less with its criticism. But, in fact, these very titles, 'Books of Moses,' 'Book of Joshua,' may mean only 'Books *about* Moses and Joshua,' and do not at all imply that the books in question were supposed to have been *written* by Moses and Joshua. We might as well infer from their titles that the 'Book of Judges' was written by the Judges, and the 'Book of Ruth' by Ruth." If all the Bishop's remarks were as moderate as the above, his work would not be so objectionable.

reject this conclusion. For if it shows that parts of the Pentateuch were written in their present form at a time when the people had made more spiritual progress, it accords with the above conclusion as to what would have been the best course for the production of those early Scriptures, as far as we can see.[7]

Doubtless this is one reason why we find in the earliest portions of the Bible traces of defective spiritual as well as scientific knowledge on the writer's part, whilst nothing remains that could lead a reader into error.

I now wish to draw the reader's special attention to the means used for the education of man in divine truth before the one which we call revelation. He will perhaps hesitate to accept the fact, especially if he does not believe in evolution; but it was a means which in the light of evolution we see to have been necessary, simple, and effectual. It accounts for important facts which have come to light in connexion with the Scripture accounts of the Creation, the Fall, and the Deluge; and even for the non-Mosaic authorship of parts of the Books of the Law. Its full significance will be seen as the later portions of this work are perused. Here I can do no more than present it briefly.

Prior to revelation there was *the overruling of men's thoughts and beliefs, the fostering of their ideas, the guiding of their traditions, the leading of these in the direction of truth.*

In predicating revelation we implicitly assert an unseen connexion between God and the man who receives that revelation. In the preceding part of this chapter we have noticed an inner and an outer contact between God and men, the outer one being the knowledge of general truths about God, which must exist before the closer communion is possible. Here in like manner we find a closer contact in

---

[7] A fuller treatment of this question is given in the next chapter.

The Writers of Scripture, etc. 77

the case of revelation, and a fainter one, but still a real one, in this influencing of the unenlightened mind. The latter, too, had different degrees; for it began in the most distant ages, long before historical times, in causing men's thoughts to go vaguely in the direction in which the truth lay, it proceeded in leading, or drawing, the mind closer and closer to the truth, until finally it merged into revelation itself. In thus preparing the mind for truth and leading up to it, we see that it prepared the way, too, for the writing of the Bible: further on we shall see that it had a still closer connexion with the writing of the Bible as regards its earliest part.

Very evidently there could not be revelation of any truth before some ideas of a similar kind had been developed in the human mind. Some such previous education was indispensable; and can we think of any other method which would have been so simple, so effectual, so natural that God should adopt, as this guiding of human thoughts and beliefs? What so natural as that He who had built up the mind of man should guide and foster the growth of his ideas and beliefs towards that truth which He was waiting to reveal? We might almost ask what other course was *possible?*

Moreover, we should consider here the ways of God, and both Scripture and Christian experience surely reveal that, in carrying out His purposes, He does not go out of the way and create special means, but He takes up *that which is at hand*, and works upon it, till what was needed has been produced. And such was the course adopted here, in this education of the human mind for the revelation that was to follow.

We have also to notice here another guiding of the mind, also unknown to the man himself, which had much to do with the production of the early Scriptures. It was the divine substitute for that miraculous inspiration which has been wrongly predicated, and which, we have seen, would not have been at all effective. Not only was the public mind thus led near the truth, but the words used by the early writer of Scripture, and his compositions altogether, were in many cases so overruled and arranged, as to present for the benefit of later readers truths unknown to, and beyond, his comprehension.

One is amazed to find what quality of work was done in the beginning of the Bible with instruments so poor as these early writers, and how the Divine Mind did what the poor human mind could not then do.

We find the writings of one, and sometimes of two or more, of these writers, so overruled and woven together (in ways obviously unknown to themselves) as to present pictures and other combinations exhibiting truths of many orders. We even find scientific truths thus hidden where they could not be clearly expressed. We find sometimes an arrangement of words such that the simple reader of early times reading them in the light of his own beliefs, and the enlightened reader of later ages reading them in the light of his knowledge, both gather the divine meaning, which is the one important thing. We find the very simplicity of the writer and of his writings so made use of that these convey, in some form or other, truths which one would find it difficult to express in the fuller light and rich language of to-day. If we want testimony to divine authorship and divine wisdom in these early Scriptures, both are there in abundance. We shall have occasion to notice many such instances.

The reader will see how such facts as these harmonize with the conclusion at which we arrived in the previous chapter—that the Bible is not, and cannot be, the Word itself, which is a portion of the Mind of God, but that it is

God's Book designed to reveal that Mind to man. Thus it is not always by the literal meaning, but sometimes by indirect ways such as those just referred to, that the Mind of God reaches the mind of man. We need not therefore shut our eyes to the defective knowledge of the human writer where it appears in these early Scriptures. It is conspicuous in the first eleven chapters of Genesis, which treat of events preceding Hebrew history, but it also appears sometimes in later writings, as we shall notice in tracing out the evolution of the knowledge of God. It may be well to notice one or two instances here.

The author of Psalm cxxxix. says (verses 21, 22) "Do not I hate them, O Jehovah, that hate thee? . . . I hate them with perfect hatred." A New Testament writer, having learnt the grace of God, would never use such language as this. But the Psalmist who lived in an age in which that grace had not yet been fully revealed, uses language more in accordance with the just principles of the Law which he *had* learnt.

Similarly, when the author of the 95th Psalm would extol Jehovah in the fulness of his heart, he says (verse 3) "Jehovah is a great God, and a great king above all gods." No one would use such language as this in the present day or in New Testament times. In the next chapter we shall have to trace out the leading of Hebrew belief from Polytheism to the true Monotheism. Here we see that the Psalmist has not been quite freed from polytheistic notions. To his mind such beings as other gods are still in existence, far inferior in power to Jehovah. The very excellence of Jehovah's power seems to him to consist in His exalted position as higher than those that are high.

One of the narratives of which we shall have to take account in its place, as being irreconcilable with facts of science, is that of the Tower of Babel in Gen. xi. Here we have only to notice the writer's anthropomorphic conception of Jehovah. The conception of an omnipresent spiritual God was not taught to the Hebrews in a generation, and it does not appear to have been in existence in this writer's time. Therefore (Gen. xi. 5—9) he represents Jehovah as *coming down to see* the city and the tower, as a man would do. Shall we look down upon this imperfect conception of God? Is it not more natural to regard the passage as a treasured record of the firstfruits of God's work in man? When as yet the full conception of God was not in existence, was not this incomplete conception precious in His sight, being the work of His own hands? We cannot now stay to discuss the divine meaning of this passage; but let us pass on to see that meaning in another passage which has been brought forward as evidence against the divine origin of Scripture.

I refer to the thirty-first chapter of Numbers. After the reader has perused the chapter, specially noticing verses 17, 18, and 35, will he turn also to Matt. xix. 8, where Christ says to the Pharisees, "Moses for your hardness of heart suffered you to put away your wives," and verse 9, where He adds, " Whosoever shall put away his wife, except for fornication, and shall marry another, committeth adultery." We know that, not only in the time of the Patriarchs, but as late as that of David and Solomon, polygamy and concubinage were largely practised. Notwithstanding, David is called the man after God's heart, and Solomon the wise man. Here we have ignorance of the principles of morality manifested in several cases, and we have Christ's authority for the fact that certain parts of the Law were adjusted to the times.

Bishop Colenso takes it as a fair estimate (from verse 35) that there would have been 68,000 women and children slain 'in cold blood'; and he asks, How could such an act and the adultery of verse 18 have been committed at the command of God? adding that the narrative itself is unhistorical. One might argue that the former act was just, perhaps; but after what has been said, the matter appears in a different light. We must recognize the customs and notions of the times as to morality and the treatment of conquered enemies, which were more or less those of the lawgiver or writer of the passage. We must recognize the custom of the times to associate Jehovah's name with the acts of those in power, which is manifest from the similar practice of their Moabite neighbours, as revealed by the Moabite inscription referred to on page 56. However honoured the position of Moses, these facts have some bearing on the character of the passage.

But now let us see the other side. We notice that the passage occurs in one of the Books of the Law, whose principle is stern justice without mercy. The object of this Scripture is, therefore, not to give a historical account; nor is it in this part of the Law to inculcate morality, that being done in *other* parts. Here it is a question of equity, "an eye for an eye." Accordingly we have in verse 2 "Avenge the children of Israel of the Midianites," and in chapter xxv. 17, 18, "Vex the Midianites and smite them, for they vex you. . . ." More particularly do we notice this feature in respect to verses 17, 18. In the previous verse (16) we have "*these (women) caused* the children of Israel, through the counsel of Balaam, *to commit trespass against Jehovah in the matter of Peor, and so the plague was among the congregation of Jehovah.*" Then follow verses 17, 18 : "Now therefore kill every male among the little ones, and kill every woman," etc. Here is the very essence of the legal principle throughout. It is "an eye for an eye, a tooth for a tooth, vexation for vexation, *death for death, adultery for adultery.*" It exhibits human

G

ignorance of the principles of morality, divine wisdom in overruling it to express in this Scripture the character of Law. If to the enlightened mind it seems to inculcate or permit immorality, that is the inevitable concomitant of the cumbersome language corresponding to the morality and notions of that age.

In such touches as these we trace the hand of God in these ancient Scriptures. These remain for instruction and admiration to-day, whilst we should never forget that their chief work was done long ago amongst the people who first received them, and to whom they were far better adjusted than they are to us. But for their first work where would now be found the enlightened minds of to-day which pass judgment on them? Not in existence, for it was only after that first work had been done that fuller light could be given, and thus upon that first work the whole was based. Rejecting them in that way is like pulling out the foundations upon which one stands.

When, therefore, we find defective knowledge manifested in these ancient Scriptures, if there is any tendency to look down upon them, it is well that we find ourselves thus confronted with a manifestation of God's handiwork. Seeing how He thus overruled such human imperfection to work out His own ends, both in the first work amongst the Hebrews and in the construction of the Bible for the use of all ages, we shall be less likely to forget that it is not a work of man's that we are handling, but the work of God, worthy of all reverence.

SUMMARY OF CONCLUSIONS OF THE CHAPTER.

The law of a gradual natural course of things holds in what we call Nature and in the spiritual work in men's hearts—two departments which fill the whole region accessible to observation. It is obvious that such a course, being more thorough, is the best; and the only reason for using miracle would be that of special necessity, or as a special proof of God's action. This accordingly we find to have been the course of Scripture history. In the spiritual work among the Hebrews (connected with the writing of Scripture) the special need was a natural and thorough work. Miracle would have done harm.

When two things have to work together, they must fit into each other in their working parts, a state of things which can only be produced by evolution. Therefore a complete Bible could not be delivered to man all at once. It must be done by a gradual process of adaptation, both Scripture and man's mind being moulded by each other, little by little. They must grow up together. So also with the Mind of God and the mind of man.

But two things cannot grow up together in mutual adjustment without being first placed in contact. Therefore man is brought sufficiently near to God for such contact to be established—he attains to a knowledge of general truths about God, such as are possessed by civilized nations. This forms a channel along which deeper Divine knowledge can flow, and in the Christian's case this does flow, and thus his mind grows together with God's Mind in a closer way.

But this general knowledge about God cannot be given without a previous basis to build it on; there *must* be some pre-existing ideas of the Deity. These were produced, partly at least, by means of the effects produced on primitive men by physical phenomena, which were so overruled by God as to form the conception of gods. God wrought this basis in all peoples on the earth, taught full knowledge of Himself by its means to the Hebrews, and then sent them to teach the already-prepared heathens.

Scripture was delivered little by little to the Hebrews; and, as they passed through great social changes and gradually progressed in knowledge, its literature differs much. It was necessary that the writers of Scripture should be like the people, and should write in the literature of the day, in order to reach the popular mind. Each increase of Divine knowledge in the people produced a writer fit to receive further revelation from God; and his writings in their turn furthered the growth of Truth in the people. This growth of the people in Divine knowledge was quite as important as the writing of the Bible; neither could proceed without the other.

We might therefore expect much ethically defective language in the early parts of the Bible; but as it was intended for the use of enlightened people afterwards, every serious defect of language has been removed, and the minor ones which remain are cancelled by later Scriptures, written in fuller light. Miraculous Inspiration of writers would not have been effective; not only would the greatest of miracles have been required for this, but it would have impeded, instead of furthering, the growth of Truth.

After dim ideas of the Deity had been formed in man in the manner before noticed, the theological beliefs of early peoples were gradually led nearer and nearer to the Truth. This was continued in the early history of the Hebrews, until amongst them its place was taken by revelation itself, for which it had prepared the way. This was a most important part of the education of man in Divine truth. It had an important connexion with the writing of the earliest Scriptures, as will be seen further on.

When man was so poor an instrument, in those days, for the writing of the Bible, God adopted many other means in conjunction with the writer's own knowledge, such as the controlling of his language in ways unknown to him.

THE WRITERS OF SCRIPTURE, ETC. 85

These conclusions agree with those of Chapter II.—that the Bible is not, and cannot be, the Word of God itself; but is God's Book, designed to reveal His Mind to man, and containing many classes of literature for that purpose.

The defective knowledge of the writers of Scripture may therefore be freely admitted.

CHAPTER IV.

SEVERAL PHASES OF THE DEVELOPMENT OF THE KNOWLEDGE OF GOD.

It has already been stated that it is very important to have some knowledge of the circumstances under which the successive portions of the Bible were produced, so as to understand, in some measure, what their first work in the hearts of men was, and how its language was necessarily adapted to different people and times. It will therefore be well to give here an outline of the development of the knowledge of God. It is indeed almost entirely with the earlier part of that development that this work has to do. But the whole subject has a most important bearing upon an attack that is made on the doctrines of the New Testament, as will appear towards the end of this chapter. For this additional reason let us proceed with our investigation.

It is natural to us all to look for the deepest and most advanced spiritual truths in the words of the Son of God—those which He Himself uttered when on the earth. It is soon found, however, that this is a mistake, for many of the deepest and most advanced truths are to be found in the Epistles. The reason is not far to seek. It lies in the fact that when Christ was on the earth the minds of those about Him were not prepared to receive such truths. After His ascension and the gift of the Holy Ghost, the Apostles were fitted to receive from God the revelation of those truths, and the early Christians were fitted to learn them from the Apostles. It may indeed be said that such truths were not uttered by the Lord to those about Him because they concern only such as have the Holy Spirit, which those about Him had not at that time. But this is only repeating in another form the reason just given.

I have noticed before that the sequence of the Scriptures —Law, Psalms, Prophets, Gospels, Epistles—illustrates the gradual delivery of spiritual truth to the Hebrews. We may be quite certain that any other order of delivery, whether possible or not, would not have been effective. Abolish slavery at one stroke without substituting a temporary paternal control over the liberated slaves, and grave ills will ensue in lieu of the greater ill of slavery itself. The liberated slaves need to be controlled and taught how to use their liberty, before they are fit to enjoy it. Show grace to an uncivilized man, and he will probably take you for a coward. In like manner, the Hebrews required a long drilling in the principle of the stern justice of the Law, before they were fit to hear the good tidings of Mercy and Grace.

The lie which Rahab tells (Josh. ii. 5, 6) in order to carry through her act of faith appears to be told in perfect unconsciousness of its being wrong. Jael's treachery to Sisera (Judges iv.) wears a like appearance; whilst the rejoicing of Deborah and Barak over the fallen foe (Judges v. 24—30) is of a character consistent with crude times. Other cases might be cited which show the moral darkness of the Hebrews at that early age, but the fact is sufficiently well known. The reader may find information on the subject in Canon Mozley's *Lectures on the Old Testament*, Dr. Stoughton's *Progress of Divine Revelation*, and other works.[1]

[1] The last-named work contains the following:—"After the

In such times God could only reveal Himself to the hard heart and darkened intellect of the early Israelite as "a jealous God, visiting the iniquity of the fathers upon the children, upon the third and upon the fourth generation of them that hate me; and showing mercy unto thousands of them that love me and keep my commandments" (Ex. xx. 5, 6).

At a later date the Prophet learns that if the sinner have a son who does righteously, the latter "shall not die for the iniquity of his father, he shall surely live" (Ezek. xviii. 14—18).

And further than this, "when the wicked man turneth away from his wickedness that he hath committed, and doeth that which is lawful and right, he shall save his soul alive" (Ezek. xviii. 27, 28). Deut. xxiv. 16, which contains language somewhat similar to Ezek. xviii. 14—18, seems, from the context, to be a command given for the Israelites to observe amongst themselves. Canon Mozley, after affirming a double aspect of the law of the second commandment, remarks upon Ex. xx. 5:—

"Ezekiel understood the second commandment in a sense different from the judicial punishments of one man for the sins of another. . . . The interpretation of an earlier age doubtless did not distinguish the didactic and judicial senses of the law of the Second Commandment. . . . Dim and confused in the first ages, the notion of desert—partly resting on the individual, partly clogged with the irrelevant associations of blood relationships and neighbourhood—struck an uncer-

settlement in Canaan, decline rather than progress was visible. The story of the people for many years was very sad. The heroes Gideon, Jephthah, and Samson, though men of faith, though God's power moved them to great exploits for the deliverance of their oppressed brethren, present a low type of moral and religious life. . . . Deborah's song, under the influence of Israelitish enthusiasm, can never be regarded as giving any Divine sanction to the act perpetrated by the wife of Heber the Kenite" (p. 122).

tain ambiguous note in man's conscience. But as the law of Sinai worked in men's minds, it gradually developed the deeper parts of his moral nature.... We recite this commandment in our churches now, but we take it in a sense which satisfies the terms of it, viz., the physical consequences."...."[2]

If for natural descent we substitute spiritual descent (as in John viii. 37—44) the judicial aspect seems to embody an important principle.

The order of delivery of the books of the Bible thus accords with the Hebrews' progress in religion, as already stated. For the man whose heart was most fully moulded to the justice of the law, and enlightened by its teaching, was the fittest person to learn from God a little of His merciful character—fit therefore to write Psalms. So, the Hebrew who had read the Psalms, and had his heart softened more, was a fit subject to learn more from God and to write Prophecy.

It appears from the Apocrypha, too, that before the coming of Christ, the teaching of the Psalms and Prophets had so far taken effect upon the people, that the writer of the Book of Ecclesiasticus says (chapter 28, verse 2) "Forgive the neighbour the hurt that he hath done unto thee, so shall thy sins also be forgiven when thou prayest." Had there not been such progress in the moral condition of the people, the fields would not have been 'white already to harvest' when Christ came. After He had *in due time* died for the ungodly, the Holy Spirit was given to the believer, and the wonderful spiritual blessings of which we read in the Epistles were revealed to, and conferred upon, him in Christ.

This is a very brief outline of the last phase of the progress of the Hebrews in Divine knowledge. Some other details will, however, be brought out afterwards.

[2] *Lectures on the Old Testament*, pp. 120, 121.

Let us now pass on to another phase, which preceded it, generally, though the two were not mutually exclusive.

Not only does it follow from the principles of Evolution that all knowledge of God must have been developed from small beginnings, and that originally all peoples must have been in darkness; but the Bible itself also testifies that the earliest Hebrews were idolaters or polytheists. At that time they had *no more notion of God* than other early nations had. All were alike in darkness.

We read in Josh. xxiv. 2, "Thus saith Jahveh (or Jehovah, as often spelt) the God of Israel, Your fathers dwelt of old time beyond the River, even Terah, the father of Abraham, and the father of Nahor: *and they served other gods.*" We also read that they served other gods in Egypt. "Put away the gods which your fathers served beyond the River, and in Egypt; and serve ye Jehovah" (Josh. xxiv. 14). So in Exod. iii. 13 we read that Moses, when about to go and declare to the Israelites "The God of your fathers hath sent me unto you," anticipates being answered with the extraordinary question, "*What is his name?*" plainly showing that the common ideas of gods, such as other nations had, were all they knew about the Divinity.

So we read of Rachel stealing her father's teraphim, or gods (Gen. xxxi. 19, 30); and it appears from 1 Sam. xix. 13-19 that such teraphim were kept in the house in the time of Saul.

Not only do we find the Israelites in the desert worshipping other gods, but all through the Book of Judges, and even throughout the two Books of Kings, we again and again read of their turning to other gods and serving them. Even the wise Solomon is not sufficiently superior to heathen beliefs to resist the influence of his wives: he, too, falls into idolatry (1 Kings xi. 4). The language of

DEVELOPMENT OF THE KNOWLEDGE OF GOD. 91

2 Kings xviii. 4, "he brake in pieces the brazen serpent that Moses had made ; for *unto those days* the children of Israel did burn incense to it" seems to imply such a practice from time immemorial.

Not until after the Captivity do we find the belief in other gods thoroughly weeded out of the nation. *A period of more than 1000 years was required to do this work.* By that time, it appears, their original belief in other gods was thoroughly rooted out. From that time forward they served the true God.[3]

There is nothing which, to my mind, shows the original darkness of the Hebrews more than the story of Jephthah. In Judges xi. 29, 32, he appears as one whom Jehovah chose to deliver Israel from the Ammonites, and afterwards he becomes their judge (Judg. xii. 7). Let us see what is the extent of his knowledge of God. From verses 23, 24, it is manifest that Jehovah is to him nothing more than one of the gods of the other nations. He says to the king of Ammon " Jahveh (or Jehovah, as oftener spelt) the god of Israel hath dispossessed the Amorites from before his people Israel, and shouldst thou possess them ? Wilt not thou possess that which Chemosh thy god giveth thee to possess ? so whomsoever Jahveh our god hath dispossessed from before us, them will we possess."

But the sequel is far more significant. *Jephthah positively believes that Jahveh takes pleasure in human sacrifices !*

In verse 30 we read, " Jephthah vowed a vow unto Jahveh, and said, If thou wilt indeed deliver the

---

[3] Canon Farrar has remarked that . . . "a pure monotheism and an independence of symbols was the result of a slow and painful course of God's disciplinal dealings among the noblest thinkers of a single nation, and not, as is so constantly and erroneously urged, the instinct of the whole Semitic race; in other words, one single branch of the Semites was, under God's providence, *educated* into pure monotheism only by centuries of misfortune and series of inspired men."

children of Ammon into mine hand, then it shall be, that whosoever cometh forth of the doors of my house to meet me, when I return in peace from the children of Ammon, it (or he) shall be Jahveh's, and I will offer it (or him) up for a burnt offering."

Our Revised Authorized Version gives, 'whatsoever cometh forth,' with 'whosoever' in the margin as alternative reading, and therefore 'it' in the latter part of the verse. But 'whosoever' is manifestly the right word; for (1) Jephthah would not expect an animal to *come forth from the doors of his house to meet him;* and (2) he would not have considered himself bound to offer up his daughter, if he had referred to *an animal* in that vow. And accordingly (verse 39) he *actually offers up that daughter in sacrifice to Jehovah!*

He was only acting according to the notions of his time. As late as Ahaz' day (2 Kings xvi. 3) the rite of offering human sacrifices was practised by the surrounding nations; and Ahaz and Manasseh offered up their own sons. Such then was the darkness of Israel in Jephthah's time, that he, their deliverer and judge, upon whom "came the spirit of Jahveh," had no better knowledge of the true God, than to believe such horrible rites to be pleasing to Him.

Ahaz and Manasseh in their wickedness practise such rites before other gods; Jephthah in his goodness thinks Jehovah is pleased with them. If the leader and judge in Israel knows no better than this, what about the rest of the nation at that time?

It was to people living in so great darkness that God sent His light, and the first and greatest work of the early Scriptures was to lighten the darkness and soften the hearts of these Hebrews of early times.

As progress is generally rhythmic, or marked by waves with alternate heights and depths, this dark period of

DEVELOPMENT OF THE KNOWLEDGE OF GOD. 93

Jephthah's time may have been preceded by a somewhat lighter one. By judging of everyone else by ourselves, we have all made the natural mistake of supposing that Moses and the Patriarchs must have possessed as full a knowledge of divine things as was only revealed long after their time. Not only so, but it is very natural to invest the individuals of Scripture history with a holy character and a perfection of knowledge, even in cases where there is nothing in the Bible to indicate these. Thus Job has been supposed to have possessed superior knowledge when he said that God "hangeth the earth upon nothing," simply because he is a Bible character. Such thoughts result from a mistaken association of ideas. We find that there is neither reason for them, nor reason in them, when the case is duly examined. For instance, if 2 Samuel iii. had not plainly stated that David had sons by six different wives, but had only used words that might imply it, would not the person who should point out the fact have been resisted in his conclusion, simply because David is presented in Scripture as a good man? In like manner one may feel called upon to defend the characters of Jael and Jephthah. But it is better to take them as Scripture presents them; it does more honour to the work of God, and the Scriptures too, to recognize frankly what these have had to do, and have done.

So with Moses. Common sense tells us that amongst such a people he would have been a more efficient servant of God with the imperfect knowledge of the times, but little in advance thereof, than any person of more enlightened times could have been. Imperfect knowledge of God on the part of Moses seems to be manifested in Exodus xv. 11, when he sings with the Israelites "Who is like unto thee, O Jahveh, among the gods?" and on the part of Aaron, when he makes a golden calf at the people's request (Ex. xxxii. 1—4). Nor must we forget the testimony of

Num. xxxi., before referred to. If there are passages from which it appears, not only that the *Law* of Moses exhibits light in advance of those early times, and not only that the *Law* of Moses emanated from God Himself, but also that the *man* Moses was supposed to have had such superior knowledge and direct interviews with God—we must not forget that the testimony of fuller light is "No man hath seen God at any time." Nor can we shut our eyes to the evidence as to the date of writing of portions of the Books of the Law in their present form. But do not the conclusions of Chapter II. of this work throw light on the matter? Was it not above all things necessary that the truths of the Law and the fact of its Divine origin should be presented in such forms as the Israelite could apprehend, and as would reach his heart? And what would have an effect upon the early Hebrew, who knew nothing of a spiritual God, and very little of any abstractions, but whose mind was only acquainted with, and capable of conceiving of, material things? Nothing so much as a picture of a man receiving his laws from a material God, a God of vengeance. Of this he could think. Of a spiritual unseen God, or of such a thing as the principle of the law, he could think little, or not at all, in those times before such conceptions were developed. In short, the *man* Moses is of little moment; the principles of the Law—they constitute the *Word of God*. If therefore in these cases Moses is the figure under which that Word is expressed; if the historical lawgiver and leader of Israel formed the centre around which were clustered some teachings of a fuller light than he ever knew, in order that the Word should reach the Hebrew mind—would not this accord with the wisdom of God, and with *all the facts* that bear upon this question, which has been so much discussed?

Before dismissing, however, a question which affects, not

Development of the Knowledge of God. 95

the inner content, but the letter, not the substance, but the form, of so many Scripture passages, let us consider some further facts bearing on the matter.

In a Tract on *The Mosaic Authorship and Credibility of the Pentateuch,* Dean R. Payne-Smith says (pp. 4, 5) :—

" The earlier books (of the Bible) were composed when the art of writing was in its infancy, when writing materials were of the simplest kind, and when but few persons could either make records of events, or read them when recorded. And it is a well-established law of the Holy Scriptures that in their outward form they were subject to the conditions of the times when they were written. . . . There is never anything magical in the Bible, and the writers of its many books are never lifted out of the moral and mental state of things among which they lived ; nor are their intellectual endowments or physical qualities changed. . . . In the Old Testament many of our modern difficulties arise from the demand, unconsciously often made, that everything should be in accordance with nineteenth century advancement. But the gift of inspiration, and the watchful care of the Spirit that in the historical books the subjects selected and the method of treating them should be for the edification of the Church, did not raise the writers above the conditions of their own times."

The above statements, considered in the light of the gradual progress of Divine Revelation, involve much.

We have the notion that whatever is legendary is of purely human origin, but the sooner we dismiss that idea the better. It has already been maintained in this work (pp. 76, 77) that the Divine leading of human beliefs and traditions has *played a most important part* in the development of the knowledge of God. We shall see this distinctly in the chapter on the Chaldean Account of Genesis. Here let us accept the fact ; and when we see how (as before affirmed) this process began in the most distant ages, long before historical times, in simply causing men's beliefs to go vaguely in the direction in which the truth lay, then gradually led the mind nearer and nearer to the truth, until finally in Hebrew times, having fully prepared the mind for revelation itself, it gave place to it—then there will appear less need to hesitate in thus applying the principle to explain the difficulties as to authorship and literal accuracy of parts of the Books of the Law. We shall see that in early Hebrew times some of their traditionary beliefs about Moses may have been thus divinely guided, so that in them the people believed things which embodied important truths, or which were even close approximations to, or peculiar forms of, historical facts;[4] that these traditions would be so firmly believed by the people as to be naturally written down side by side with other records of Moses and legal ordinances, so completing the Books of the Law in their present form. Lastly, if we fully bear in mind that the important thing is what *God's thoughts* are, not what those of *any man* such as Moses were, or what he did; we shall see how the whole Law, being associated with Moses, is, scripturally considered, Mosaic, in a characteristic sense. It is not *the man* Moses, but the Mosaic dispensation, its spirit and principles, with the active work of God in fostering these among the Israelites, and the Divine care and protection specially accorded to them in those times—*all as being of God*—that are essential. Nothing would impress these upon the Israelite of old so well as the language of the Books of Exodus to Deuteronomy; nothing would so well convey the idea of the reality of God's actions in their midst.

All is of Divine origin, all expresses Divine truth; but that truth is necessarily expressed in a somewhat crude form in some parts.

---

[4] For an instance of this see pp. 100, 101; see also pp. 157, 158.

DEVELOPMENT OF THE KNOWLEDGE OF GOD. 97

Indeed there is a profound truth in the term 'Divine Myths' used by an accomplished exegete in reference to some of the earlier parts of Scripture.

Upon the subject of 'progressive revelation' Canon Mozley writes [5] (it need hardly be said, in defence of the letter of Scripture, and without reference to the question as affected by Evolution):—

"It was the peculiarity of the Jewish dispensation that it was both present and prospective in its design; that it worked for a future end, while it provided also for the existing wants of man. . . . Scripture was progressive: it went from lower stage to higher, and as it rose from one stage to another it blotted out the commands of an inferior standard and substituted the commands of a higher standard. This was the nature of the dispensation as being progressive; it was the essential operation of the Divine government as it acted in that period of the world. The dispensation then, as a whole, did not command the extermination of the Canaanites, but a subordinate step did; and this step passed from use and sight as a higher was attained. . . . God allowed, during all those ages, rude men to think of Him as one of themselves, acting with the rudest and dimmest idea of justice. But He condescended at the moment, to prevail and conquer in the end. In entering into and accepting their confused ideas, He grappled with them. Through what a chaos of mistakes did final light arise, and the true idea of justice make its way in the world! And God tolerated the mistakes, and allowed His commands to go forth in that shape, but the condescension was worth the result. It is the result alone which can explain those accommodations; but the result does explain them, and brings them out as successful Divine policy."

The above remarks require one addition, so that the mind may not associate God's name with evil :—The intermediate, half-enlightened, human agent sometimes enacted in God's name what God Himself never could have commanded.

In regard to the exterminating of the Canaanites it may be added, What a faithful picture it presents of the

[5] *Lectures on the Old Testament*, pages 250-253.

H

necessity for giving no quarter to enemies of another kind in the human heart. Such is the economy of Scripture, many of these old passages having been designed for the double purpose of yielding (1) instruction to the Hebrew of old, (2) types and figures, and instruction, too, for to-day.

We have now to notice a striking instance of the Divine policy which dealt so successfully with the heathen darkness of the earliest Hebrews. It throws light on many facts in the history of those times.

Why does Jephthah regard Jehovah in the same light as Chemosh, the god of the Ammonites? Why does Moses sing with the Israelites, "Who is like unto thee, O Jahveh, among the gods?"[6] Here is another and more important question:—*Why, all through the Old Testament, is God spoken of under the name of Jahveh* in the Hebrew writings? For wherever in our Revised Authorized Version the name 'the Lord' is in capitals, it is 'Jahveh' in the Hebrew. (See marginal note to Gen. ii. 4, and paragraph I. in the Appendix between the Old and New Testaments). The answer to all these questions is the same.

When God began to reveal Himself to the Hebrews they had not the remotest idea of His omnipresent, omniscient, or spiritual nature. This conception had to be developed little by little, just as all things in the organic world and mind itself are developed. They had some notions of Beings superior to themselves, which they called gods, just as the surrounding nations had.

It was in the likeness of these gods, and under the name of one of them, that God introduced Himself to the Hebrew people.

---

[6] It does not necessarily follow, however, that one who used this language must have regarded Jehovah in the same light as another god. It might possibly have been used simply in recognition of the fact of surrounding Polytheism.

DEVELOPMENT OF THE KNOWLEDGE OF GOD. 99

This conception of gods, such as it was, was the raw material, which had to be modified, developed, purified, into that conception of God's Being which in the present day we all learn in our childhood from those who educate us. Therefore, in the first instance, God introduces Himself first to the Patriarchs, as god, simply, as a Being of that description, but without identifying Himself with any god in particular; and, later, in Egypt, He introduces Himself as the peculiar god of the Hebrews, ' Jahveh.'

To the Patriarchs He is (not God Almighty as we conceive Him, but) El Shaddai, 'the Powerful.' See Gen. xvii. 1, xxxv. 11, and more particularly Exod. vi. 2, 3, Revised Authorized Version, marginal readings; where we read " And God spake unto Moses, and said unto him, I am Jahveh : and I appeared unto Abraham, unto Isaac, and unto Jacob, as El Shaddai, but by (or as to) *my name Jahveh* I was not made known to them." (See also the answer that Moses was to give to the question of the Israelites, " What is his name ? " in Exod. iii. 13—16.)

There was originally a plural conception in the name Elohim (translated God), of which there are traces here and there in some of the very oldest writings. See, for instance, Gen iii. 5 and Gen. xxxi. 53, where (R. A. Version) the alternative reading 'gods' is given in the margin for 'God,' as if two different gods had been referred to in the preceding words of this latter verse by Laban, the speaker. Later on that plural conception passed away, and when the names Elohim and Jahveh were used, the One God was understood, though it was long ages before He was known to be the only real God, and the conception which was attached to these names took that form.

Thus we have the command in Exod. xx. 3, 4, " Thou shalt have none other gods before (or beside, margin) me. Thou shalt not make unto thee a graven image, nor the likeness of any form that is in heaven above, etc.," which may perhaps signify that the Israelites had been in the habit of making images of Jahveh himself. Certain it is that "after the attempt of Jezebel to introduce the Baalim of Sidon into the northern kingdom, Jahveh was still regarded as the national god, and that the worship carried on at the high places, idolatrous and contrary as it was to the law, was nevertheless performed in His name."[7] This would be about 400 years after the Exodus.

Dr. Goldziher writes respecting the Hebrews of earliest times (*Mythology among the Hebrews*, pp. 246, 247):—

"The Hebrews . . . called every power which they regarded as divine El and Shadday. 'the Powerful;' and as these Powers (which they also called Elôhîm, i.e. 'the Worshipped' or 'the Feared') were seen [in imagination] by them on the dark sky, El was also called Elyôn, 'the Highest.' To the Hebrews these names were not yet exclusively theological. . . . Many synonyms of the terms in question are found among the Phenicians as religious terms, and among the Hebrews (when the words are equally native there) in a completely appellative sense, e.g., Ba'al 'Lord,' Kabbîr 'Great, Powerful.' . . . Besides El, Elôhîm, Elyôn, Shadday, even Ba'al received worship from the Hebrews in Canaan. . . ."

Thus, in the very beginning, God was thought of in the Hebrew mind simply as god, or as the gods, later on as one of their gods identified as 'Jahveh,' in no way different from the others; then as Jahveh, a particular god superior in might to their other gods; then as 'Jahveh,' their own peculiar god and their only one; then as the only real god existing (the gods of the other nations being no gods); and lastly as God as we ourselves conceive of Him.

How admirably the passage quoted above from Exod. vi. 2, 3, embodies this historical fact that the Hebrews first knew God only, and how dimly, as Elohim or El Shaddai, and later on as Jahveh—a fact, be it remembered, which no

---

[7] *Fresh Light from the Ancient Monuments*, by Sayce, p. 77.

Development of the Knowledge of God. 101

Israelite could have known from experience or even from tradition. For the period covered was too long for knowledge by experience, and such facts are not transmitted by tradition. If, however, God had guided their traditions, so that according to one of them this colloquy had taken place as recorded between Him and Moses, we see Divine Action and Divine Wisdom in thus expressing the foregoing truth in the Book in such terms that the people could and would grasp it.

On the other hand, which of us really believes the letter of Exod. vi. 2, 3, and at the same time the letter of Gen. xiv. 22; xxvi. 22; xxviii. 16; xxiv. 27; xxvi. 28, 29?—where the Jahveist writer, when writing passages where God's name comes in, very naturally uses the name Jahveh to which he is accustomed, rather than Elohim which he seldom uses.

We believe that we believe the letter everywhere until we are confronted directly with such cases; then we wisely conclude that "it is all right," knowing that it *must* be so. Unfortunately, however, there are many who conclude that it is all *wrong*. They see such difficulties plainly enough, whose existence no honest mind can deny, whilst they do not see the case in all its bearings, some of which are of vital importance to the forming of a correct judgment. To such the present investigation may, it is hoped, be of some assistance.

One more point here. It is suggested above that parts of the Books of the Law were presented in their present form in order that their truths might be apprehended by the Hebrew of old. But how far is their form of presentation adapted to the mental constitution of the Englishman of to-day? The tenacity to the letter which is manifested, even in cases where Science has swept the letter away, with the abandonment of the *spirit* which Science has not touched, seem to show that the presentation of truths by means of concrete pictures, of which we have so many examples in the beginning of the Old Testament, is wisely adapted to meet the needs of to-day, as well as those of the Hebrew of old times. That is not all. How much is there, of which we think we have a perfect comprehension, of which we have only such an approximate one as is possible in the present constitution of things? However much of God's mind is revealed through grace, how little is known of the nature of His Being. Omnipresence in space is perhaps the best approach that can be made to a true conception of it, but undoubtedly that is only an approximation after all. What is this but ignorance when viewed in the light of a fuller knowledge to come? And yet—ignorant inconsistency—we regard this conception as knowledge and the old anthropomorphic conception as ignorance!

It may be added that a full knowledge of God is by no means necessary to the performance of acts of faith, or to such progress in divine things as we find manifested in the character of David and others. Also that some sections of the nation were always in advance of others; some few individuals perhaps very far in advance of the majority. Therefore before God was known as Jahveh, when He was conceived of as Elohim, there was surely faith in patriarchal times.

Nor do I mean to imply that God never spoke to man by signs, nor communicated definitely with him in those times. If however He communicated with him, not by a physical appearance, but in the way in which He spoke to Philip in Acts viii. 29, by a motion of the intellect or heart, or both; there would be then no language in which to record the fact in literal terms. Here, too, let me once more call attention to the wide difference in respect of language between New Testament times and those early days. In

DEVELOPMENT OF THE KNOWLEDGE OF GOD.

New Testament times abstractions and ideas of spiritual things were developed in the Jewish mind, and there *were words and phrases existing* wherein to express those ideas literally, as we say. In the earliest times, however, such truths could only pass into and out of the mind when associated with, and attached to, ideas of material things. This is the fact that makes *so wide a difference between the letter of the New Testament and that of the early parts of the Old.* So great is the difference that (if actions do speak louder than words) the reader often reads as much of the Divine mind by the perusal of a single verse of the one, as by that of a whole chapter of the other.

Doubtless many readers will object that it is not permissible to depart from the letter of some of the early Old Testament Scriptures in this way, notwithstanding the impossibility, or at least *extreme difficulty*, of maintaining it. To such it may be remarked—in addition to what has been said, and much more that should have been said if the subject were fully treated—that the principle is not a new one, but an extension of one that is adopted where the literal meaning of the text is obviously untenable. Thus Dr. Kinns says in reference to the work of the fourth day in Gen. i. "This does not describe the creation of the Sun and Moon, but their appointment to special offices, etc.," (*Moses and Geology*, 1889, p. 14). Thus Dr. Stoughton, referring to the Biblical account of the Confusion of Tongues, says (*Progress of Divine Revelation*, p. 39), "The only way in which that history comes before us here is in reference to the Divine intervention to scatter the proud builders on account of their presumption. It is described in human language, and according to human forms of thought. *In what other mode could any revelation of God's ways and purposes be revealed?*" And then he adds an argument quoted from Lange, that our most philosophical language would have been no improvement upon the terms which are used, and which suggest such crude conceptions. Thus, (in the same work, p. 78, 79) he explains away the difficulty, before referred to, about the names Elohim and Jehovah in Exod. vi. 2, 3. It is not necessary to cite other cases. In these we see how, when there has been due reason for it, the letter has been consciously rejected. Ofttimes the *letter* counts for nothing; the *spirit* of the passage is everything.

The conceptions of gods entertained by all peoples are more or less coloured with man's own characteristics. Even in the present day the nomadic tribes of Arabia, whom we do not regard as savages, conceive of God as a Powerful Nomad Sheikh—at least much more like that than anything else. The Zeus of the Greeks and the other gods over whom he exercises authority are very like the members of the Greek governments in early times. Naturally, unless better instructed, man must regard his gods as more or less like himself, only superior as regards power, place of residence, etc. The early Hebrews were no exception to this rule. One instance has been given where the idea of a man-like form appears. The anger of God was inevitably conceived of as hot and impulsive like the passion of man. They could conceive of it only in such terms, and it was perhaps well that it was so for the time being. Truer knowledge in this respect is manifested in the Psalms. There, too, the notion of a man-like form has given place to the truer one of a God omnipresent in space (see Psalm cxxxix. 1-12), who knows all about man. There is additional meaning in this beautiful Psalm when one thus finds that its author has learnt from God the truths which he writes, some of them new to man and greater than any of the discoveries of Science.

No real Monotheism has been discovered in any other nation. There is an approach to it in the Grecian theology, where there are a number of subordinate gods with Zeus exercising authority over them. It would seem that this stage is as far as the natural mind can go in the direction of Monotheism. Beyond this stage, except in the Hebrew nation, men found that their gods did not take any active part in the affairs of men, and that their very existence was unproved, having originated in the thoughts of their primitive ancestors.

How markedly contrasted was the case of the Hebrews. *Their Theology stood the test.* They found their Divinity was a real Person, and so their religion took deeper root than ever. They had begun to prove that reality when their ideas of the Divinity were very crude indeed; and the nearer those ideas approached to the truth, the more real did they find their God to be. It is a marvellous sight, this little nation, slowly learning during more than a thousand years the true conception of God, and during that time and four or five hundred years more, a fuller knowledge of Himself; watched over and protected in the midst of powerful neighbours, whose actions were overruled to the furthering of the growth of Truth; and then to see that Truth spreading over and conquering the whole civilized world. To lead that people from darkness into light was the first work the Scriptures had to do. Thus did the growth of Truth and the writing of the Bible proceed side by side, each vitally necessary to the progress of the other.

One other feature of this spiritual training of the Hebrews should be noticed here—the ritual of sacrifice and the priesthood. It is a mistake to suppose that these institutions were *specially designed* and appointed by God for the Israelites. We find institutions more or less like them amongst other nations. We read of burnt offerings in the very ancient 'sacred book' of the distant Hindus, the Vedas. Parallel too with the Hebrew Levites, we find among other ancient peoples special families with the exclusive right of exercising 'sacred' functions. In the Bible we read of priests in Egypt (Gen. xlvii. 22), and that Moses' father-in-law was priest of Midian (Exodus ii. 16), before we hear anything about the Israelites' own ritual being ordained.[8]

Not only so, but just as we find Phenicians or Canaanites having deities similar to those of the earliest Hebrews, so there is strong evidence that they practised the same Sacrificial Ritual, and had similar High Places, sacred groves, etc. The Sacrificial Tablet of Marseilles, of Carthaginian origin, discovered in 1845, and certain existing Carthaginian Sacrificial documents, furnish information respecting the system of priests and sacrifices which prevailed among the Phenicians (since Carthage was a Phenician colony). These are very similar to those described in part of the Book of Leviticus.

But these ceremonies were of the greatest importance. In Hebrew ix., x., we read that Christ is the only true Sacrifice, it being impossible that the blood of bulls and of goats should take away sins; and in Hebrew vii. we read that He is likewise the true Priest.

But what meaning would these all-important truths have had in the eyes of the Jews if their minds had not been prepared for them through the Ritual to which they were accustomed? None whatever. The knowledge of the true

---

[8] So also with portions of the Mosaic Law. Thus Canon Mozley says (*Lectures on the Old Testament*, p. 201) that the case of the Avenger of Blood under the Law of Goel " is an instance of an unwritten law of the East, which was incorporated in the Mosaic dispensation, as the new conditions which were annexed to it, and by which it was partially modified, show."

DEVELOPMENT OF THE KNOWLEDGE OF GOD.

nature of sin, that it could be purged only by the death of a victim—the very essence of the doctrine of the Atonement—could never have been apprehended or understood at all by them, nor by mankind in general who have learnt it through them, but for the ancient Sacrificial Ritual, by means of which, little by little, the perception of such truths was developed.

We now pass on to another phase in the evolution of the knowledge of God—the third to be treated of here, but the first in the order of time. For the benefit of the reader who is unacquainted with the subject, I will begin with stating a few of the facts of Mythology. No pretence is made to an exhaustive treatment of the subject, the object being merely to illustrate in a general way how the conception of gods first arose in the mind of man.

When we were children and looked upwards to the sky we did not know that there was only empty space above us, with Sun and Stars at almost infinite distance, and thin vapours but a few hundreds of yards away. We thought that all was at about an equal distance, and that somewhere far away on every side the sky extended downwards to the ground. In like manner primitive men mixed up together the phenomena of clouds, celestial bodies, and dome of heaven, placing all in the same region—the region that is *above*, the place to which one cannot get.

Therefore, when we were children, we could only look up at the wonderful things above, and make some crude interpretations of our own as to the nature of what we saw.

So too did primitive men.

But what course did our thoughts take? *We noticed that in certain ways the things above were like some of the things around, and we therefore concluded that the things above were of the same sort, or partly so, as the things around.*

This is just what primitive men did; and this, as we shall soon see, was the source of their mythology.

Those white pillared clouds were like hills in outline, white and soft in substance, more like snow than anything else we had ever seen. So we thought they were a sort of white, soft, snowy, hills—delightful places to tumble about in, if one could only get there. In some brilliant sunset scene we saw something like a road—it was the golden highway to Heaven. Other clouds looked more like the common hills on earth. Some of us thought the moon was a man's face; and there are even some still who see the outline of 'the Man in the Moon' with a thorny bush on his back. We saw now and then a cloud in the shape of a sheep, a bird, or some other animal—we thought it was a real one. Or we *began to think so*, till our myth-making was cruelly nipped in the bud by some wise Elder.

But there was no wise Elder near to correct primitive man when he had such thoughts, and so his myth-making developed fully, bearing a rich fruit of fancy.

It was in such scenes as the thunderstorm, especially the violent tropical one, that he was most impressed. Totally ignorant of causes, with a mind weak as a child's, helpless in the scene, no wonder that he was so powerfully impressed by all. Let us try to be 'primitive' for a moment, and take our place beside primitive man. We see the terrible commotion going on above and around us, knowing nothing. The fearful, rolling, roaring noise reminds us of the roaring of a wild beast, because we have never heard the like produced by any other cause. Some dreadful living thing must be above us who makes that fearful noise. And the dashing, furious, pounding storm, what is it? We only know that it also comes down from above, and in its motions it, too, is like something alive; or something hurled down upon us by a powerful living thing up there. The wind too that blows so fiercely, raging so madly, swaying the trees, breaking the branches, tearing up root and all, destroying our huts, threatening to sweep ourselves away—what is it? We can only think of some awful unseen living thing whose all-powerful breath causes the raging blast. But what is the next thing? Two of us suddenly fall dead! The tree under which we stood is split to pieces; and in the same instant a more fearful roar than ever!

What does it all mean? Surely it is a fearful battle that is being waged by those Powers above! It is one of their stray shots that has killed our friends, or they are the victims of their raging passion. Terrified we fall on our faces and pray the Thunderer to be merciful, and the covering Night-god to hide and so protect us.[9]

The reader's own superior knowledge and strength of mind will have been an effectual barrier to his entrance to the scene. But the picture will give some idea of it, and of how the myths arose.

In describing such scenes there was no system : each one spoke of just what he saw, or imagined ; so that the same celestial phenomenon, seen in twenty different lights, gave rise to as many different myths. It was later on that such stories were woven into a system. The lightning was a heavenly bird darting about; or it was fire. The Sun was a fire, for it warmed the earth and the people. And the Fire itself, which cost them such labour to kindle with the boring stick—what was that?

[9] One of the most dramatic and profoundly true pictures in Victor Hugo's *Toilers of the Sea* is that in which the hero, after using his powers of knowledge and skill to the utmost, is suddenly baffled by the strength of the storm—he falls down and prays. For in all ages prayer has been the resource of men who have reached the limit of their human powers. These limits have been extended in each succeeding age as the conquest of nature has become more and more thorough ; but still at the limits of their natural endeavours the men of to-day are true to the instinct of their ancestors, and fall down and pray.

They had seen him come down from above, in the lightning; they saw the Sun-Fire always there in the sky. Therefore Fire must have his home in the sky: he had come down from on high to bless mankind. When the wood did ignite, the flame appeared suddenly, and it often disappeared as suddenly. Its motions altogether were mysterious. They thought it was alive, and called it Agni. He had come down from above, and now he dwelt in the wood. He loved the rubbing, when they worked their fire machine; it tempted him to come forth. But often he required a deal of such coaxing before they could induce him to come out.

But the Sun, what was that? They saw him come up from behind the hills in the morning, and after his day's journey on high he in like manner disappeared at night. Of course he was alive, or he would not move like that. But where did he pass the night? Their friends who lived by the sea could tell, for at sunrise they had actually seen him come up out of the water. Others had seen him go down into the water. It was there that he passed the night; he took a journey under the water. He was the All-seeing One. His rays were locks of golden hair. When he disappeared behind a thick cloud, he was swallowed by the Storm-god, or the Storm-serpent, as in some cases it was conceived to be. Because he came up after the Dawn, he was the son of the Dawn; as the Dawn coming after the Night was brought forth by the Night. (Here probably the idea of producing arose before that of mere sequence.) Or again, as the Day gave place to the Night, it was thought that the two were fighting for the mastery, and that Night was victor and slew the Day.

The tendency of the human mind, when beginning to elaborate its first percepts and concepts, to regard the objects as alive, is shown by the notions of savages to-day, who

DEVELOPMENT OF THE KNOWLEDGE OF GOD. 111

are always in fear of the 'spirits' of their own imagining. The so-called Fetishism is in many cases a worship, not of the inanimate thing which we see, in a stone for instance, but of the 'spirit' of the stone. Not, however, that their idea of a spirit is the same as ours; it is of a less abstract and spiritual nature.

To the reader unacquainted with the subject two objections have very likely occurred :—(1) Where is the evidence that these things are true? (2) Men never invented gods like that in a day.

In reply to the first objection—the striking resemblance of myths found in all parts of the world gives the clue to their origin; the names of the gods, the features of the myths, and other things adding their confirmation. Let us also notice here a passage from the most primitive writings on earth, the Vedas. Max Müller says (*Lectures on the Origin of Religion*, p. 216), " We find in the Veda hymns addressed to Vâya, the Blower, and to Vâta, the blast. . . . Though the Wind is not often praised, he, when he is praised, holds a very high position. He is called the king of the whole world, the first-born, the breath of the gods, the germ of the world, *whose voices we hear, though we can never see him* (Rig-Veda x. 168)." The Vedas abound with these mythical deities.

The second objection is quite correct. The conception of gods was a slow growth. The lofty and inaccessible position occupied by celestial phenomena, and their inscrutable character, would at once tend to make them objects of curiosity, and of a measure of veneration. The activities manifested in them, such as the changes from night to dawn, dawn to sunrise, the sun's course through the sky, motions in other celestial bodies, the specially active changes in the wind and storm—all these could be accounted for only by comparing them with the only other known source of activity—Life. The names they received from men expressed these activities, their high position, their brightness; and the very use of such names would strongly tend to place them together in the mind in a class apart from ordinary things. They would be regarded as the bright ones, or the high ones, and the actions recorded of them, such as already noticed, would ever tend to associate them in the mind more and more with living things. But more especially did this take effect as time went on, and men in succeeding generations became accustomed to phenomena, and perceived their purely physical nature. The old stories still continued to be told, still retaining their character as relating to the Wonderful, the High, the Bright, the Active, the Living Ones. Retaining this character, and being no longer associated with the physical phenomena which gave them birth; what could the later generation think, but that the subjects of these stories were real Living Beings of a superior order—inhabitants of an Upper Region, Invisible, Powerful, Active, Living, doing the same things as men did. There being nothing else but man (and occasionally animals) to supply the form in which they should be conceived of in the human mind, we can see how the conception took the form of what we call gods.[10] It was at a far later date that men, finding no traces of their reality, dared to question the existence of such gods.

Thus, and in other ways [11] which need not here be dis-

[10] If it seem that such was the natural and necessary result, however, we must remember that we judge of what is natural by our own thoughts, which are in a sense the offspring of the thoughts of our predecessors. Thus if an opposite effect had followed, we should regard that as natural for the same reason. We cannot infer that the above result would have followed without a special control and fostering of man's ideas by God.

[11] According to Professor Huxley, "the Fetishism, Ancestor-worship, Hero-worship, and Demonology of primitive savages are all different manners of expression of their belief in ghosts, and

cussed, arose the conception of, and belief in, gods; and long after the original myths were forgotten, these gods remained as objects of belief and worship amongst mankind, as they are to this day among those who have not been taught the truths of Monotheism.

The reader will perceive that in all this there was no devil-worship, nothing of what we call idolatry, nothing necessarily debasing. It was only ignorance and mis-directed reverence. It was not altogether mis-directed either, for it was in the direction of better things, as near an approach to an idea of the true object of reverence as men could then form. We may even say that in such guises they ignorantly worshipped God after a fashion in those early days.

It was at the later stage, when men thought the gods had evil passions like their own, and then set these debased gods as their own examples, that the system became corrupt. In some of the myths there were certain features which gave this tendency, through a natural misinterpretation; but these matters do not here concern us.

Let us note, that in the beginning the myth was not sinful,[12] that the conception of the god was a most important step, an indispensable step, towards the conception and know-

of the anthropomorphic interpretation of out-of-the-way events which is its concomitant." He maintains that one of the most clearly demonstrable articles of the theology of the early Israelites was "the article which is to be found in all primitive theologies; namely, the belief that a man has a soul which continues to exist after death for a longer or shorter time, and may return, as a ghost, with a divine, or at least, demonic character, to influence for good or evil (and usually for evil) the affairs of the living." (*The Evolution of Theology*, Nineteenth Century, March, 1886, pp. 360-362.) Other writers take account of both the myth and spirit-worship, and also of other forms. Probably in some cases spirit-worship has served as a steppingstone to mythology.

[12] Of course we cannot assert that there was no evil in the myth-makers; what we see is that there was nothing essentially wrong in the myth-making itself, and how different it was from a sensual or debasing idolatry.

ledge of the true God; and that therefore this perfectly natural process was undoubtedly made use of by God to prepare man's mind for the revelation of Himself.

As to the necessity for this preparation, the following quotation may help to present the matter in a clearer light than has been done in preceding pages :—[13]

"It is easy to understand that, even if a complete grammar and dictionary had suddenly come down from heaven, they would have been useless to beings that had not themselves elaborated their percepts into concepts, and that had not themselves discovered the relation in which one concept may stand to another. They would have been a foreign language, and who can learn a foreign language, unless he has a language of his own? We may acquire new languages from without: language and what it implies must come from within. The same with religion. Ask a missionary whether he can efficiently preach the mysteries of Christianity to people who have no idea of what religion is. *All he can do is to discover the few germs of religion which exist even among the lowest savages,* though hidden, it may be, beneath deep layers of rubbish; to make them grow afresh by tearing up the weeds that had choked them, and then to wait patiently till the soil in which alone the natural seeds of religion can grow, may become fit again to receive and to nurture the seeds of a higher religion."

It has already been stated that all peoples on the earth have passed through more or less of this myth stage; which, under God's overruling Hand, has resulted in a development of their ideas, a preparation of their minds to receive a knowledge of Himself, when the truth should be carried to them by their fellow-men after it had been fully taught to the Hebrews.

Although in the early history of the Hebrew people we find them, like the nations round about them, believing in

---

[13] *Lectures on the Origin of Religion,* by Max Müller, p. 263.

gods, yet it is evident that in the infancy of the nation they were myth-makers as well as others. Whence it appears that their notions of gods were derived partly from their neighbours and partly through direct development from their own myths. Some of the people appear to have had more advanced notions than their contemporaries.

We find traces of such myths in the ancient Book of Job. It appears from Job's answer to Bildad, in chap. xxvi., that his own ideas of God are somewhat mythological. In verse 8 he refers to the waters in the clouds; and by the sea in verse 12 he probably means the upper waters, which among the early Hebrews were regarded as a sea, and which he calls, in Job ix. 8, "the high places of the sea." And then he says, "By his understanding he smiteth through Rahab ... his hand hath pierced the fleeing serpent." Comparing this with the myth of the sun fighting with the storm-serpent (referred to on page 110), of which serpent Rahabh was originally the name—we find that Job supposed Jahveh to have been the one engaged in this conflict with the serpent in the clouds, and to have overcome him.

Such notions on the part of Job are not only quite consistent with the uprightness and spiritual-mindedness attributed to him, but they are just the sort of twilight knowledge we should expect to find in those early days, when the Hebrews were slowly learning the true nature of God. It is better to take him as we find him than to begin with the foregone conclusion, simply because he is a Bible character, that he must have been possessed of superior knowledge. Not only does much of the language of the book then possess *a meaning*, which otherwise it has not; but, when we see what sort of people the Scriptures had first to teach, we have some idea of the wonderful work they have done, and why their language must sometimes differ in character from our own. If it be thought that Job's words in verse 7 of this chapter prove a knowledge superior to that of his times, we must remember that in the Vedas we have words very like them: "Savitri has fastened the earth with cords, he has established the heaven without a support."[14] Let us also ask ourselves, "For what possible purpose should Job have received any revelation of scientific truth beyond his time?" and we shall see the utter gratuitousness of such a theory. It is merely the result of association of ideas, without examination of what they involve, what they consist of, and what they lead to.

The case is different, however, when we find Jehovah's answer to Job containing similar expressions; and one cannot here so readily affirm mythological notions. Yet it is just in this answer that we have two such non-existent monsters (Behemoth and Leviathan) described, that *no one does believe in the literal meaning* of the passage. Here semi-consciously our minds find a way out of the difficulty, by concluding that God did not mean what He was saying, but only adopted that language for His own reasons. In doing this we do not see that we are no more insisting on the letter than if we had concluded that God for His own reasons had the passage placed in the Bible as it stands. And upon due consideration we see that the latter is the most reasonable conclusion of the two, more especially after all that has been said in foregoing parts of this work.

For it is evident that at that time, as the Hebrews were learning the Almightiness of God, they were seeing it in those physical phenomena, like the whirlwind, in which they believed Him to be personally present. Naturally therefore, and at the same time most beautifully, language corresponding to those ideas is used everywhere. We shall have

---

[14] Max Muller's translation of this extract from the Veda.

occasion to notice in another place that the Hebrews certainly did believe in the existence of those two monsters. Whether, therefore, we believe that God conveyed the *truth* of His power and greatness in mythological language, through the intermediation of a partly-enlightened writer for the benefit of *many* readers of those days, or conveyed it by speaking such mythological language with His own mouth out of the whirlwind for *Job's benefit alone*—in either case we assert that *He adapted His language to the people and the times.*

It need hardly be repeated here that this principle is most important to the subject of the present inquiry, and clears away a host of difficulties. It is the principle before suggested as removing the difficulties as to the date and Mosaic [15] authorship of parts of the Pentateuch, and one that will be applied still more when we are treating of the first eleven chapters of Genesis.

In the foregoing remarks the *poetical* character of the Book of Job is not considered; but this should on no account be overlooked. Many of the phrases may have been used as mere figures of speech; and, as part of the same poem, it was necessary that Jehovah's answer to Job should be in character with the rest of the book.

In the expressions used here and there in the Psalms and elsewhere, there are traces of former myths. Naturally the Psalmist used the current expressions of his day; and some of these originally had mythological significations, which they had lost by the time he used them. It is not necessary here to trace out these.

Having seen then that the Hebrews were myth-makers

---

[15] By 'Mosaic' here I only mean actually written by Moses. Of course, scripturally considered, the Law is all Mosaic, being associated with, and delivered in, his name.

like other nations, we may just notice one other use which God has, perhaps, made of the myth for preparing the mind for truth.

In the storm-myth and certain others, primitive men expressed their belief in certain supernatural beings, who were opposed to each other; and we see that this belief was derived from the apparent antagonism between certain physical phenomena. They considered the actions of such Beings as good or bad according as they appeared to affect the welfare of man. To nomadic people abundance of rain was a blessing, because it produced pasture for their cattle. But to agricultural people these relations were inverted, for the sun ripened their crops. Therefore to the nomad, the Storm-god was good and the Sun-god wicked; and he rejoiced when, at sunset or the overclouding of the sky, the Sun-god was slain by his opponent. But to the agriculturist, the Storm-god, or it may have been the Storm-serpent, was the bad party, and his myth celebrated the *other's* victory.

When the Lord said to the Jews, "Destroy this temple and in three days I will raise it up," no one understood Him, until after His resurrection the disciples remembered that saying (John ii. 19-22). When He spoke to them of their adversary Satan, could they have understood Him, or have had the faintest idea of His meaning, if they had had no previous notions of such a being? Yet if the saying "Forewarned is forearmed" be true, it was important that they, and all Christians, should know something about him. He is mentioned a few times in the later parts of the Old Testament, but seldom, if ever, in its earliest-written books.[16] In Genesis iii., when there is occasion to refer to him, this is achieved by an allegory, which, in the

---

[16] He has an important place in the introductory part of the Book of Job, however.

Development of the Knowledge of God. 119

simple reading of the narrative, conveys no such idea as an evil *spirit*. Where we have in the Revised Authorized Version 'demons,' it appears to refer to the gods of the nations, as in Deut. xxxii. 17. The Book of Chronicles was written later than the Books of Samuel; and accordingly 1 Chron. xxi. 1 mentions Satan (or an adversary) whereas the parallel passage 2 Sam. xxiv. 1 does not. Not until such ideas existed in the Hebrew mind did they perceive that he was the being meant by 'the serpent' of Gen. iii. (See Wisdom ii. 24 and Rev. xx. 2). The development of such conceptions was, doubtless, a much slower and more difficult work than we are apt to suppose, and in the beginning of the process God may have utilized crude ideas such as those described on the preceding page.

Summary of Conclusions of the Chapter.

In order to understand the work which the Scriptures had first to do, we must know the condition of the Hebrews at different periods. Rahab, Jael, and others, show that in their age they were a crude people, who required a long drilling in the Law before they were fit to hear the tidings of grace. The Hebrew thus drilled was fit to learn a little of God's merciful character, and then to write, or to appreciate, the Psalms. Later on the one who had been instructed and softened by the Psalms was fit to learn more of God, and to write such truths as we find in the Prophetical Books. These latter further prepared the Hebrews for the teachings of Christ.

Moses had but imperfect knowledge of God, but was well fitted for his work among such people. There is reason to suppose that portions of the Books of the Law are the expressions of traditionary beliefs, which were so guided by God as to embody important truths, and present them in a form such that the early Hebrew could most readily apprehend them. In the earliest times such truths could enter the mind only when associated with ideas of material things; neither abstract ideas of spiritual things nor the language wherein to express them then existed. Therefore in the beginning of the Old Testament many truths are conveyed by means of narratives; whereas in the New Testament truths are literally expressed. But the former method of reaching the mind is most useful for people in the present day, as well as for the early Hebrews.

But the Hebrews were originally Polytheists, with *no more notion* of the true God than other nations had. The story of Jephthah shows their original darkness very strikingly. They were over 1000 years in learning to worship the only true God, and in giving up polytheism.

God introduced Himself to the early Hebrews under the name, and in the likeness, of one of their gods, Jahveh. Their conception of the god was the raw material which had to be purified and developed into that of the true God. The Hebrews at first only knew God dimly as Elohim, or the Elohim (plural); then as Jahveh; finally as God as He is. But full knowledge of God was by no means necessary to the acquisition of much spiritual truth, or to saintliness of character; so that we find such qualities in Moses and David, and faith in the patriarchs.

All the theological systems of other nations broke down when tested, because they were human; but it was just at that critical point that the Hebrew theology manifested its Divine origin; it stood the crucial test and took deeper root than ever. The ritual of sacrifice and priesthood prepared Hebrew ideas for the True Sacrifice and Priest. For this important work they were essential.

DEVELOPMENT OF THE KNOWLEDGE OF GOD. 121

The original worship of gods was an ignorant form of worship of the true God; it was in part God's own work, achieved by natural means, chiefly through the effects produced upon primitive men by physical phenomena. It was as men grew in sin that this was turned into corrupt idolatry. It was the only channel through which man could acquire acquaintance with the true God. Job had mythological notions. In Jahveh's answer to him we find, whichever way we look at it, that God adjusted His language to the people and the times.

There are, however, two sides to most questions, and from some of the foregoing facts conclusions opposite to the above have sometimes been drawn. The *false logic* of a few of these is illustrated below. But, to prevent misapprehension, let me distinctly state that these conclusions are not given as being an average specimen of the beliefs of sceptics. They represent the logic of *unbelief*, rather than that of unbelievers. They are placed here solely in order to expose the fallacies that underlie them, and to illustrate how inconsistently the mind is apt to run to and fro in such reasonings. Indeed some of them are given in their extreme form, in order the better to show their true nature. In the second column the reader will recognize for himself (1) what has actually been concluded, (2) what should consistently have been concluded, (3) what premisses or conclusions are in direct opposition to previous premisses or conclusions, (4) how some of them are disproved by a practical application, as No. 3 to the Hebrews. Each paragraph in the second column should be carefully compared with the one bearing the same number in the first column; paragraph 2 in the second column should also be connected with paragraph 1 in the same column.

Logic of Faith.	*Logic of Unbelief.*
1. The Bible teaches that once in history certain supernatural events occurred, for special reasons.	1. We have studied the Universe as far as it is accessible to man, and everything proceeds in the natural way. Therefore it could never have been otherwise; not even on a particular occasion.
2. It is clear that without natural laws all would be chaotic confusion. They are necessary to man's very existence, and are wisely appointed. But laws previously unsuspected have been from time to time discovered, and are still being discovered. Man cannot possibly see the ultimate cause of phenomena. Unknown forces may well have been brought into operation on special occasions. Still the general course of God's manifestation of Himself to man was clearly a natural one, obviously because that was the best. The Power in Nature and the God of Religion are the same. Both work in the same manner.	2. Whatever is natural must be of human origin. *i.e.* We cannot believe that Divine power was manifested supernaturally on special occasions, where necessary; but it would have been so manifested throughout the general process of teaching man Religion, where this was unnecessary. Or otherwise, Since some theologians hold that the evidence of divine action consists in supernatural occurrences, which theory we have proved to be false; we will *base our own inference*, in this matter, *on their error*, and so draw this true conclusion:—As there were no supernatural occurrences, there was no divine action. Therefore Religion is of man.

3. God chose out one nation through which to reveal Himself to man. Some religious notions were indispensable to other peoples, before they could possibly receive the knowledge of God when brought to them through the Hebrews.

3. Where there is a high or low religion there is a high or low morality in the people. Therefore men make their own religions, which correspond to their morality. Thus the *original darkness* of the Hebrew produced the *Light* of Christianity; his *immorality* produced its *purity*; his *barbarity* produced its *gentleness*; his belief in *many* gods *similar* to those of other peoples, produced the belief in *one* God *totally different* in Being and in character from all others. And so on.

4. The peculiarity, sole success, efficiency, entire superiority, of this Religion stamp it as Divine. All others failed when tested, because they were of man. But it was just there that this one especially began to make its way.

4. Notwithstanding the fundamental difference between this and all other religions, we conclude that it also is human, and will end like others.

5. It is the Divine element in this Religion that has raised and keeps the civilized world above immorality, and also keeps our social state stable. We are all so imbued with its precepts, that our

5. Since "the tranquillity of society depends so much on the stability of its religious convictions,"[17] Religion has not helped man. But because some of its false representatives have been irreligious,

[17] *History of the Conflict between Religion and Science*, 1887. Preface, page vii.

philosophers who repudiate it *owe much of their own morality to it.*	notoriously in the Romish Church, in estimating what Religion has done for man, we must take into account only what the irreligion of those men has done.[18]
6. Many of those who have made the Bible their guide know, in their own experience, that it leads man to the knowledge of God.	6. Not having sought God in that way, but having *confined our experience to something totally different*, we can form a true judgment of such experiences, and pronounce them imaginary.

Lest this Logic of Unbelief should seem unfair, I would again remind the reader that it is not given as an average specimen of the beliefs of sceptics, but rather of the reasonings of prejudiced unbelief. Let the reader beware of these. When traced to their root they will exhibit some such fallacy as above. One cannot do more here than expose a few of them. They originate largely through the natural tendency of the mind to occupy itself with its familiar concepts, passing over the deeper and greater realities of spirit; whilst the Enemy will leave no stone unturned to misdirect all such reasonings. Before closing the chapter, however, attention may be directed to one other fallacy that may have an effect on some readers.

Having seen how the first religious emotions and ideas arose in close connexion with mythological ignorance, it

---

[18] *History of the Conflict between Religion and Science*, chap. x. and pp. 325, 326. Here and elsewhere Dr. Draper estimates what *Science itself* has done, and what the *Representatives* of Religion have done, for man. If his interesting work had been entitled 'History of the Conflict between Science and the Representatives of Religion,' superficial readers would not be so likely to overlook the results of true Religion itself, whilst occupied with the failings or sins of those who have professed it.

may be argued, notwithstanding what has been said, that that ignorance was the origin of Religion. Not at all. The beginnings of Religion were the *truths* that were present in the mythological ideas; such as the idea of a Superior Power, his position above that of man (though not above in space), the reverence due to him, etc. These *truths* were the work of God's own Hand, *they* were the beginnings of Religion, whilst those ignorant forms which they could then alone assume were erroneous, and have therefore passed away. (It might be added that the Power which primitive men supposed to be *in* the elements was the Power who formed and owned the elements, and so the worship was perhaps nearer the truth in the direction it took, as well as in purity, than the idolatry of after ages was. Professor Sayce remarks about a Babylonian psalm, "in reading it we do indeed feel that even in the darkest ages of ignorance and heathenism God was still moving the hearts of men, 'that they should seek the Lord, if haply they might feel after Him and find Him'"; whilst the different tones of the Babylonian and Hebrew writings show how the latter people had found what the former was dimly seeking.) The Origin of Religion is God Himself, from whom it all flows. It began to flow in those primitive times when the human mind became capable of receiving it, and throughout the progress of divine revelation it continued to flow in ever-increasing waves, till attaining its full depth in Apostolic times. From that same origin it flows to-day.

SUPPLEMENT TO CHAPTER IV.

THE BOOK OF ENOCH.

An unavoidable defect of all works of this description is that the wider their scope the more new difficulties do they introduce to many readers, in the endeavour to remove such for the help of others. This section refutes the arguments against portions of the New Testament which have been based on the Book of Enoch. It has very little connexion with the subject of this work, and is intended only for those readers who are affected by the aforesaid arguments.

We now pass on to one other phase in the evolution of divine knowledge; a most important one.

There are prophecies relating to the Messiah in the Old Testament, and a few references to life beyond the grave. But, not only was the last book of the sacred canon written about 400 years B.C. according to the chronology appended to our Bibles, but those Scriptures also show that the Jews of that day were in a spiritual condition widely different from that of their descendants in New Testament times. They possessed most meagre ideas—practically none—on these important subjects.

But it was different when Christ was on earth. "Art thou He that should come?" "Wilt thou at this time restore again the kingdom to Israel?" He was asked. We read in Jewish history that many false Christs presented themselves after the true One had come, and Gamaliel's speech (Acts v. 36, 37) may signify that some such had appeared before Him. From these facts, from other passages in the New Testament, and also from another source to be named presently, we know that the Jewish mind was full of expectation of the Messiah's coming at the time when He came. We also know that it was much occupied with thoughts of another life and another world. So much had these subjects been discussed, that a sect had risen up who contended that there was no resurrection, or that its existence could not be proved from the Law (Matt. xxii. 23-29).

Clearly these two things were of the utmost importance to the issue of the Lord's coming and teaching. If no one expected Him, no one would have believed on Him when He did come. Still more apparent is this when we remember that the manner of His coming was a disappointment to the Jews. His work was of a nature different from what they expected and desired. He had to turn their hopes from temporal to spiritual and eternal things—a change not at all palatable to the natural man. Few believed on Him during His lifetime, and there was no triumphant manifestation of His resurrection to allure the many, even when His work was done. Would He have had a single follower from first to last, had He come to the Jews of the Old Testament with such teaching? We may almost venture to say that He would not. All the seed would have fallen on stony ground had He offered Himself as the Christ to a people who knew nothing about any Christ; or had He preached the doctrines of Christianity and the hope of a future life to a people whose thoughts were entirely occupied with the present; who had no belief in, and no ideas of, any other life. Indispensable as we have seen all the previous preparations of the human mind to be, before man could acquire a knowledge of God, this preparation was undoubtedly equally indispensable, and yet more deep and full.

There is some reason to believe that one great (perhaps the ultimate) object of the captivities, first of the ten and then of the two tribes, was to sift the nation thoroughly; so that the most spiritually and suitably minded of them (or of their descendants) might be in Palestine afterwards, when the Gospel should come to the nation. Such would be those who had to traverse vast countries under difficulties and to meet further difficulties and trials on their arrival in their native land (see Amos ix. 9, 10). The carnal-minded would not return, but would prefer to stay where they were. These were not the only siftings of the people, as we learn from their history in the period between Old and New Testament times.

The Old Testament Scriptures had done much, the siftings and trials of the captivities and subsequent wars did more; but obviously much still had to be done, and was done, during the 400 years preceding the coming of Christ.

The reader will by this time agree with me, not only that such a work required the power of God to accomplish it, but also that it was necessary, or at least very desirable, that it should be done, not by miracle, but by a natural, gradual, and therefore more heart-pervading, process. We also see that, inasmuch as such truths were in advance of Old Testament teaching, the Old Testament Scriptures were not adequate to the work. How then was it accomplished?

Clearly, writings for the people's perusal were the necessary accompaniments of the spiritual work in the heart. We look down upon the books of the Apocrypha which existed among the Jews at that period, (1) because they are not Scripture, and (2) because we find much in them that does not commend itself. The latter character, however, does not apply to the whole of their contents. Undoubtedly, as they were both written and read by Jews of that period, they were made use of by God—though not Scripture—to further the work in their intellects and hearts. But the books commonly bound together as "the Apocrypha" do not contain very much literature calculated to develop ideas so far in advance of, so different from, those of present things. Something else was needed surely. At any rate, here we come upon something else; and something extraordinary—*the Book of Enoch*.

As this book is not much read by the public, I give the following brief account of it, preparatory to answering the arguments based on it.

It represents itself as being the work of the antediluvian patriarch Enoch, and consists of his visions and prophecies. From the number and character of the allusions to its contents in the New Testament, there can be no doubt that it was known amongst the Jews before the books of the New Testament were written. It seems that it was generally accepted as the genuine work of Enoch and as the Word of God. No reader amongst ourselves could well believe it to be, *as a whole*, either of these—certainly not the work of Enoch; and, although it contains spiritual truth, certainly not a work of the same class as the Scriptures.

Archbishop Laurence, who translated the book from the Ethiopic in 1821, concluded, that it made its appearance amongst the Jews in the first century B.C.; that it was written by a Jew residing at a distance from Palestine, perhaps a member of one of the tribes carried away by Shalmaneser; and that, being thus brought to Palestine from a distant place, its true origin was not discovered by the Jews. The author of the Introduction to the latest edition of this translation (1883), maintains that there is no doubt as to its Hebrew-Chaldee origin, though he says the Archbishop's conclusion as to the writer's place of residence, has been questioned. In any case it must have been written by one well acquainted with Jewish history down to about one or two centuries B.C., and one who was deeply imbued with religious beliefs far in advance of those of Old Testament times. This seems to me a

THE BOOK OF ENOCH. 129

serious objection to the theory that it was composed by an Israelite of the ten tribes. Resurrection life and heavenly glory are depicted in glowing language as the reward of the righteous; and for the wicked, or the wicked angels, there is so much of hell-fire as almost to make one tremble.

The Advent of the Son of Man, the Elect One of the Ancient of Days, is announced much more definitely and emphatically than in the Old Testament Scriptures; while accounts of the actions and dwellings of good and bad angels fill a large portion of the book.

The striking feature, to my mind, is the high moral tone of the work. The Coming One is not represented as an earthly prince coming to deliver the Hebrew people from their national enemies and reign in earthly glory over them. He is the Holy One who is coming to deliver the righteous, to bless and reward them, and to judge the wicked. (In the writer's mind *the righteous* may, however, have been identical with the Hebrew people). Iniquity is reproved on the ground of its essential character, in a manner which, one feels, could not have been assumed by any wicked impostor. Yet intermixed with all this is a vast amount of fabulous description of supernatural visions, and of unscientific astronomy.

Whilst, therefore, it is a complete mistake to regard the writer as an ordinary impostor, the English mind finds it difficult to understand how any man could have produced such a work and presented it as the words of the Patriarch Enoch. But the book does not appear to be all the work of one hand, or if so, it was not delivered complete in its present form. We find three or four chapters recording a vision of Noah, as the speaker, not Enoch. Chapters xviii. verses 13-16 and xxi. 1-4 are evidently duplicate accounts of the same vision, differing slightly. The first half of the 68th chapter appears to be another version of chapters vii. and viii. The end of verse 1 and beginning of verse 2 in chapter xxxvii. appear as the words of a later writer, probably the real writer of the vision. Whence it seems likely that there were several detached compositions in circulation, which were finally united and preserved as one whole. The author of the Introduction suggests that the writer may have "through the accidental synchronism of some prearranged sign, personated Enoch in the conscientious conviction that he was piously fulfilling the will of the Deity." But the following statements made by Professor Huxley upon another subject, Saul's interview with the witch of Endor, seem to throw light on the matter. He says, (*The Evolution of Theology*, Nineteenth Century, March, 1886):—

K

"Saul goes to this woman, who, after being assured of immunity, asks, 'Whom shall I bring up to thee?' whereupon Saul says, 'Bring me up Samuel.' The woman immediately sees an apparition. But to Saul nothing is visible, for he asks, 'What seest thou?' And the woman replies, 'I see Elohim coming up out of the earth.' Still the spectre remains invisible to Saul, for he asks, 'What form is he of?' And she replies, 'An old man cometh up, and he is covered with a robe.' So far, therefore, the wise-woman unquestionably plays the part of a 'medium,' and Saul is dependent upon her version of what happens." (After quoting 1 Sam. xxviii. 14–20, he continues)—
"The statement that Saul 'perceived' that it was Samuel is not to be taken to imply that, even now, Saul actually saw the shade of the prophet, but only that the woman's allusion to the prophetic mantle and to the aged appearance of the spectre convinced him that it was Samuel. . . . . Nor does the dialogue between Saul and Samuel necessarily, or probably, signify that Samuel spoke otherwise than by the voice of the wise-woman— the Septuagint does not hesitate to call her a ventriloquist, implying that it was she who spoke. . . . *It is most probable that, in accordance with the general theory of spiritual influences which obtained among the old Israelites, the spirit of Samuel was conceived to pass into the body of the wise-woman, and to use her vocal organs to speak in his own name*—for I cannot discover that they drew any clear distinction between possession and inspiration."

I quote the above for the sake of the sentence which I have given in italics, without expressing any opinion as to the correctness of Prof. Huxley's application of this 'general theory of spiritual influences' to the case of the witch of Endor. For if this theory of spiritual influences was general among the old Israelites, we can clearly see that the author of the Book of Enoch was no 'impostor,' but believed himself to be the recipient of supernatural communications from the patriarch Enoch, whose spirit had taken possession of him for the time-being. He believed that Enoch was speaking in him and by him. He was therefore only acting in accordance with one of the beliefs and practices of his time; whilst, as the seer of such visions, he must have been of a class very much superior to that of the wizards, or dealers with familiar spirits, of earlier times—of a class totally different from these.

Thus the writer, or writers, must have believed himself or themselves, to be inspired; and, as before remarked, the Jews read the work with the same conviction.

It is, however, an utter mistake to suppose that any man *invented* all the contents of the work, as the said author of the Introduction, although an Evolutionist, seems to imply; for no man conceives a world of new ideas in that way. He can only re-arrange, modify, and develop, the notions he has received from his predecessors: he may add something to them; but, in the evolution of such ideas as these, he can only do this when he has pre-existing materials.

And, accordingly, in this case the passage in Genesis vi. about the 'sons of God' is present, but much enlarged upon; there is the Coming of the Messiah, many times referred to in the Old Testament (and in 2 Esdras); the language of Joel ii. 1, 2, 30, 31, of Malachi iv. 1, as to the great and terrible day of the Lord, is enlarged upon and added to; the new heavens and new earth of Isaiah lxv. 17, and the imagery of Daniel are there; and the resurrection life of Daniel xii. 2, 2 Esdras vii. 32, 43, xiv. 35, etc. (But as to the actual date of the latter I cannot speak with certainty, since verses 28, 29 of chapter vii. are doubtless a later interpolation).

There is nothing about the Atonement; no consciousness manifested of any need of it. But the Coming of the Elect One; the judgment of the wicked, and future blessings of the righteous; the descriptions of good and bad angels and their habitations; the spirits of the righteous dead separated from those of the wicked dead, and regarded as in some sense now living; the resurrection life on earth or in heaven—are all so amply enlarged upon as (combined too with the composite character of the book) to convince me that these subjects were somewhat familiar to the Jews of that period.

At the same time no one can reasonably doubt that the Book of Enoch, although not (as a whole at least) sacred writ, was much used by God to deepen these sentiments in Jewish minds before the Coming of Christ. In the present day we often know of cases where the preaching of hell-fire, although not a truly scriptural kind of preaching, is used to awaken sinners and prepare them for a reception of the Gospel. In the same manner, doubtless, was this work made use of by God to prepare the Jews for the Coming of Christ, and for the preaching of Christ and His apostles. God uses whatever agency He chooses, when He works.

This is not all; the book undoubtedly contains Scriptural truths, although closely mixed up with wrong ideas and accounts of fabulous visions; out of which compound mass these truths were separated, and incorporated with the New Testament Scriptures, in a later day.

Thus, as a well-known instance, and the most striking one there is, the writer of Jude 14, 15, sharing with his contemporaries the belief that Enoch was the author, introduces the subject of the Lord's Second Coming in words almost identical with those of chapters ii. and xxvi. 2 of the Book of Enoch, from which no one can doubt he was quoting. Here of course it is unimportant whether or not such a *man* as Enoch ever spoke the words in question. The important thing is what God has to say to the reader in that passage. Doubtless it is there for a purpose. And when we notice the words "the *seventh* from Adam" applied to Enoch, and connect them with his pleasing God and his translation, there seems a connexion in a characteristic sense. The latter usage is common in Scripture. Thus the description of Melchisedech in Heb. vii. 3, contains features which are not stated about him in Gen. xiv. 18-20, but are characteristic of the manner in which he there makes his appearance. A holy character is essentially a testimony against and judgment of sin, and perhaps also a prophecy of its consequences.[1] So the one who "walks with God" judges the one who "speaks hard things against Him." Nor must we forget that the manner in which the truth of the Lord's coming is introduced in that passage, was probably well suited to the people whom the writer was addressing; who believed, as he himself did, that the patriarch had written the book which bore his name. Similarly, it may be recognized that the language of the Old Testament, which sometimes offends the refined mind, was suited to an unrefined people.

Mr. J. N. Darby has remarked (*Synopsis*, p. 19) that "Enoch—who has his portion in heaven, and who bears witness to the world of the coming of Jesus—and Noah, on the other hand, warned for himself, preaching righteousness and judgment, and passing through the judgments to begin a new world—are figures of the Church and the Jews in connection with Christ's coming." As we shall see, more fully, further on, the *important thing* in the case of many of these early Old Testament characters, is not the man himself, but the spirit manifested in his character, or the figure or type which he presents. Doubtless this is the case with Enoch; and we here find that the character which he presents in the Old Testament is completed by this trait of prophesying of the Lord's coming, which is given in the Epistle of Jude.

Further on in the present work we shall notice a good many instances in which the simplicity of the writer of Scripture has clearly been made use of by God, so that in writing what he himself believed to be ordinary historical fact, he expressed historical spiritual fact, or other spiritual truth. Since there are these cases in the beginning of the Old Testament, it is not surprising that we find one such case in the New. This is, no doubt, the explanation of this quotation by the writer of Jude.

---

[1] "The testimony of Jesus is the spirit of prophecy" (Rev. xix. 10).

In other instances we find the language of the Book of Enoch used in the New Testament as the common expressions and beliefs of the day. But some of these expressions may not have been originally obtained from the Book of Enoch; they were perhaps current expressions before the book was written, and thus naturally adopted by its writer or writers; or the passages which contain them may have been placed amongst the other parts of the work when the whole was completed in its present form, long after the original book was written—a sort of thing which seems to have occurred in those days.

Its whole contents, original and derived, seem to present the notions of Eschatology and the unseen world which prevailed amongst the Jews when these subjects were first taking a large hold on their mind. They are somewhat crude notions. One labours in vain to unite the different passages which seem to treat of the same subject, so as to find a system. The fallen angels seem to be of a semi-material nature, for they marry women, beget children, and are cast into a chasm in the desert and covered up with stones. Resurrection life sometimes seems to be on earth and sometimes in heaven. Sometimes the raised saints seem to have material bodies; sometimes they are spirits; and whether they are to dwell together with the righteous of a later day on earth (xxxix. 1), or to have a place apart, it is difficult to gather by making all passages agree. Satan is not the leader of the fallen angels, but Azazyel or Samyaza is. Where the name Satan occurs, it does not at all convey the notion of the One Great Enemy and the god of this world, as he is revealed in Scripture. There is no being corresponding to him in the book. But one feature is unmistakable—the old-world notion of the structure of the Universe. It is in a material heaven where we see the clouds and stars above us, that God and the angels dwell, so that when the latter descend to earth they alight on a mountain. The luminaries are closely related to angels; sometimes they are identical with them; but generally they are rather regarded as controlled by them. In that region God, the good and bad angels, the stars, the clouds, and sometimes the saints, are all mixed up together, i.e. all represented as existing there.

Out of this chaos of ideas truer ones were gradually evolved, under divine guidance, on those points where better knowledge was necessary for Christian welfare, and for the writing of certain portions of the eschatological and prophetic parts of the New Testament. The Book of Enoch served to introduce some, and further the growth of others, of such ideas in the Jewish mind, thus preparing the way for something better. Then its work was done, and it gradually fell out of use.

We may notice here one or two instances which illustrate

the fact already stated, that the Book of Enoch introduced to the Jewish mind only approximations to certain truths; after which, through Christ's teaching and through revelation, the truths themselves were made known.

The Book of Enoch knows nothing whatever about that essential doctrine of Christianity—the Atonement; nor about a first and second Coming of Christ. It only teaches that such an One is coming, and that He is coming to deliver the righteous and judge the wicked. The Jewish mind being, through this and the Old Testament prophecies, led to expect Christ, He comes in due time, reveals that He is coming twice, in the first case to die for man's redemption, and in the second case to judge.

In Enoch x. Azazyel is to be bound hand and foot, blinded, cast into an opening in the desert, and covered with stones; there to remain for ever, and in the day of judgment to be cast into the fire. Samyaza and the other angels are to have all their sons slain, then to be bound for seventy generations underneath the earth until the day of judgment, then to be taken away into the lowest depths of the fire in torments, and in confinement to be shut up for ever. How different is Rev. xx., where it is "the dragon, the old serpent, which is the Devil, and Satan," who is to be bound and cast into the abyss, that he should deceive the nations no more during the thousand years; then to be loosed for a little time, once more to deceive the nations; and finally to be cast into the lake of fire and brimstone and tormented day and night for ever and ever.

In Enoch lxvi. we find the doctrine of Purgatory, which has no place in the New Testament.

In the New Testament the language used on the subject of Eschatology is necessarily figurative, as it also is in all the prophetic parts of the Book of Revelation. When we see the extreme difficulty of conveying adequate ideas on such matters, we are impressed with the *absolute necessity* for some such literature as the Book of Enoch; the mind must be familiar with such subjects before those Scriptures which treat of them *could* be written in a suitable form. It may be added that, whereas future punishment is brought before the sinner as a solemn warning in the Bible, such is not the course Scripture usually takes for reaching the heart of man. It addresses his conscience, whilst it presents the Gospel as the greatest of blessings, for his acceptance.

Had the One who came from God, to do the will *and work of God*, and who required such a forerunner as John the Baptist, had no harbinger of another kind, He would not have found the 'fields white already to harvest.' After tracing, as we have briefly done, the work of God in man's heart from the very beginning, we are not at all surprised to find—but should rather be surprised if it was not so—that He had duly prepared the way for the crowning revelation of His Son, and the gift of the Holy Spirit. We may, indeed, be surprised that He should have used, amongst others, such an instrument as this Book of Enoch. But He who, seeing the end from the beginning, so overruled the action of 'natural selection' and other agencies as to produce results so marvellous in the Evolution of Life—and who even makes use of the Evil One to work out His purposes—was doubtless well acquainted with the intricacies and peculiarities of the Semitic mind, and knew how to deal with it. So indeed, in the education and sanctification of His people in the present day: He often brings them through strange trials and experiences, brought about by many different and unexpected agencies.

But on one point the foregoing observations are not, perhaps, sufficiently explicit. The author of the Introduction to the Book of Enoch argues that "if the author was not an inspired prophet, who predicted the teaching of Christianity, he was a visionary enthusiast whose illusions were accepted by Evangelists and Apostles as revelation—alternative conclusions which involve the Divine or human origin of Christianity."[2]

The answer is very simple. The boundary-line between that which is of God and that which is not, corresponds neither with the line which divides books from each other,[3] nor with the line which divides men from each other. It may, indeed, correspond in places with these rough divisions, but in others it cuts through both books and men. Therefore not only are some parts of the Book of Enoch God's work, but part of the mind of its writer was of God too.

We often err in supposing that those divisions which present themselves to our senses are fundamental divisions. Even whilst doing this we sometimes indirectly and semi-consciously perceive where the true dividing line is. Instead of trying to prove this principle, and then apply it to the case before us, it will be better to take an example. I find one close at hand.

I have stated that the author of the Book of Enoch must have believed himself to be 'inspired,' that he wrote largely

---

[2] Introduction to the Book of Enoch, p. 42.
[3] Perhaps it should be said this does not relate to the difference between the Bible and other books. In what manner the Bible is God's work, and what is the Word of God, are questions dealt with elsewhere in this work.

of fabulous visions and unscientific astronomy, and yet that he wrote in a high moral tone—I think I may add here, in an unimpeachable spirit generally, though not everywhere. I do not suppose that the reader questioned those statements, but even if he did, they illustrate this matter. For if we ask, Was that high moral tone, was the spirit thus manifested, of God, or of man? there is only one answer, for it *could* only be of God.[4] Yet the mental peculiarities with which they so closely co-existed were of man!

We need not, therefore, inquire how some of the writings of this 'visionary enthusiast' could have been of God, or how the Spirit of God could have pervaded a man of such mental peculiarities, since we have just stated that in one respect *it was so*. However fine and untraceable such dividing lines may appear to our eyes, they are most real; *they are fundamental.*

Just in as far, therefore, as this writer was pervaded by the Spirit of God, was his work of God; no more, and no less.

God uses what instruments He chooses, to what extent He chooses, and in what way He chooses.

Concerning the Book of Enoch we conclude then:—

(1) That it was an important harbinger of Christ Himself.

(2) That it was a most useful agent in leading Jewish thought from the present life to the unseen world, and the subject of Eschatology; whilst it also developed their pre-existing conceptions and introduced new ones, forming a crude structure of ideas ready to be moulded into truer ones by the Holy Spirit.

(3) That together with the intellectual peculiarities of the writer, such a spirit is manifested as could only be of God: that his visions were sometimes overruled by God to take the direction of truth, so that they sometimes express an adumbration to certain truths, or even a closer approach.

(4) That when the Books of the New Testament were being written, that which was of God, and also was intended to be taught to people of subsequent times, was placed in the New Testament Scriptures. In the latter there are seldom complete extracts; but there is considerable alteration, as if the essential part were taken out and put in its proper place and connexion.[5]

---

[4] If the foregoing account has not conveyed the impression that the author of the Book of Enoch wrote in a spirit such as could only be of God, it was intended to do so.

[5] Perhaps the reader will compare this with the remarks on pp. 74, 75, as to the course of production of parts of the Bible.

THE BOOK OF ENOCH. 137

The Book of Enoch then presents no difficulty when the facts are understood. It is also a strong confirmation of the principles maintained in this work—that God habitually worked in those days as now, by natural means and not by miracle; that He therefore revealed truth to the writers of Scripture only as their minds became prepared to receive it, whilst they naturally embodied it in their writings only as their readers were ready for it, and in the language to which they were accustomed; and that thus the growth of truth in the mind of the people proceeded *pari passu* with the writing of the Scriptures, in a beautiful and orderly manner.

But it strikes the death-blow to the theory of *wholesale miraculous* inspiration.

It has already been remarked that some sections of the Hebrew people were further advanced in truth than others. It appears too from Dr. Edersheim's *Sketches of Jewish Social Life*, that even in the time of Christ there was much difference between the several sections of the people in regard to their religious tenets and in some other respects. Of course there could not be such an interchange of thought amongst them as amongst ourselves, where books are so abundant. It seems extremely probable from these and other facts, that in the evolution of the knowledge of divine truth amongst the Hebrews, certain sections of the people made progress in some branches of truth, and others in others, for a long time before such truths became common to all. Doubtless the scattered state of the Hebrews during the latter part of their history furthered this condition of things.

A parallel may be noticed here. Before the beginning of revelation, the human mind was being led in the direction of truth, as already stated, and as will be more apparent further on. In like manner the Jewish mind had been led near to the divine truths of the Apocalypse, before these were delivered to the early Christians. It may still seem doubtful to the reader that God would use such a man as the writer of the Book of Enoch. But when we realize that God habitually *uses what is at hand* to carry out His purposes, whilst this writer was merely acting in acccordance with one of the beliefs and practices of his time, that God should use a spiritually-minded man possessing peculiarities presents no difficulty. If the writer had been a *wicked* man the case would be different.

We have seen, moreover, that much of the Book of Enoch consists of fabulous stories about angels, false astronomy, etc.; from which some have inferred that no *other* parts of the book should have a place in the Bible, as expressing Divine truth. But the argument is, in reality, in the opposite direction. For there can be little doubt that the whole book was accepted by the Jews as of Divine origin; and therefore the fact that none of this fable or false astronomy was transferred to the Bible, though the other extracts were so transferred, is *most significant*.

CHAPTER V.

INSPIRATION AND THE GENERAL STRUCTURE OF THE BIBLE.

WE have not yet examined the question, What Scriptural authority have we for the assertion, that the writers of Scripture were habitually endowed with knowledge in a manner involving the setting aside of the laws of Nature? and particularly for the extreme view, that this occurred not only in cases where we might suppose it to have been helpful, but even where (for reasons given in this work,) it would have been useless and injurious to the work of God? It was thought well to defer that inquiry to this place, because foregoing facts facilitate its discussion, and put us in a better position for arriving at the truth of the matter.

Let us notice a few texts that seem to bear upon the question. The Apostle Peter writes (2 Pet. i. 21), "no prophecy ever came by the will of man; but men spake from God, being moved by the Holy Ghost." Also in his speech (Acts ii. 30, 31) he says of David that "he foreseeing spake of the resurrection of the Christ," etc. But both these passages refer to *prophecies*, and are not general statements relating to writers of Scripture. So with 1 Peter i. 10-12.

The Apostle Paul writes (Gal. i. 12) that he received the knowledge of the Gospel not from man, but "through revelation of Jesus Christ," and (Eph. iii. 3) "by revelation was made known unto me the mystery," etc., which latter revelation he probably received on the occasion referred to in 2 Cor. xii. 1-8.   Here, in the first place, we have clearly something *special and unusual*. He has a special call from God at the beginning of his Christian career, on account of the important position he has to fill. In like manner certain divine truths are revealed to him—and what a fitting subject he was for such an honour—in a case where we may say it was quite necessary, or at any rate altogether suitable, for the communication of those truths to the Church. But that is not all; for there is every reason to believe his own mind was fully prepared beforehand for comprehending those truths, so that through enlightenment of the Spirit he could receive them naturally and without miracle.   He says also (2 Cor. xii. 2, 3) that he did not know whether he was in the body or out of the body. There is no occasion therefore to affirm, even in this special case, any miraculous transportation of his body. If he was 'in the Spirit' in the same manner as the Apostle John in Rev. i. 10, iv. 2, there seems little reason to suppose there was miracle in his case, more than in the Apostle John's. The same applies to the visions of prophets. In all these cases such wonderful communications from God seem to be quite possible without any miracle in that sense of the word in which I always here use it,—without any setting aside of the law that all perceptions imply some mental preparation, some ideas of a congruent character. In any case these are special exceptions, which do not at all apply to the general course of things.

But what have we in 2 Tim. iii. 16? "Every Scripture inspired of God also profitable for teaching," etc. This is a general statement at any rate. But what does it say? We may—if we have been accustomed to read it so—see in it the proposition at the head of Chapter II. of this work, and perhaps even the additional assertion that the writers of Scripture were miraculously 'inspired.' But it cannot be said to contain either of these assertions—the second would be a quite gratuitous attachment to it; the first we saw upon analysis to be in reality, not a true proposition, but a pseudo-proposition. We might perhaps say that it expresses the truth dwelt on at length on page 43, namely, the connexion between the written word and the real Word, which is God; or the important truth that God is the author of every Scripture, having produced such for teaching, etc. These things satisfy completely the terms of the passage. But let it be specially noted that it says *nothing* as to the manner in which the writers of Scripture were enabled to perform their task; which is all that concerns us in this inquiry.

Are we to infer miraculous inspiration, or unlimited revelation, in the case of writers of the New Testament, because they sometimes, when referring to Old Testament passages, say things which we ourselves cannot find in those Old Testament passages? When, for instance, the Apostle Paul states that Enoch, before his translation, "had witness borne to him that he had been well-pleasing to God" (Heb. xi. 5), is it implied that he knew this by revelation? No, for in the Septuagint Version, which was in use in the Apostle's days, we read "Enoch was well-pleasing to God" (Gen. v. 24). The mention of the names Jannes and Jambres is another case. Comparing the passage (2 Tim. iii 6-8) with Num. xxv., we find that the man Zimri agrees in character with these two men; and on referring to the Septuagint Num. xxv. 6, 14, we find that, instead of one man Zimri, it speaks of two men—a man and his brother— one of whom was named Zambri, the other name not being given. It seems most likely, therefore, that that was the event referred to in 2 Tim. iii. 6-8, and that Zambri and Jambres are two forms of the same name.

Similarly with other cases : they are simply references. Scripture does not teach that there was any such *useless* revelation to the Apostles.

Whilst, however, we do not find, as we have no right to expect, that miracles were largely performed on behalf of the writers of Scripture, what do we find ? That Moses was learned in all the wisdom of the Egyptians, and Paul was " brought up at the feet of Gamaliel, instructed according to the strict manner of the law "—both men chosen by God, well fitted by natural means for the work which they had to do. Because some of the Apostles were fishermen we have inferred that they were poor and ignorant. But it was the custom of well-to-do Jews to have their children brought up to useful trades, so that even Paul is said to have been a tent-maker (Acts xviii. 3). The Apostles John and James were the sons of a fisherman who owned a ship and had hired servants. The writer of the Gospel of Luke and (as supposed) of the Acts was a physician, and naturally well fitted, one would think, for his work of writing those two books. Other cases might be cited, where such writers of Scripture were chosen by God as were naturally qualified for their work.

It was stated in a former place that, in cases where such natural qualification of the writer of Scripture was not complete, owing to the times in which he lived, God used a substitute for it. We may here notice a few instances which illustrate this fact, which we shall find of great importance in treating of Gen. i. to xi. I refer to cases where there is a scriptural signification in passages which appear at first sight to be merely historical, and where it is obvious the writer of the passage had only the historical facts before his own mind.

Did the writer of the narrative of Abraham offering up Isaac, see what an affecting typical picture he was drawing of the One who delivered up His only begotten Son (but who was not, like Abraham, released at the last moment), and of the Son who was made the Victim? There is no reason to suppose he had any such light.

Careful searchers into the treasures of Old Testament Scriptures have found in Elijah and Elisha representatives of law and grace, as manifested in some of their characteristics.

In the killing of the lamb in Exod. xii. 21--24, and the striking of the blood upon the doorposts, what a beautiful figure we have of the sacrifice of Christ, and the safety of the believer who has in like manner trusted in His blood and in the Word of God that declares it to be all-sufficient.

Safety in the Ark of Gen. vi. to viii. from surrounding judgment prefigures safety in Christ. In the narrative of Numbers xxi. 9, where the serpent-bitten man looks and is cured, are prefigured the lifting-up of the Son of man, and the look of faith that saves (John iii. 14, 15).

In none of these cases, nor in many similar ones that might be given, is there the least reason to attribute to the writers *any idea* of the special significance of what they were writing. Here we trace the Hand of God, who so directed the action of the human writer, unknown to him, as to express His own Mind in those passages.

This is further supported by 1 Cor. ix. 9, 10, "it is written in the law of Moses, Thou shalt not muzzle the ox when he treadeth out the corn. Is it for the oxen that God careth, or saith he it altogether for our sake? Yea, for our sake it was written; because he that ploweth ought to plow in hope, and he that thresheth, to thresh in hope of partaking." Here it appears that the author of Deut.

xxv. 4, did not at all understand the significance which *God* attached to his words.

Nor is it only in historical parts of the Bible and in the Law that we discover this unseen process. We even find it in prophetical parts, where in some cases the writers did not intend their words to be prophetic. In John xix. 36 we read " these things came to pass, that the Scripture might be fulfilled, A bone of him shall not be broken." Where is that Scripture? We find in Exod. xii. 46, a command relating to the Passover, " neither shall ye break a bone thereof," with its parallel passage Num. ix. 12. There is also Ps. xxxiv. 19, 20 :—" Many are the afflictions of the righteous : but Jehovah delivereth him out of them all. He keepeth all his bones; not one of them is broken." One of these passages is doubtless the prophecy referred to ; and in neither of them is there anything to show that its writer had his thoughts fixed on Christ, or that he intended his words as a prophecy.

Several parallel cases may be found by comparing John xix. 24 with Ps. xxii. 18; John xix. 37 with Ps. xxii. 16 and Zech. xii. 10 ; Matt. ii. 23 with Amos ii. 11 and Judg. xiii. 5 ; Matt. ii. 17, 18 with Jer. xxxi. 15—17 ; Matt. xiii. 35 with Ps. lxxviii. 1, 2. Also in Matt. ii. 15 the prophetic words " Out of Egypt did I call my son," relating to Christ's return from Egypt, are taken from Hosea xi. 1, " When Israel was a child, then I loved him, and called my son out of Egypt." In all these cases there is much reason to believe that the writers did not consciously prophesy of the things named in the New Testament passages, but that when they wrote, their words were so overruled and directed by omniscient God as to express these prophecies.

Again in Matt. xii. 39, 40, we read " there shall no sign be given to it but the sign of Jonah the prophet; for as Jonah was three days and three nights in the belly of the whale;

INSPIRATION & THE STRUCTURE OF THE BIBLE. 145

so shall the Son of man be three days and three nights in the heart of the earth." Here we find the whole narrative of Jonah and the whale to be a prophecy, of which fact there is not the least reason to suppose the writer was aware. (It is, however, true that in the parallel case, Acts ii. 30, 31, before cited, the apostle Peter believed David to have foreseen the resurrection of Christ.)

We read also in John xi. 51, 52, that Caiaphas uttered a prophecy "not of himself, but being high priest that year " His words (John xi. 50) do not read like any such prophecy as verses 51, 52 give ; and he seems to have thus prophesied both involuntarily and unconsciously. This last instance seems to give an insight into God's own ways and thoughts ; and when we have realized that the men whom God used for the production of the Bible were not immaculate or inspired to an unlimited extent, it appears that such may have been His way of producing prophetic writings to a greater extent than is here affirmed. God may use 'exceeding greatness of revelations' and the miracle, for special purposes now and then ; but a work is *just as much of God* —and how much more like His work in Nature—when it takes the gradual, quiet, and more effectual course. Nor does it matter in the least how much, or how little, God enlightened His human agents who wrote the Bible. The only important fact for its reader to-day is that He *was* its author, from Gen. i. to Rev. xxii.

The reader may, perhaps, think it a mistake to insist, as has been done in this work, on the imperfect condition of the human writers of Scripture, although their very excellence consisted, in the first instance, in their likeness to the people for whom they wrote. I should quite agree with him if this work was intended for those who know little or nothing about the difficulties that form its subject. It is unquestionably better that they, missing enlightenment on matters

L

relatively unimportant, can read their Bibles believing in the letter (or what appears to them to be the letter) everywhere. But the case is totally different for those who know the serious nature of those difficulties. For it is this common belief, that the divine origin of the Bible and the perfect knowledge of its human writers, must stand or fall together, that has so fatal an effect in the present day. It is therefore of vital importance to remove this error on which so many mistakes are built up ; and to build on what we have here seen to be the only true and sure foundation.

This imperfect knowledge of the human writer must inevitably show itself more or less in such a work as the Bible, in the same manner that his Oriental peculiarities must show themselves.

It has been shown that there is no such thing as expressing truths in language outside of mind, because the ideas are the realities, which language only serves to convey, and language does not exist until the mind makes and uses it. Truths must be conceived in the writer's *mind* before they can be transmitted through his writings, and this process must be repeated in the case of every writer through whom these truths are transmitted to posterity, unless he simply transcribes a well-known language. We have seen, too, that in the evolution of such knowledge as we have in Scripture, the people of early times can perceive only an approximation to many of the truths, and therefore their writings can directly express only such an approximation. In the course of ages, as these approximate perceptions approach nearer and nearer to the reality, the language used also expresses those clearer thoughts. Let us take an instance. A Hebrew of early times has vaguely apprehended that God is angry with the nation for their sins. Not only does he represent his God as in human form, but he can think of His

INSPIRATION & THE STRUCTURE OF THE BIBLE. 147

anger only as hot, impulsive, unreasoning, as his own passions are. It is impossible to read Exod. xxxii. 7–14 without perceiving a difference between the character of Jahveh as depicted there and that of the God of the New Testament. So also the author of the Book of Judges relates that "the anger of Jahveh was hot against Israel" (or "kindled against Israel" R. A. V.). A truth is expressed, but crudely ; it could not be expressed otherwise till more enlightened times. As an instance of another kind, we may take the Flood. We know that a universal flood of water is not the exact signification of that Scripture, for such never occurred. Later on we shall see reason to conclude that that truth is of a nature such that the early Hebrew could not represent it to himself in thought. But a universal destruction of men by a flood of water is an approximation to it such as he could conceive of. Here we have an instance of the guiding hand of God, working with the human ignorance displayed in the details of the narrative. The approximation to the divine truth which God wished to have expressed in that passage could *then* be presented in writing only through the medium of human ignorance, which alone could produce such a story. In the first of these two cases any possibility of a misapprehension to-day of the character of God is prevented by the light of later Scriptures, which confirm the truth of the passage and cancel its concomitant inaccuracy. In the second case both the scriptural truth and the accompanying scientific error remain, for at the time the Bible was completed men were still ignorant of geology, and Scripture does not teach science. Here science will not upset Scripture, but aid it, or should do so if the question is properly approached, by enabling us to approach nearer to the scriptural truth of the passage than our predecessors could do.

Most of the truths expressed in the Bible are of a nature

such that a writer could not express them without presenting a large proportion of his usual thoughts; more than he would present in expressing facts of common knowledge. For divine truths are almost entirely *truths of mind.* They can be conceived by the writer only in terms furnished by, and composed of, his own thoughts, with which they are thus *most closely associated.* Therefore he can express the truth only by expressing those very thoughts. Therefore if those thoughts are Oriental, otherwise peculiar, or ignorant, the Orientalism, other peculiarity, or ignorance, must inevitably be expressed in the very act of conveying the divine truth. The ignorance need not appear in every case, but in some cases, because there is so wide a range of truths expressed in the Bible.

In foregoing pages we have noticed many facts which justify the language and structure of the Bible. To my mind, the above important fact furnishes the final vindication of the Bible.

We observe an Orientalism, and say, "Of course that is expressed in the writer's words." It is equally "of course" that his so-called ignorance does. The one is not, essentially, more derogatory to Scripture than the other is, but we are so ignorant ourselves that we are very slow to perceive this.

I have before remarked upon the *relative* character of ignorance. The reader will excuse my doing so again here, and more fully. The diagram on the next page illustrates the matter. The lines *a, b, c, d, e, f,* represent the upward progress of man. No distinction is made here between religious and scientific or other progress, nor are the lines meant to be in exact proportion to the reality. If we take our standpoint at *f,* making *f* the standard to judge by, all predecessors *a, b, c, d, e,* are ignorant; but *e* is less so than the others before it, and so with *d, c,* and *b.* If we stand at *b, c, d,* or *e,* we can only see that our predecessors are shorter than (in-

Inspiration & the Structure of the Bible. 149

ferior to) ourselves; we cannot see our longer (superior) successors, for they are not yet come into existence. Therefore neither of these positions furnishes a true view of the matter. The proper standpoint is O. As we look at *a* we must cover up all the other lines *b*, *c*, etc., for *they do not exist* at this time. Then, truly, *a* is a marvel. So, when we come to it, is *b*. *c* is a still greater marvel, and so on to the end.[1]

Thus, it is the short-sightedness and self-complacency of *e* that makes it regard *d* and the other shorter lines as ignorant or low. The ignorance is not an absolute quality, but only a relative one. The ignorance is applicable to *e* just as well as to *d*, only in a less degree. It is merely the act of looking down that produces the idea of ignorance (as derogatory) on the part of predecessors.

From the proper standpoint O, *each is wise, and wonderful.*

Of course we cannot "step out of the rank and take a look at our-

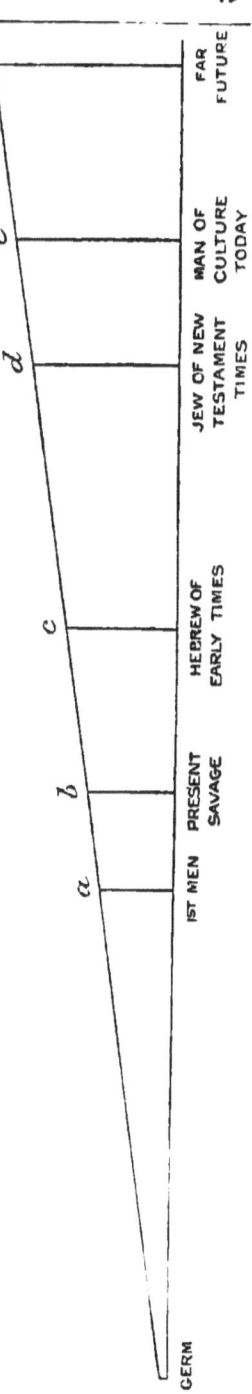

---

[1] Perhaps it should have been said that the height at O forms the true standard whereby to judge the other lines; since, if the eye were actually placed at the angle, all the lines would appear the same length.

selves" after the manner of the Irishman's suggestion. We cannot see with the first man's eyes, or make a true comparison of the Amœba with the Man; but we, at least, possess the representative faculty in a sufficient degree to get many of our natural false impressions removed by such reflections. And, in some measure, we are certainly enabled to approach to a true view of the facts.

However important the above fact, we should remember that it does not at all affect the truths of God, but only the biblical literature which merely serves to convey them to our minds.

But, while seeing that, theoretically, that literature should be no defect to the Book of God, we yet *feel* that it is so; because of our own mental constitution, which finds it difficult to look down (as it cannot well help doing at inferior knowledge) on the literature, and, in the same act, to hold in due reverence the divine element which is so closely associated with it. At the same time we see that it could not be otherwise, unless God had chosen to wait till man had ceased to progress in knowledge, before delivering His Book, or, at least, before completing it. However well this might have suited our successors, *we* have cause to be glad that God did not choose that course.

It has been stated before that, as knowledge of divine truths progressed among the Hebrews, abstract ideas of such truths gradually came into existence, accompanied by abstract terms for their expression. This culminated in New Testament times. It therefore follows that New Testament writers expressed themselves in abstract terms to a much greater extent than former writers had done; the result of which is, that less of the New Testament writer's *own mind* is presented in proportion to the divine truth he expresses, than in the case of the Old Testament writer.

INSPIRATION & THE STRUCTURE OF THE BIBLE. 151

But even in the New Testament the writer's own mind is inevitably expressed in some degree, with its Orientalisms, and, occasionally, with its—as we call it—ignorance.

Perhaps the reader has demurred to the assertion that abstract ideas of divine things did not exist till New Testament times. We have, for instance, the abstractions 'good' and 'evil' as early as the second chapter of Genesis. In Babylon the idea of 'spirits' existed long before Hebrew times. In Greece there were psychological abstractions at an early period. The answer is that the above is a general statement respecting the progress of such ideas in the Hebrew people alone; that, as before stated, progress differed in different sections of the Hebrew people, so that some abstractions appeared long before others, for this reason, as well as for the reason that this would be the natural course of things; that when we analyze the Babylonian conception of a spirit, we find indications that it was of a material nature, as to-day among savages. In the illustration of Merodach delivering the Moon-god from the evil spirits, given in the *Chaldean Account of Genesis*, p. 101, the evil spirit is represented as an erect animal. Doubtless there are, however, other indications known to students of Babylonian literature, which show what their conception of spirits was like.

As to the progress in Greece, more remains to be said. Under the successors of Alexander the Great, Greek culture spread over South-Western Asia and Egypt, where many Jews had settled. It continued to do so after their kingdoms had come under Roman power. In the time of Christ it had made its way in Palestine. The Apostles used (often, but I think not always) the Greek translation of the Old Testament which is called the Septuagint. The New Testament was written in the Greek language. The Hebrews did not study science much, but confined their studies to theology. What resources the Hebrew (or the Aramean) language has in expressing abstract ideas I do not well know, but there is no doubt that it is less rich than the Greek in this respect. Did not the Greek language, then, come into use among the Hebrews just when it was needed, to facilitate the final development of abstract ideas of spiritual things in the Hebrew mind, and furnish, at the same time, language for their expression?[2]

But there is another fact. The progress of Christianity was westwards. It has had its stronghold among Indo-European people. How immense has been the advantage to the latter that the truths of Christianity—the grand truths of the Bible—were originally expressed in one of their own tongues (the Greek), instead of in the tongue of a Semitic race, such as the Hebrew. Here we see distinctly how God had prepared the best of means to facilitate the progress of Truth over the civilized world, in this spread of the Greek language over so large a portion of the world of those days, including Palestine, the cradle of that Truth. Here, once more, we see that it was *in due time* that Christ died. Here, once more, we recognize natural development and not miraculous interference as God's way of working. Just as God prepared the way for the progress of the truths of Christianity among the Jews, as we saw in the last chapter, so He also prepared the way for their diffusion among the Europeans.

No doubt the Hebrews were a very suitable nation to be taught the truths of God, for several reasons. For one thing, they were a small people and young in knowledge, and therefore their ideas could be readily moulded to the truth as they developed; whilst they were aided by some of

[2] Of course it is not meant that the Greek religious ideas and psychology would exactly fit the Hebrew, but that they were of a kindred nature and more extensive.

the literature of Babylon, as we shall see in the next chapter; also doubtless by that of Egypt.

Probably two difficulties have occurred to the reader long ere this :—(1) However satisfactorily the foregoing arguments may account for the presence of ignorant statements in the Bible, how can we always be sure that we are believing the divine element, and not the human? Or if the divine truth is not in some cases what it, at first sight, appears to be, how are we to know what it really is? (2) If the early parts of the Bible are devoted to the rudiments of the knowledge of God, and were written specially for the early Hebrew, are they not uselessly present in the Bible for this age?

The first difficulty is a much smaller mountain than it appears to be. It resolves itself into this, "If God has been so careful to have His truths placed in the Biblical literature in a form such that the ignorant could not fail to apprehend them, how can the cultured man manage to apprehend them?" When put thus, in its true form, the difficulty is ludicrous. But there is another point in regard to the second part of the above question. The believer cannot, perhaps, arrive at the exact divine truth in such cases; but, seeing what his predecessors believed who believed the letter of the passage, he may be sure that that belief produced in their minds as near an approximation to the exact truth as was necessary. If that approximation has sufficed all these ages, there is no doubt that the exact truth is *one of a similar order*, and if he himself cannot get nearer to it, *that is quite sufficient for him to know*. Unbelief may see a host of difficulties, but they vanish before the eye of simple faith. Or if they do not all vanish, we can rest assured that God will provide for the difficulty in some way.

As to the second difficulty. Has the simple literature in

which the earliest Old Testament truths are conveyed, been of no use since the completion of the Bible? (1) Was it of no use when the Civilized World was passing from Paganism to Monotheism and Christianity? (2) Is it of no use to the missionary in heathen lands to-day? (3) Is it of no use in the Christian education of children amongst ourselves? The missionary can best answer the second question. Any Christian mother can answer the third. How much of the rudiments of the knowledge of God did we ourselves learn in the beautiful narratives of Joseph, or David, or in the Story of the Garden? It was stated on an earlier page that the simple language in which the Gospel is expressed constitutes the gateway leading to deeper truths within. The child can go in by it, and after entering he can gradually apprehend the more advanced truths of the Epistles, etc. So with the Bible as a whole. Its truths enter the mind as the tide gradually floods the bay, as the wedge cleaves the oak. Genesis is the margin of the water, or the thin end of the wedge; the New Testament is the deep water, or the thick end of the wedge. We have overlooked it, very likely; but, much as the Hebrews did of old, so have we, got into the depths by beginning at the shallows. There is no other way.

This water-side-like, wedge-like, evolution-like, structure of the Bible may offend the dignity of the proud, or stagger the unbelief of the sceptic, perhaps, who see their objections, but do not see the vital aspect of the case. But to my mind, and I hope to the reader's mind, this structure of the Bible is divine in its simplicity, perfect in those very imperfections which so perfectly fit the deepest needs of imperfect man.

Does the reader recognize this extract? "Let us try to get hold of a few ideas about these interesting subjects; and first let us remember that in the Introductory Primer we have been taught the meaning of the words solid, liquid, and gas. . . . Before we begin to study the chemistry of air, water, and earth, let us start with FIRE, about which you have not learnt much." Childish language! And what does the writer mean by such inconsistency as to say, "*We* have been taught in the Primer," and then, "*You* have not learnt much." This change from "we" to "you" can only be the work of a poor composer, can it? And his words are not correct, for *he* certainly did not learn from the Primer. How can one read the works of such a writer with any confidence? or without feeling his inferiority?

Professor Roscoe, the words bear your name; what is the meaning of this?

Yet the work which contains them, and is in the same strain throughout, is an admirable one, *being written for children*. It is not beneath the dignity of our most learned men to come down to the child's level, that being the *best way* to impart knowledge to them. Still less is it concluded that they never wrote such words. But somehow—though upon what grounds I know not—such a state of affairs in regard to the Bible is not to be thought of. There such language is clear evidence that the book is not of God!!

Let me make one more remark about these early Old Testament Scriptures. They are not limited to the teaching of those simpler truths, but are replete with others. He who reads them, searching for the mind of God, will read them many times before they are exhausted. More probably what God has to say through them will be found inexhaustible.

Some readers may see a difficulty about the fact so often insisted on in this work, that God adjusted the language of Scripture to the people and the times. For in certain cases where it is seen in more enlightened times that language is used which cannot be reconciled with known facts, the question may be asked, Is this consistent with the Truth of God? The following remarks throw light on the matter.

Dr. Stoughton writes in his Introduction to *The Progress of Divine Revelation*, page 6 :—

"We should bear in mind, all the way through, the distinction between the *objective* and the *subjective* aspects of revelation. . . . Truth has existence independent of man. It is what it is, let mortals apprehend it as they may. As to its fulness, richness, and splendour, it is not to be estimated according to the clearness and depth of human perceptions. . . . At the back of a truth revealed, there may lie an immense amount of meaning unrevealed; and the conscious apprehension of a revelation may lag behind the revelation itself."

Applying this principle to the case before us, we see how, in the revelation of a certain truth to a man, nothing but the unalloyed truth passes from the Divine to the human mind; but the man can apprehend it only by fusing it with his own ideas, which may be defective in many ways, and when he expresses it in writing he must express it *as he has apprehended it.* Here, moreover, we see the admirable fitness of using the intermediate human writer, so that, whilst the unalloyed truth comes from God, the writer presents that truth to his contemporaries dressed in a form that is both suitable and absolutely necessary for their apprehension of it. Upon this reasoning, then, the Divine truth alone that is in Jehovah's answer to Job attaches to the Divine Person, and the mythological part of that answer attaches to the human agent. And if it be argued that the use of incorrect language is inconsistent with truth, it is better to read the passage in this way than to regard it as spoken by God Himself.

As a matter of fact, however, the use of incorrect language is perfectly consistent with truth; for it is in the *heart's emotion* that in man's case usually co-exists with wrong statements, that the falsehood lies. That is the evil, and that alone. We see this when we remember how Christ used parables and symbols, how we ourselves use figurative language, or language adapted to children, as in the elementary work on chemistry just referred to, and in many other ways.

Something further remains to be said on the question of miracles. Some of those presenting most difficulty find a simple explanation in the principles maintained in the second chapter of this work; chiefly in the fact that the old Hebrew notion of a miracle would have approximately its true equivalent in modern English thought in a special divine action accomplished by natural means. For instance, Dean R. Payne-Smith has remarked, " The plagues of Egypt are found generally to be based upon natural phenomena, happening usually at long intervals. . . . This knowledge of Egypt and Egyptian customs and phenomena is now generally granted." Clearly the only important fact in regard to the frogs, or the lice, is that God caused these to increase at an extraordinary rate, so as to plague the Egyptians. Let us assume, for the sake of argument, that this enormous increase was brought about by perfectly natural means. Could the Hebrew of that age *possibly* represent to himself a spiritual God, controlling natural agencies in this way? Surely not. How then was this special interference of God on behalf of Israel to be conceived of and recorded? There was but one way :—" And Aaron stretched out his hand over the waters of Egypt; and the frogs came up, and covered the land of Egypt." . . . " And Aaron stretched out his hand with his rod, and smote the dust of the earth, and there were lice upon man and upon beast " (Exod. viii. 5, 6, 16, 17); in both cases at the command of Jahveh. Translate the material Jahveh and the act of his servant Aaron, into the spiritual God and His unseen control of natural agencies, causing the frogs and the lice to multiply —the crude Hebrew idea into the more accurate modern one—and difficulty disappears, but the vital truth remains. This truth, the *Word of God*, forms the centre of every one of these ancient Scriptures, often expressed in a thick covering of verbal signs or crude ideas. Strange that we should be so quick to see the outer crudeness, so slow to perceive that that is but a vehicle for the inner reality ; so quick to see the difficulty, so slow to see the simple explanation.

Such considerations as these have, doubtless, an important bearing on the general difficulty in regard to miracles, though we need by no means infer that they apply to all.

Again, the pillar of fire and cloud (Exod. xiv.) clearly implies special divine protection of Israel. Such a visible pillar would hardly be in itself a complete safeguard ; it appears to be a concrete picture of the divine protection accorded—of God's decision in regard to the Egyptians :— " Thus far and no further." This barrier would be alike invisible to Hebrew eyes, and inconceivable to Hebrew minds, but in its *effects*, of the utmost consequence.

It has been suggested that parts of the Books of the Law are the expressions of divinely-guided Hebrew traditions, embodying spiritual truths in concrete language and familiar ideas. Such instances as these plagues and this pillar of fire and of cloud, illustrate this guiding of traditions by the Hand of God, and show how they would embody historical truth of the highest order. Scripture history is thus for the most part a spiritual history, expressed, in its early parts, in the language of material things.

Inspiration & the Structure of the Bible. 159

SUMMARY OF CONCLUSIONS ABOUT THE BIBLE.

LANGUAGE is only a system of conventional signs used for the communication from mind to mind of ideas, feelings, etc. There is no inherent meaning in words, all the meaning which they possess being lent to them by the mind. The mental states are the all-important realities; not the language by which they are conveyed.

This applies to the Bible. The two all-important factors here are the Mind of God and the mind of man, the Bible being necessarily nothing more than a store of verbal signs adapted for the communication of the former mind to the latter. Thus the real *Word of God* is quite distinct from the language of the Bible: it is that portion of God's *mind* which He desires to communicate to man.

If, therefore, the language of the Bible is in places defective, this does not at all affect the *Truths of God*, which its office is only to convey, and which it most effectually does convey.

This is its high mission, and not the teaching of scientific truths, which man can acquire by other means.

The Bible was not specially prepared for any one class of readers, such as ourselves; but was intended for all mankind; and has therefore to meet the needs of minds of all orders in all ages. These minds differ very much; for there are educated and uneducated, people who think accurately and people who think loosely, people in different states of society, of different races—people of widely-different capacities of thought and modes of thought.

The *Truths of God* are of a nature different from ordinary knowledge (at least until they have become part of ordinary knowledge), and they are of various kinds. Since, therefore, the Bible's mission is to teach truths of this *high order*, and of *various kinds*, to *minds of all classes, its excellence must essentially consist in its suitability for this purpose.*

The first duty of an author is to make himself understood. If all are to understand the Truths of God, the man of small intellectual capacity must do so, amongst others. If, therefore, the Truths of God are presented in a form suitable for him, the wiser man must not charge the Bible with that as a defect, but as an excellence.

The Bible, moreover, was not first delivered to ourselves, but to the Hebrews; and the Truths of God are therefore presented in literature better adjusted to them than to ourselves, or any other people. There were also considerable differences between the Hebrew of early and crude times and the Hebrew of late and more cultivated times, who also spoke a language more like our own; and therefore there is a corresponding difference between the early parts of the Bible and its later and more important part, the New Testament. If, therefore, the Divine Truths delivered in its earliest portions are conveyed in literature suitable to crude times, but which is also intelligible to us, this is no defect in the Bible, taking its whole work into account.

But there is a more important factor to be taken into account. Language does not exist until it is made; ideas must come into existence first, and language to suit them after. So with the language that expresses Divine Truths. The writing of the Bible therefore involved the teaching of the Hebrews those Divine Truths. This was necessarily a process of Evolution. The development of this knowledge and the writing of Scripture proceeded together, the progress of each depending on that of the other. In the beginning the Truths of God could only gain access to the mind when associated with ideas of familiar things; therefore, in the

INSPIRATION & THE STRUCTURE OF THE BIBLE. 161

beginning of the Bible they are conveyed almost entirely by means of narratives and concrete pictures. As divine knowledge progressed, the abstract ideas came into existence, and therewith language corresponding to them, and this state of things culminated in New Testament times. Therefore the divine truths of the New Testament are delivered in language more appropriate, and better suited to ourselves.

The Truths of God have thus come to us in the Bible through the minds of men; these men could apprehend them only by grafting them upon, or fusing them with, their own natural ideas; they could express them in writing only as they had apprehended them; therefore in doing so they must bring out in some measure their own natural ideas; and if these are Oriental or defective, in so wide a range of Truths as there are in the Bible the Orientalisms or defects must inevitably appear in some cases. From the facts stated in the last paragraph it follows that inaccuracies resulting from this will be most numerous in the early parts of the Old Testament, and fewest in the New Testament, where Divine Truths are conveyed to a much greater extent in their own proper language, so that less of the writer's own mind appears, and that mind is better instructed, both in natural and Divine things. Miraculous Inspiration for the avoidance of such things would not have been at all effective; it would have impeded rather than helped the progress of the work. But other means have been used to reduce these inaccuracies to a minimum, and to prevent evils resulting from them, whilst in very many cases they have been turned to useful account in different ways.

Thus, proceeding from Genesis to Revelation, we find the Bible like water which is shallow at the edge and gradually deepens beyond human depth. We have over-

M

looked the advantage which this has been to ourselves, and is to all learners in the present day, as well as in the Hebrews' day. Instead of being a defect, this structure of the Bible is seen to be its excellence, when we judge it by the only true standard, its fitness for the work for which it was designed.

CHAPTER VI.

THE CHALDEAN ACCOUNT OF GENESIS.

IN Heb. i. 1, 2, we read, "God, having of old time spoken unto the fathers in the prophets by divers portions and in divers manners, hath at the end of these days spoken unto us in his Son."

In former chapters of this work we have noticed, too, how in later days God spoke to the Hebrews in the language of spiritual abstractions and terms relating to a future life : how, before these were in existence, He spoke in language referring to this present life only, reaching their hearts by the moral lessons drawn from their own experience and that recorded of their ancestors : how in early times He purified, developed, and moulded into the Law their crude precepts, amongst other things teaching them by their notions about sacrifice the true significance of Atonement : how, when He would give them a knowledge of His own Person, He began by introducing Himself in the likeness of one of their gods. In all these cases we see how God took up such crude materials as already existed amongst them (albeit of His own producing), worked upon their own ideas and beliefs, and, later on, developed from these what was new and progressive.

Is it natural then to suppose that, when God had occasion to teach them certain other important truths—

truths relating to the origin of things—He would adopt a totally different course? Evidently not.

Wonderful results were obtained by means of their historical beliefs, the experience of the nation supplementing that of the individual; and when these were being committed to writing, the selection and grouping of events was sometimes overruled so as to embody a meaning of which the writers were not distinctly conscious.

But before they had a history—what was there then to work upon? We have seen that at about this time the Hebrews had ideas of gods, and of right and wrong, which God turned to wonderful account. So had they also unhistorical traditions, and traditions partly historical—myths and legends *which they held as most sacred*. These could be worked upon, as well as their other ideas and beliefs. Looking at the matter then from this position, we should naturally expect to find that God made use of these beliefs, moulding them into forms suited to convey those other divine truths which He had to teach them, and mankind after them.

This brings us again, therefore, to the position already referred to on one or two occasions. In the light of evolution, and in that of God's usual way of working, we see that there could be no revelation before the human mind was duly prepared to receive it—comprehending the new truth by assimilating it with pre-existing ideas, in the manner in which all knowledge is acquired. That preparation of the human mind for revelation was two-fold. The first and most important preparation consisted in the genesis and growth of conceptions of the Deity, and of religious sentiments generally. The second consisted in the genesis and growth of traditionary beliefs about the Creation of all things, and about the dealings of the Deity with man in pre-historic times, and also included certain of the Hebrew

The Chaldean Account of Genesis. 165

people's traditionary beliefs about His dealings with them in particular. The first of these has been briefly treated of in the third and fourth chapters of this work; and in the same chapters the divine guiding of the strictly Hebrew traditions has been suggested as an explanation of difficulties as to the authorship of parts of the Books of the Law. It is not my intention to deal further with either of these matters in this work. But the genesis and growth of the general traditionary beliefs about the Creation, etc., have an important bearing on the subject of the following portion of this work—the first eleven chapters of the Book of Genesis. Some consideration of these traditionary beliefs is essential to a correct understanding of those Scriptures, and the difficulties attending them. I shall, therefore, give in this chapter a brief account of the traditions of this description which were current among the nations of Antiquity.

The many ancient inscriptions which have been dug up in the East and deciphered, of late years, have thrown much light on the history of the ancient Hebrews, and on the Old Testament Scriptures. An interesting account of several of these inscriptions is given in Prof. Sayce's *Fresh Light from the Ancient Monuments*. Amongst others there are the Monument of a Hittite King, the Moabite Stone, the Inscription of Sennacherib, etc. Some of these inscriptions relate events of which we have the counterparts in the Old Testament, and they unmistakably corroborate some of its records. Indeed, some of them were executed by, or by the orders of, men who were actors in those very events.

There are also certain inscriptions of another class, of which an outline is given in the above-named work, and which are discussed more fully in the *Chaldean Account of Genesis*. Thus we find an Account of the Deluge, extracts from an Account of the Creation, sundry statements which undoubtedly refer to a Story of the Fall, and other matter relating to pre-historic events recorded in Gen. i.–xi. Here, however, the records are not composed by actors in the events related; they are merely ancient Chaldean or Accadian legends.

Can we, therefore, accept their testimony as corroborating the Genesis narratives in the same manner that the other class of inscriptions testify to the later events of Hebrew history? Manifestly not. We cannot give to them, on their own merits, the credence which is due to authenticated history; we can only place that amount of faith in *them* which can be placed in such legends generally.

But further remarks would be premature before the reader has examined the contents of these inscriptions. They are given below, from *Fresh Light from the Ancient Monuments* by Sayce, and *The Chaldean Account of Genesis* by G. Smith, revised by Sayce. I also give some extracts from the writings of the Babylonian historian Berosus, and a number of legends of other ancient nations, which have come down to us through different channels.

It should be remarked that the original inhabitants of Chaldea were the Accadians, a non-Semitic race, who were conquered by the Semitic Chaldeans (the kinsmen or ancestors of the Hebrews) between 3000 and 2000 B.C. The Accadian language became extinct as early as 1800 B.C.[1]

The Story of the Flood is given first, as its resemblance to the Genesis narrative is the most striking. It is well known that the Biblical account is composed of the amalgamated versions of two different writers—the Elohist and Jehovist, as they are called. I have noted in the margin of the Chaldean account below, the parallel passages in Genesis; the texts belonging to the accounts of these two

[1] *Chaldean Account of Genesis*, pp. 20, 21.

writers are, with one or two exceptions, placed one under the other, in cases where they both occur.

THE CHALDEAN OR ACCADIAN STORY OF THE FLOOD.
(From *Fresh Light from the Ancient Monuments*, pp. 27-32.)

This "formed the subject of more than one poem among the Accadians. Two of these were amalgamated together by the author of a great epic in twelve books, which described the adventures of a solar hero whose name cannot be read with certainty, but may provisionally be pronounced Gisdhubar. The amalgamated acccount was introduced as an episode into the eleventh book, the whole epic being arranged upon an astronomical principle, so that each book should correspond to one of the signs of the Zodiac, the eleventh book consequently answering to Aquarius. Sisuthros, who had been translated without dying, like the Biblical Enoch, is made to tell the story himself to Gisdhubar. Gisdhubar had travelled in search of health to the shores of the river of death at the mouth of the Euphrates, and here afar off in the other world he sees and talks with Sisuthros . . . . . . :—

'Sisuthros speaks to him, even to Gisdhubar: Let me reveal unto thee, Gisdhubar, the story of my preservation, and the oracle of the gods let me tell to thee. The city of Surippak, the city which, as thou knowest, is built on the Euphrates, this city was already ancient when the gods within it set their hearts to bring on a deluge, even the great gods as many as there are—their father Anu, their king the warrior Bel, their throne-bearer Adar, their prince En-nugi. Ea, the lord of wisdom, sat along with them, and repeated their decree: "For their boat! as a boat, as a boat, a hull, a hull! hearken to their boat, and understand the hull, O man of Surippak, son of Ubara-Tutu; dig up the house, build the ship, save what thou canst of the germ of life. (The gods) will destroy the seed of life, but do thou live, and bid the seed of life of every kind mount into the midst of the ship. The ship which thou shalt build, ... cubits shall be its length in measure, ... cubits the content of

Gen. vi. 5-8.
Gen. vi. 11-13.

Command to build an ark.
Gen. vi. 14.
Gen. vi. 19-21.
Gen. vii. 2,3.
Dimensions.
Gen. vi. 15, 16.

its breadth and its height. (Above) the deep cover it in." I understood and spake to Ea, my lord: "The building of the ship which thou hast commanded thus, if it be done by me, the children of the people and the old men (alike will laugh at me)." Ea opened his mouth and said, he speaks to me his servant: "(If they laugh at thee) thou shalt say unto them, '(Every one) who has turned against me and (disbelieves the oracle that) has been given me, . . . I will judge above and below.' (But as for thee) shut (not) the door (until) the time comes of which I will send thee word. (Then) enter the door of the ship, and bring into the midst of it thy corn, thy property, and thy goods, thy (family), thy household, thy concubines, and the sons of the people. The cattle of the field, the wild beasts of the field, as many as I would preserve, I will send unto thee, and they shall keep thy door." Sisuthros opened his mouth and speaks; he says to Ea, his lord: "(O my lord) no one yet has built a ship (in this fashion) on land to contain the beasts (of the field). (The plan?) let me see and the ship (I will build). On the land the ship (I will build) as thou hast commanded me." . . . On the fifth day (after it was begun) in its circuit (?) fourteen measures its hull (measured); fourteen measures measured (the roof) above it. I made it a dwelling-house (?) . . . I enclosed it. I compacted it six times, I divided (its passages) seven times, I divided its interior (seven) times. Leaks for the waters in the midst of it I cut off. I saw the rents, and what was wanting I added. Three *sari* of bitumen I poured over the outside. Three *sari* of bitumen I poured over the inside. Three *sari* of men, carrying baskets, who carried on their heads food, I provided, even a *saros* of food for the people to eat, while two *sari* of food the boatmen shared. To (the gods) I caused oxen to be sacrificed; I (established offerings) each day. In (the ship) beer, food, and wine (I collected) like the waters of a river, and (I heaped them up) like the dust (?) of the earth, and (in the ship) the food with my hand I placed. (With the help) of Samas [the Sun-god] the compacting of the ship was finished; (all parts of the ship) were made strong, and I caused the tackling to be carried above and below. (Then of my household) went two-thirds: all that I had I heaped together; all

---

Gen. vi 19-21.
Gen. v 2, 3.

Making the Ark.
Gen. vi. 22.
Gen. vii. 5.

Coating with pitch.
Gen. vi. 14.
Taking food in.
Gen. vi. 21.

that I had of silver I heaped together; all that I had of gold I heaped together; all that I had of the seed of life I heaped together. I brought the whole up into the ship; all my slaves and concubines, the cattle of the field, the beasts of the field, the sons of the people, all of them did I bring up. The season Samas fixed, and he spake, saying: "In the night will I cause the heaven to rain destruction. Enter into the midst of the ship and close thy door." The season came round; he spake, saying: "In the night will I cause the heaven to rain destruction." Of that day I reached the evening, the day which I watched for with fear. I entered into the midst of the ship and shut the door, that I might close the ship. To Buzursadi-rabi, the boatman, I gave the palace, with all its goods. Then arose Mu-seri-ina-namari [The Water of Dawn at Daylight] from the horizon of heaven (like) a black cloud. Rimmon in the midst of it thundered, and Nebo and the Wind-God go in front; the throne-bearers go over mountain and plain; Nergal the mighty removes the wicked; Adar goes overthrowing all before him. The spirits of earth carried the flood; in their terribleness they sweep through the land; the deluge of Rimmon reaches unto heaven; all that was light to (darkness) was turned. (The surface) of the land like (fire?) they wasted; (they destroyed all) life from the face of the land; to battle against men they brought (the waters). Brother saw not his brother; men knew not one another. In heaven the gods feared the flood, and sought a refuge; they ascended to the heaven of Anu. The gods, like a dog in his kennel, crouched down in a heap. Istar cries likes a mother; the great goddess utters her speech: "All to clay is turned, and the evil I prophesied in the presence of the gods, according as I prophesied evil in the presence of the gods, for the destruction of my people I prophesied (it) against them; and, though I their mother have forgotten my people, like the spawn of the fishes they fill the sea." Then the gods were weeping with her because of the spirits of earth; the gods on a throne were seated in weeping; covered were their lips because of the coming evil. Six days and nights the wind, the flood, and the storm go on overwhelming. The seventh day when it approached the storm subsided; the flood which

Entering the Ark.
Gen. vii. 7-10.
Gen. vii. 13-16.

Shutting the door.
Gen. vii. 16.

Coming of the Flood.
Gen. vii. 10-12.

People destroyed.
Gen. vii. 21, 22.
Gen. vii. 23.

Duration of Deluge.
Gen. vii. 12, 24.
Gen. vii. 17.

EVOLUTION AND SCRIPTURE.

<small>Waters subside.
Gen. viii. 1.
Gen. viii. 2.</small>

<small>Opening the window.
Gen. viii. 6.</small>

<small>Ark rests on a mountain.
Gen. viii. 4.</small>

<small>Birds sent out.
Gen. viii. 6-12.</small>

<small>Leaving the Ark.
Gen. viii. 18, 19.</small>

<small>Altar built. Sacrifice offered.
Gen. viii. 20.</small>

<small>Smelling the savour.
Gen. viii. 21.</small>

<small>The rainbow.
Gen. ix. 13-17.</small>

had fought against (men) like an armed host was quieted. The sea began to dry, and the wind and the flood ended. I watched the sea making a noise, and the whole of mankind was turned to clay; like reeds the corpses floated. I opened the window, and the light smote upon my face; I stooped and sat down; I weep; over my face flow my tears. I watch the regions at the edge of the sea; a district rose twelve measures high. To the land of Nizir steered the ship; in the mountain of Nizir stopped the ship, and it was not able to pass over it. The first day, the second day, the mountain of Nizir stopped the ship. The third day, the fourth day, the mountain of Nizir stopped the ship. The fifth day, the sixth day, the mountain of Nizir stopped the ship. The seventh day when it approached I sent forth a dove, and it left. The dove went and returned, and found no resting-place, and it came back. Then I sent forth a swallow, and it left. The swallow went and returned, and found no resting-place, and it came back. I sent forth a raven, and it left. The raven went and saw the carrion on the water, and it ate, it swam, it wandered away; it did not return. I sent (the animals) forth to the four winds, I sacrificed a sacrifice. I built an altar on the peak of the mountain. I set vessels [each containing the third of an ephah] by sevens; underneath them I spread reeds, pine-wood, and spices. The gods smelt the savour; the gods smelt the good savour; the gods gathered like flies over the sacrifices. Thereupon the great goddess at her approach lighted up the rainbow which Anu had created according to his glory. The crystal brilliance of those gods before me may I not forget; those days I have thought of, and never may I forget them. May the gods come to my altar; but may Bel not come to my altar, since he did not consider but caused the flood, and my people he assigned to the abyss. When thereupon Bel at his approach saw the ship, Bel stopped; he was filled with anger against the gods and the spirits of heaven: "Let none come forth alive! let no man live in the abyss!" Adar opened his mouth and spake, he says to the warrior Bel: "Who except Ea can form a design? Yea, Ea knows, and all things he communicates." Ea opened his mouth and spake, he says to the warrior Bel: "Thou, O warrior prince of the gods, why, why didst thou not consider but causedst a flood? Let the doer of sin bear his sin, let the doer of wickedness bear his wickedness. May the just prince not be cut off, may the faithful not be (destroyed). Instead of causing a flood, let lions increase, that men may be minished; instead of causing a flood, let hyænas increase, that men may be minished; instead of causing a flood, let a famine happen, that men may be (wasted); instead of causing a flood, let plague increase, that men may be (reduced). I did not reveal the determination of the great gods. To Sisuthros alone a dream I sent, and he heard the determination of the gods," When Bel had again taken counsel with himself, he went up into the midst of the ship. He took my hand and bid me ascend, even me he bid ascend; he united my wife to my side; he turned himself to us and joined himself to us in covenant; he blesses us (thus): "Hitherto Sisuthros has been a mortal man, but now Sisuthros and his wife are united together in being raised to be like the gods; yea, Sisuthros shall dwell afar off at the mouth of the rivers." They took me, and afar off at the mouth of the rivers they made me dwell.'" <small>Sin caused the Flood. Gen. vi. 5-7. Gen. vi. 11-13. Noah spared for his righteousness. Gen. vi. 8. Gen. vii. 1. Never to be another Flood. Gen. viii. 21, 22. Gen. ix. 11. Noah warned. Gen. vi. 13. Enoch, not Noah, translated. Gen. v. 24.</small>

The Account of the Flood which has come down to us through the Babylonian historian Berosus reads much like an abstract of the above story. It also states that Sisuthros was translated for his piety, and that the place where the ship rested was in the land of Armenia.

Traditions of a Flood have been found among many other nations. Sometimes it is a universal, sometimes a partial one. In one of the Greek accounts (for there are two) it appears that the object of the Flood was to destroy 'the brazen race' for their wickedness. The only righteous man, with his wife and pairs of different kinds of animals, were saved in a vessel which he had made. Here the vessel is made to land on Mount Parnassus. The Phrygian legend has probably been adopted from the Biblical story. The Indian and Mexican legends somewhat resemble the

Chaldean one.[2] Professor Delitzsch remarks that nearest to the Biblical record stand the Flood-legends of the West Asiatic circle of nations. In Persia, India, and China, there is a second group peculiar to the countries of Eastern Asia. A third group is formed by the legends of the Grecian circle; and a fourth by the legends of nations lying beyond the intercourse of the ancient world, as the Welsh, Mexicans, Peruvians. The legend of the Mexicans and Islanders of Cuba agrees with the Biblical account in respect of the dove and raven. The legend of the Macusi-Indians in South America states that the only man who survived the Flood repeopled the earth by changing stones into men. According to that of the Tamanaks of Orinoko it was a pair of human beings, who cast behind them the fruit of a certain palm, and out of the kernels sprang men and women. There are legends among the Tahitians and other Society Islanders which bear some resemblance to those of Asia. The inhabitants of Raiatea show, as a proof of the Flood having taken place, the corals and mussels, which are found on the highest summits of the island.[3]

It is to be remarked that, except in the Hebrew account, the ship, where there is one, is made by the narrators to rest on some mountain in their own country. There is no known Egyptian Flood legend.

The Chaldean Legend of the Creation.

(From *Fresh Light from the Ancient Monuments*, pp. 22-24.)

There were two or more of these legends, one of which, writes Prof. Sayce:—

---

[2] These facts are taken from extracts given by Bishop Colenso from various writers. *The Pentateuch*, pp. 380–382.

[3] These remarks are quoted by Bishop Colenso from Delitzsch. *The Pentateuch*, p. 383.

"bears a striking resemblance to the account of the Creation in the first chapter of Genesis. . . . We possess, unfortunately, only portions of it, since many of the series of clay tablets on which it was inscribed have been lost or injured. The account begins as follows :—

1. 'At that time the heavens above named not a name,
2. Nor did the earth below record one:
3. Yea, the deep was their first creator,
4. The flood of the sea was she who bore them all.
5. Their waters were embosomed in one place, and
6. The flowering reed was ungathered, the marsh-plant was ungrown.
7. At that time the gods had not issued forth, any one of them,
8. By no name were they recorded, no destiny (had they fixed).
9. Then the (great) gods were made,
10. Lakhmu and Lakhamu issued forth (the first),
11. They grew up . . . .
12. Next were made the host of heaven and earth,
13. The time was long (and then)
14. The gods Anu (Bel and Ea were born of)
15. The host of heaven and earth.'

"It is not until we come to the fifth tablet of the series which describes the appointment of the heavenly bodies— the work of the fourth day of Creation, according to Genesis —that the narrative is again preserved. Here we read that the Creator 'made beautiful the stations of the great gods,' or stars, an expression which reminds us of the oft-recurring phrase of Genesis: 'And God saw that it was good.' The stars, moon, and sun were ordered to rule over the night and day, and to determine the year, with its months and days. The latter part of the tablet, however, like the latter part of the first tablet, is destroyed, and of the next tablet —that which described the creation of animals—only the first few lines remain. 'At that time,' it begins, 'the gods in their assembly created (the living creatures). They made beautiful the mighty (animals). They made the living beings come forth, the cattle of the field, the beast of the field, and the creeping thing.' What follows is too mutilated to yield a connected sense.

"There is no need of pointing out how closely this Assyrian account of the Creation resembles that of Genesis. Even the very wording and phrases of Genesis occur in it, and, though no fragment is preserved which expressly tells us that the work of the Creation was accomplished in seven days, we may infer that such was the case, from the order of events as recorded on the tablets. But, with all this similarity, there is even greater dissimilarity. The philosophical conceptions with which the Assyrian account opens, the polytheistic colouring which we find in it further on have no parallel in the Book of Genesis. The spirit of the two narratives is essentially different.

"The last tablet probably contained an account of the institution of the SABBATH. At all events, we learn that the seventh day was observed as a day of rest among the Babylonians, as it was among the Jews. It was even called by the same name of Sabbath . . ."

In the fragments of the work of Berosus that have come down to us, we read of "a time in which there existed nothing but darkness and an abyss of waters," and that Belus divided the darkness, and separated the heavens from the earth, and also "formed the stars, and the sun, and the moon, and the five planets."[4]

Bishop Colenso quotes the following from Von Bohlen :—

"The most intimate relationship may be observed between the myth of Genesis and the Zend representation of Creation, which was composed near the same locality, and has a similar outline and succession of development. The universe is created in *six* periods of time by ORMUZD (Ahura-Mazda) in the following order : (1) the Heaven, and the terrestrial Light between Heaven and Earth, (2) the Water, which fills the deep as the sea, and ascends up on high as clouds, (3) the Earth, whose seed was first brought forth by Albordj, (4) trees and plants, (5) animals, and (6) lastly, Man, whereupon the Creator rested, and connected the divine origin of the festivals with these periods of Creation. We must remember, however, that Zoroaster had taken the old Magian system as the foundation of his reform, and had modified it to suit his purposes,— that, consequently, his cosmogony, is the *old Chaldean*, which

---

[4] *Chaldean Account of Genesis*, pp. 34, 36.

very probably spread from the times of the Assyrians into Western Asia. But the Bible narrative, apart from this common basis, far surpasses the description of the Zendavesta in simple dignity...."

He also quotes from *Aids to Faith* by Dr. M'Caul:—

"The *Etruscans* relate that God created the world in six thousand years. In the first thousand, He created the heaven and the earth,—in the second, the firmament,—in the third, the sea and the other waters of the earth,—in the fourth, the sun, moon, and stars,—in the fifth, the animals belonging to air, water, and land,—in the sixth, man alone."

CHALDEAN REFERENCES TO THE STORY OF THE FALL.

(From *Fresh Light from the Ancient Monuments*, pp. 25, 26.)

"No account of the FALL OF MAN, similar to that in Genesis, has as yet been found among the fragments of the Assyrian libraries. . . . It is, nevertheless, pretty certain that such an account once existed. An archaic Babylonian gem represents a tree, on either side of which are seated a man and woman, with a serpent behind them, and their hands are stretched out towards the fruit that hangs from the tree. A few stray references in the bilingual (Accadian and Assyrian) dictionaries throw some light upon this representation, and inform us that the Accadians knew of 'a wicked serpent,' 'the serpent of night' and 'darkness,' which had brought about the fall of man. The tree of life, of which so many illustrations occur on Assyrian monuments, is declared to be 'the pine-tree' of Eridu, 'the shrine of the god Irnin'; and Irnin is a name of the Euphrates, when regarded as the 'snake river,' which encircled the world like a rope, and was the stream of Hea, 'the snake-god of the tree of life.' The Euphrates, we must remember, was one of the rivers of Paradise.

" *The Site of Paradise* is to be sought for in Babylonia. The garden which God planted was in Eden, and Eden, as we learn from the cuneiform records, was the ancient name of the 'field' or plain of Babylonia, where the first living creatures had been created. The city of Eridu, which the people of Sumir called 'the good' or 'holy,' was, as we have seen, the shrine of Irnin, and in the midst of a forest or garden that once lay near it grew 'the holy pine-tree,' 'the tree of life.' The rivers of Eden can be found in the rivers and canals of Babylonia. Two of them were the Euphrates and Tigris, called by the Accadians *id Idikla,* 'the river of Idikla,' the Biblical Hiddekhel, while Pishon is a Babylonian word signifying 'canal,' and Gihon may be the Accadian Gukhan, the stream on which Babylon stood. Even the word *cherub* is itself of Babylonian derivation. It is the name given to one of those winged monsters, with the body of a bull and the head of a man, which are sometimes placed in the Assyrian sculptures on either side of the tree of life. They stood at the entrance of a Babylonian palace, and were supposed to prevent the evil spirits from entering within. . . .

"Like cherub, ADAM also was a Babylonian word. It has the general sense of 'man,' and is used in this sense both in Hebrew and in Assyrian. But, as in Hebrew it has come to be the proper name of the first man, so, too, in the old Babylonian legends, the 'Adamites' were 'the white race' of Semitic descent, who stood in marked contrast to 'the black heads,' or Accadians, of primitive Babylonia."

It seems clear, however, from Gen. ii. 13, that the river Gihon is the Nile, since 'the same is it that compasseth the whole land of Cush'; and so Josephus understood it. Pison has been taken to mean the Indus. Josephus remarks that 'running into India, it makes its exit into the sea, and is by the Greeks called Ganges' (*Ant.* I. i.).

The flaming sword of Gen. iii. 24 has its parallel in the flaming sword of Merodach, of Chaldean mythology.[5] The Chaldeans made use of the Euphrates for artificial irrigation. The present desert character of the country, where rain falls only during a small portion of the year, and where trees grow only on the river banks, powerfully calls to mind the description in Gen. ii. 5, 10.

The following accounts of the Persian and Chinese myths

---

[5] *Chaldean Account of Genesis,* pp. 84, 86.

are extracted by Bishop Colenso[6] from Kalisch's Work on Genesis :—

THE PERSIAN.

"The first couple, the parents of the human race, *Meshia* and *Meshiane*, lived originally in purity and innocence. Perpetual happiness was promised to them by Ormuzd, the Creator of every good gift, if they persevered in their virtue. But an evil demon (*Dev*) was sent to them by Ahriman, the representative of everything noxious and sinful. He appeared unexpectedly in the form of a serpent, and gave them the fruit of a wonderful tree, *Hóm*, which imparted immortality, and had the power of restoring the dead to life. Thus evil inclinations entered their hearts; all their moral excellence was destroyed. Ahriman himself appeared under the form of the same reptile, and completed the work of seduction. They acknowledged him instead of Ormuzd as the creator of everything good; and the consequence was, that they forfeited for ever the eternal happiness for which they were destined. They killed beasts, and clothed themselves in their skins; they built houses, but paid not their debt of gratitude to the Deity. The evil demons thus obtained still more perfect power over their minds, and called forth envy, hatred, discord, and rebellion, which raged in the bosom of the families.—(*Zendavesta, Kleuker's Ed.*). . .

"The Chinese also—have their age of virtue, when nature furnished abundant food to the happy men, who lived peacefully surrounded by the beasts, exercised virtue without the assistance of Science, and did not yet know what it meant to do good or evil. The physical desires were perfectly subordinate to the divine spirit in man, who had all heavenly, and no earthly, dispositions; disease and death never approached him; but partly an undue thirst for knowledge, partly increasing sensuality, and the seduction of women, were his perdition: all moderation was lost; passion and lust ruled in the human mind; the war with the animals began; and all nature stood inimically arrayed against him. . . .

"The *Greeks* believed that, at an immense distance beyond the Pillars of Hercules, on the borders of the Earth, were the Islands of the Blessed, the Elysium, abounding in every charm of life, and the Garden of the Hesperides, with their golden apples, guarded by an ever-watchful serpent (Ladon). But still more analogous is the legend of the *Hindus*, that, in the sacred mountain Meru, which is perpetually clothed in the golden rays of the Sun, and whose lofty summit reaches into heaven, no sinful man can exist,—that it is guarded by dreadful

[6] *Bishop Colenso on the Pentateuch*, p. 341.

dragons,—that it is adorned with many celestial plants and trees, and is *watered by four rivers*, which thence separate and flow to the four chief directions.

"Equally striking is the resemblance to the belief of the *Persians*, who suppose that a region of bliss and delight, the town Eriene Vedsho, or *Heden*, more beautiful than all the rest of the world, traversed by a mighty river, was the original abode of the first men, before they were tempted by Ahriman, in the shape of a serpent, to partake of the wonderful fruit of the forbidden tree *Hôm*. The 'tree of life' has analogies in the 'king of trees,' *Hôm*, which the Persians believed to grow at the spring Ardechsur, issuing from the throne of Ormuzd, and in the tall *Pilpel* of the Indians, to which was also ascribed the power of securing immortality and every other blessing."

The following Calabar legend is given by Dr. Goldziher from Bastian:—

"The first human pair is called by a bell at mealtimes to Abasi (the Calabar God) in heaven; and in place of the forbidden tree of Genesis are put agriculture and propagation, which Abasi strictly denies to the first pair. The fall is denoted by the transgression of both these commands, especially through the use of implements of tillage, to which the woman is tempted by a female friend who is given to her."

CHALDEAN REFERENCE TO THE TOWER OF BABEL.

(From *Fresh Light from the Ancient Monuments*, pp. 35–37.)

"Mr. George Smith discovered some broken fragments of a cuneiform text which evidently related to the building of the Tower of Babel. It tells us how certain men had 'turned against the father of all the gods,' and how the thoughts of their leader's heart 'were evil.' At Babylon they essayed to build 'a mound' or hill-like tower, but the winds blew down their work, and Anu 'confounded great and small on the mound,' as well as their 'speech,' and 'made strange their counsel.' The very word that is used in the sense of 'confounding' in the narrative of Genesis is used also in the Assyrian text. The Biblical writer, by a play upon words, not uncommon in the Old Testament, compares it with the name of Babel, though etymologically the latter word has nothing to do with it. Babel is the Assyrian Babili, 'Gate of God.' . . .

"The confusion of tongues was followed by the DISPERSION OF MANKIND. The earth was again peopled by the descendants of the three sons of Noah—Shem, Ham, and Japhet. Shem is the Assyrian Samu, 'olive-coloured;' Ham is Khammu, 'burned black;' and Japhet Ippat, 'the white race.' The tribes and races which drew their origin from them are enumerated in the tenth chapter of Genesis. The arrangement of this chapter, however, is geographical, not ethnological; the peoples named in it being grouped together according to their geographical position, not according to their relationship in blood or language. Here it is that the non-Semitic Elamites are classed along with the Semitic Assyrians, and that the Phœnicians of Canaan, who spoke the same language as the Hebrews, and originally came from the same ancestors, are associated with the Egyptians."

In *The Chaldean Account of Genesis*, p. 163, Prof. Sayce writes:—" Both Alexander Polyhistor and Abydenus [through whom Berosus' fragments are preserved] state that the building of the Tower of Babel was known to Babylonian history. . . . The legend of Etana . . . seems to imply that the Tower was supposed to have been built under the superintendence of this mythical hero." Lines 12 and 13 in the legend : "In his anger also (his) secret counsel he pours out : [to] confound (their) speeches he set his face," are closely parallel to Jehovah's self-communing (if such it be) in Gen. xi. 6, 7.

The words in Gen. xi. 3, "they had brick for stone, and slime (i.e. bitumen, margin) had they for mortar," also point to Chaldea (where bitumen is still found) as the origin of the story; and imply that the writer of the Biblical account resided in a place where stones and mortar, not bricks, were used for building.

In *The Chaldean Account of Genesis*, pp. 309-311, Prof. Sayce writes:—

"The dynasty of gods with which Egyptian mythical

history commences, resembles in some respects the list of antediluvian kings of Babylonia given by Berosus, as well as the list of antediluvian patriarchs in Genesis. This dynasty has sometimes seven, sometimes ten reigns, and in the Turin Papyrus of kings, which gives ten reigns, there is the same name for the seventh and tenth kings, both being called Horus, and the seventh king is stated to have reigned 300 years, which is the length of life of the seventh patriarch, Enoch, after the birth of his son."

It may also be noticed that in the fragment of Berosus which has come down through Apollodorus, there is a parallel, not only to the *ten* antediluvian patriarchs, but also to the passage in Gen. vi. 3:—" yet (or therefore, margin) shall his days be an hundred and twenty years." It says, " So that the sum of all the kings is ten; and the term which they collectively reigned an hundred and twenty sari."

I have devoted considerable space to the foregoing extracts, as they have an important bearing upon the subject of this work. Notwithstanding, they are but a brief outline, especially in the case of those legends which are not taken from the cuneiform inscriptions. A more complete account might have been given of the latter if the subject had been fully dealt with; but the foregoing is quite sufficient for the present purpose.

The reader cannot fail to have perceived the striking resemblance between these legends and the narratives in Gen. i. to xi. Many other points of resemblance in the cuneiform accounts, besides those before mentioned, are noticed by Professor Sayce in the *Chaldean Account of Genesis*, where the subject is more fully discussed.

Besides this general resemblance, there is another important fact to be observed—that all the events which are described in Gen. i. to xi. find their parallels in these legends, with the exception of the Story of Cain and Abel, one or two genealogies, sundry details in the life of Noah, etc. We are thus at once brought to the conclusion that the Biblical narratives and these legends must have had a common origin; and it becomes an important question, Where was that origin? Prof. Sayce has no doubt that it was not in Palestine, but in Chaldea; and, as the reader will have observed, Prof. Sayce is no enemy to the Word of Truth. Whilst finding more or less of detail which is unquestionably incorrect in the Biblical stories he undoubtingly believes in their essentially historical character.

There are four important things to be considered in deciding as to the origin of these stories. (1) Which are the more ancient, the cuneiform inscriptions or the relevant parts of Genesis? (2) Which nation, the Hebrew or the Chaldean, was the older, the greater, the more influential, and, therefore, the more likely to have been the source, not only of these Hebrew and Chaldean accounts of the Creation, the Deluge, etc., but also of all those legends which, in some form or other, were common to the surrounding Eastern nations? (3) Can we trace any connection between the Hebrew and the Chaldean nations which is likely to indicate the course by which these legends passed from the one to the other? (4) Is there anything in the Biblical stories which suggests that Chaldea was the place where they were originally composed?

The second question may be confidently answered in favour of Chaldea. This was the great source and centre of Eastern civilization; and, during early Hebrew history, the seat of the Capital of the world. The Hebrews, on the other hand, were never more than a small nation.

As regards the first question, Prof. Sayce shows in *The Chaldean Account of Genesis* (pages 178, 20, 21), that the Deluge legend is an Assyrian translation of an Accadian original, which latter was composed at least as early as 2000 B.C. The Creation legend, in its present form, is not older than the 7th century B.C., though the story itself was undoubtedly more ancient.[7] The Sabbath was an Accadian institution.[8] (The Accadians, the reader will remember, were the original inhabitants of Chaldea.) The fir-cones shown in the representations of the Tree of Life may point to the conclusion that the Accadians brought that tradition from their original home in the mountains of Media.[9]

The Exodus from Egypt took place in the reign of Meneptah II., who ascended the Egyptian throne about B.C. 1325,[10] so that we cannot assign nearly so old a date as B.C. 2000 to the composition of Gen. i. to xi. The Chaldean legend of the Deluge is therefore older than the Biblical narrative of the same, and there is every reason to believe that the original Chaldean legends of the Creation and the Fall were also older than the parallel accounts in Genesis.

Thirdly, we know that the Hebrews were of the same race as the Semitic Chaldeans, that the latter were in possession of Chaldea before the time of the Hebrew patriarchs, and that the languages of the two nations were as closely allied as two modern English dialects are.[11] And, according to Gen. xi. 28-31, xii. 5, the Hebrew Patriarchs were natives of the Chaldean city of Ur, who had migrated to Haran, and thence to Canaan. Some have thought that Ur of the Chaldees was in Mesopotamia, near Haran, so that it is marked there in the maps in our Bibles; wrongly, as

---

[7] *Chaldean Account of Genesis*, pp. 56, 57.
[8] Ibid., p. 89.   [9] Ibid., p. 85.
[10] *Fresh Light from the Ancient Monuments*, pp. 60, 61.
[11] Ibid., p. 19.

Prof. Sayce shows.[12] It may also be remarked that the Septuagint Version of Gen. xi. 31 reads, "... led them forth *out of the land of the Chaldees*, to go into the land of Chanaan, and they came as far as Charrhan, and he dwelt there." This speaks of Charrhan, or Haran, as in a different country, and at a distance, from Chaldea, the land of their nativity: not at all as if Haran and Ur of the Chaldees were near together in Mesopotamia, as shown in the aforesaid maps. Ur is well known to have been where Mugheir now stands, in Southern Chaldea, where it is also marked in our maps. It was one of the most ancient cities of the land, once the capital, and one of the first occupied by the Semitic Chaldeans. It appears, therefore, that the Chaldeans were the parent nation, the Hebrews being descendants of colonists from Chaldea, who settled first in Mesopotamia or Syria. We know, moreover, that writing was practised in Ur in very early times, as is shown by the cylindrical signet of its ancient king Uruch, one of the oldest relics found there. The Hebrew colonists may, therefore, have taken with them written copies of these legends (which were most sacred in their eyes), and their descendants may have preserved them till the time when the earliest portions of Genesis were written. Or, possibly, since these stories seem to have passed by tradition to many of the other nations of Western Asia, they may in like manner have passed into the hands of the ancient Hebrews. The close agreement, however, of the Chaldean Deluge legend with the Biblical narrative seems to imply that a written copy, and not a verbal tradition, was the means of its passage into Hebrew hands.

Lastly, the language of the Biblical stories furnishes internal evidence that they were *composed in Chaldea* and

---

[12] *Fresh Light from the Ancient Monuments*, pp. 44, 45.

were modified in their new home in Palestine. Attention has already been called to such an implication in the words of Gen. xi. 3, " They had *brick* for *stone*, and *bitumen* had they for *mortar*." In like manner the reference to bitumen or pitch in the Deluge narrative, the dates of commencement and termination of the Flood as given by the Elohist writer (which agree with the periods of inundation by the Babylonian rivers), and other details, point clearly to Chaldea as the place where the original story was composed ; whereas the term têbâh, 'a coffer,' substituted for 'ship,' indicates the work of an inhabitant of an inland country. The phraseology of the Story of the Fall still more strikingly suggests a description of Chaldean scenery and surroundings ; and in the Genesis account of the Creation there are traces of the former existence of mythological language, which was removed or altered during the compilation of those passages.

Thus we are brought irresistibly to the conclusion that, with one or two small exceptions, the stories which form the subject matter of the first eleven chapters of Genesis, were all ancient Hebrew traditions, originally obtained and probably inherited from the Chaldeans.

It is hardly necessary to assert, much less to dilate on, the difference in character between the Biblical narratives and the foregoing legends. As Sayce remarks, the spirit of the two is essentially different.

But another feature should be mentioned here—the terse and finished character of the Biblical stories as compared with these legends. Moreover, when the legends are compared with each other, it seems clear that the Chaldean stories, more than any others, resemble those in the Bible, and that the Chaldean legends are more developed than those of the Hindus, Chinese, and other nations racially more distant. In considering this question we must remember that the Persian accounts of the Creation and the Fall are, in all probability, modifications of the Chaldean; and, in judging of the latter, these Persian legends should, therefore, be taken into account, in conjunction with the cuneiform inscriptions. Now, if the Semites, Indo-Europeans, and Mongolian peoples dwelt together, or not far apart, at some very distant date; if, at a later date, the Semites and Indo-Europeans remained near each other after their separation from the Mongolian races; and if, finally, the different Semitic nations alone remained together at a still later date, the above-named features of these legends would be most simply accounted for. For we should conclude that they had a common origin; we should place that origin in the first of these periods, trace their growth through the second, and their full development in the third. This would make their origin very very old, perhaps incredibly old; but if they were thus handed down, we may be sure they had acquired a *most sacred* character in the people's eyes long before Hebrew times. At any rate, we may safely say that the genesis and growth of these legends agreed, generally, with the course suggested above, in that they originated in *very* early times, and grew up to their final form by little and little, ever growing in sacredness in the people's sight.

How deeply interesting is this matter when we see in it the then unseen Hand of God. For we see here the laying of the foundations of the Book of God. (See pp. 163, 164.) How crude is the first material; how slowly is it shaped, as nearer and nearer the *ideas* and the *beliefs* approach to their ultimate Divine form as expressed in our Bible. In a former chapter we saw how closely connected was the evolution of Divine knowledge among the Hebrews with the writing of the Scriptures. Here we find a like connection and interdependence, in these dim distant ages, between the growth of theological sentiments and ideas, by means of which came the Divine knowledge, and the growth of traditionary beliefs about the actions of the Deity, etc., out of which began the writing of the Bible.

Readers who mistake names for realities, or cannot look beneath the surface, will, perhaps, be alarmed at such words as myth and tradition when thus associated with the Person and Book of God. But the student of Nature will see that— as in the sculpturing of the statue, and as throughout the whole realm of Nature, the rude form must exist before the finished, so here—before there could be revelation and the written Word, there must be the crude religious ideas and beliefs. Before there was revelation (in its proper sense, though we might call this revelation on account of its Divine origin,) the writing of the Scriptures was a very different thing from what it was in the full light of apostolic times. But these opening chapters of the Bible are most important Scriptures; and we here see that special provision was made to ensure their efficiency, the Hand of God doing almost of itself what the hand of man could not then do. We see that it was necessary, first, to form the raw material of public theological conceptions and beliefs; then, whilst purifying, guiding, and developing these *conceptions* little by little, to shape the growth of the concomitant traditional *beliefs*, until they arrived at the desired form;. when the old Hebrew writer, in writing the treasured and sacred record, as it was in the people's eyes, expressed—though still, as we shall see, in rather crude form—the sacred truths of the Living God.

If the reader hesitates to accept this conclusion, will he pause and try to answer the question, What other course would have been so effective as this for the propagation of divine truths? Indeed, what other course *could* have been taken?

It would be well if we could realize the utter impossibility of imparting truths to a people who possessed *no* ideas and

The Chaldean Account of Genesis. 187

beliefs of a similar kind. If we think of miraculous inspiration of a writer as a means, we must instantly reject it. No one could comprehend his words: no one would accept them.

Again, let us remember, (1) how natural it would be that the One who had built up the human mind, should thus, in preparation for the revelation that was to follow, influence, regulate, and foster the growth of its ideas and beliefs; (2) that it is God's way to use what is at hand for carrying out His purposes; *not* to go out of the way and create special means. Then let us realize the whole position, and we shall never again hesitate to believe that the truths of Gen. i.-xi.—and probably some of those in the Books of the Law—were communicated from God to the Hebrews by the guidance of traditionary ideas and beliefs.

The internal evidence of the Divine origin of these ancient Scriptures cannot be given here, in further support of this conclusion, but some of it will come under notice in the remaining part of this work.

Of course after this guiding of primitive traditions had been limited to the Semitic and then to the Hebrew, in the manner outlined above, the original traditions would naturally still continue to develop in different forms among the remaining nations, so producing the various forms of such beliefs which have been discovered in that part of the world. It is of little importance to the foregoing conclusion, whether the *first beginning* of all such primitive beliefs was an entirely natural product of the human mind, or whether it was the result of a special Divine interposition; it suffices that the traditions undoubtedly were specially directed in their *development*, more particularly in their later course as they passed into Chaldean and Hebrew hands.

The association of tradition with these early Scriptures is

not altogether new. Several Christian commentators have concluded that some of them were traditions handed down from the first man to Mosaic times, the first man having received his knowledge direct from God. This is in part parallel to what is here asserted, namely, that these beliefs were handed down traditionally from the earliest times, the truths coming indeed from God Himself, though by a very different process.

These Scriptures, we must remember, were thus produced at a very early period in Hebrew history; and therefore at a time when the Hebrew's knowledge of God, if not also his natural knowledge, was in its infancy. Although intended also for the use of all mankind afterwards, they were primarily designed to meet the needs of a people who possessed neither abstract ideas of spiritual things, nor language for their expression, though the germs of these they doubtless had. We have before remarked upon the difficulty of bringing Divine truths home to such minds, and the necessity for concrete pictures for that purpose. Add to this the facts :—that even in New Testament times Christ often taught by parables, that the Bible closes with a book of symbolic language, and that God often so overruled the Old Testament writer's words as to invest his work with important truths in types and figures. We then have strong reason to conclude that the *essence* of these oldest Scriptures lies more or less in their symbolic meaning; or in such spiritual truths as must pass into the mind when the narratives are being read and believed as historical fact. There are, however, different kinds of truths in Gen. i.-xi., and it is therefore natural to expect some parts to be symbolic, and others not so, or not wholly so. For instance, we should hardly apply the principle to Gen. i. as a whole; whilst, as we shall see further on, there is much reason to apply it to Gen. ii., iii., and some subsequent passages.

But here we seem to be met by a grave difficulty. For although as long ago as the date of the Book of Wisdom, the Jews had perceived a connexion between the serpent of Gen. iii. and the Devil (Wisdom ii. 24); still it is manifest that the Story of the Fall and all Gen. i.--xi. were regarded as historical by the Jews of New Testament times, the writers of the New Testament Scriptures included. The difficulty is only apparent, however.

For if these narratives had well fulfilled their purpose of conveying their included *divine truths* to Hebrew readers of all times, late as well as early, there was no reason why those of the later age should have been specially taught to read them, or portions of them, in a different light. In fact we need but ask, How else were they to read them, who knew nothing of the facts revealed by Science in these days? and the answer is plain. And that their natural strong tendency would be to cling to their forefathers' manner of reading them, we see very plainly, by the desperate tenacity to the traditional view which is manifested in these days, even after the very foundations of parts of these stories have been swept away.

But if we find the Lord Himself apparently treating them in the same light? The answer again is simple. He who came *from* God to teach them *spiritual* truths would have no occasion to correct any of their imperfect knowledge of other matters; especially where their very manner of reading those old Scriptures was not a hindrance, but a help, to their apprehension of divine truth. Whether there be other reasons or not, this is reason enough, for His quoting from those old Scriptures as they were.

That, however, is not all. Wherever we find those Scriptures quoted in the New Testament, the *very substance* of the extract is seen to consist in *the moral truth* which is contained in the Old Testament passage. Very different in this respect are the reproductions of those narratives which we find in the Apocrypha. It may be added that in one instance Christ, in quoting from one of them, departs distinctly from the letter of the story, putting Adam's words into the mouth of God (Matt. xix. 4), whilst selecting two conspicuous *divine truths* from different passages (Gen. i. 27 and ii. 24), and joining them together as if they had been one quotation.

We ourselves often quote from the parables somewhat as if they were historical. Thus we talk of the events in the parable of the Prodigal Son, saying that the son did so-and-so, and that on his return, "his father saw him, while he was yet afar off, and . . . ran and fell on his neck, and kissed him." We repeat these *words*, well knowing in our own minds the rich depth of meaning which lies beneath them. In the same manner may Christ have quoted the old passages in Genesis, seeing Himself their full meaning, whilst those around Him saw only as much as it was essential that they should see. He said much to the multitude of which He revealed the meaning only to His disciples. When these asked Him about things which it was not necessary for them to know, rather than answer such questions, He at once directed their attention to what *was* essential (Acts i. 6-8; John xxi. 21, 22). Once when they had totally failed to apprehend Him, He supplemented His explanation with the significant statement "The words . . . . . are spirit" (John vi. 63). So too are the words of Genesis.

In teaching children, we do not always speak in words that are perfectly accurate, for our aim is to present certain truths in a form adapted to the child-mind. Was not the matchless Teacher in a similar position?[13]

---

[13] Perhaps it should not be overlooked that those who recorded Christ's references to the Old Testament could not, without a

Nor must we forget that, whilst these old Scriptures are unhistorical *as narratives*, they are yet spiritually historical, expressing thus the deepest of all historical truths. If then the writers of the New Testament quoted them simply as they stood, they in doing so were stating the truth, and the deepest of truths; only in their form of expressing it they were not, as they could not be till more enlightened times, accurate.

Further remarks would be superfluous here, as the bearings of these questions will be more clearly seen by the reader as we pass under review these first eleven chapters of Genesis. At first sight it doubtless appears a serious difficulty; but I am certain that the more fully the matter is investigated, the more it will be manifest that the course taken in this matter as we find it in our Bible, was both necessary, and the outcome of deepest Divine wisdom.

miracle—a miracle with, at most, distant utility—free themselves from their own thoughts on the subject. Whilst, therefore, they were well qualified as regards spiritual knowledge, and, with the help of inspiration, undoubtedly were enabled to give a spiritually perfect report of the teachings of Christ, it is possible that in these cases they used forms of expression not identical with those which He Himself used.

CHAPTER VII.

THE CREATION.

The object of Gen. i. 1 to ii. 4 is to give man an account of the Creation as it seemed in the eyes of God—to convey to man God's thoughts on this important subject. It is of vital importance to keep that fact always in remembrance.

But, as the account is given for man's instruction, it does not necessarily present *all* God's thoughts about the works of His hands.

Thirdly, whilst the account was designed for all people in all ages, it possesses many special features, because it was designed more particularly for the early Hebrew people. It was given them when science was unknown, and when the knowledge of God was in its infancy. Its divine truths, therefore, both the general and the special, are clothed in the crude language corresponding to the crude ideas of that age.

As we saw in the first chapter of this work, man's view of the Creation, derived from a scientific investigation, differs in certain particulars, either from the Divine view itself, or from certain things which the language used in Gen. i. has led most readers to believe, but which are no part of the Divine view itself—or perhaps, we may here add, it differs from both of these. Our object now is to ascertain, as far as possible, in the chief of those cases

THE CREATION.

where this difference occurs, what is the Divine view, and what are the erroneous beliefs which have generally been associated with it; and also to give a satisfactory reason why the language is such as to generate those beliefs.

As we proceed, the Divine view will perhaps seem to us in certain respects ideal. As to this, if we refer to Rom. iv. 17, "God who ... calleth the things that are not as though they were," we at once find a Scriptural reason for this apparent Divine idealism. Lest, however, we should entertain the notion that our own views are in entire accord with the reality, and therefore essentially preferable to the Divine views, let us pause awhile and briefly examine the nature and foundation of our own knowledge of objective reality.

Psychology, then, forces upon us—without possibility of escape—the conviction that, whatever the material things around us may be in themselves, they are not what *to us* they seem to be. All that we know, or can know, about them is conceived in terms of the sensations which they excite in us. When we perceive an object the first effect is that a group of these (presentative) states of consciousness is called up. The second effect is that another group of (representative) states of consciousness is thereby called forth from the recesses of the mind. The union of these two groups forms a complete mental picture of the object; the discerning of a relation among these states of consciousness constitutes our perception of it. Thus what we are conscious of is an affection of *our own mind*. Why should these states of consciousness which are parts of our *mind* be in any degree like the *external object* which has merely served to excite them? The object is certainly adequate, under the circumstances, to cause them to come up in the mind, and that is all we can venture to assert. But we have abundant proof that the object is *not like* the sensations which it excites. Colour furnishes a simple case. It is not easy to conceive that a green leaf is not green in itself. Yet what we are conscious of is the *sensation of green;* and if we insist that this greenness is not entirely within the mind, we must attribute it *not at all to the leaf,* but to the *light* which the leaf reflects, whilst absorbing the other-coloured rays.

A simple instance of another kind may be given. We take a smooth cylindrical piece of wood, small and long, and call it 'a stick,' or 'piece of wood.' But if we use it habitually for a few weeks for guiding the pen in drawing straight lines, what is it then? It is not merely a stick. It is a much more important entity: it has become a RULER. Yet in itself there has been no change. This illustrates the fact that many of the supposed properties of our familiar things really consist in the *uses* which we make of them.

In these two instances, which might be multiplied indefinitely, we see how qualities which really appertain almost exclusively to our minds are habitually attributed exclusively to the objects around us. And this process is carried to a far greater extent than we have any idea of, till we pursue the analysis. Then we are obliged to admit that our knowledge of any object consists entirely of feelings (or states of consciousness) excited in us by an unknown and unknowable substratum. Mr. Herbert Spencer writes (*First Principles,* 1887, pp. 68, 69):—

"The conviction that human intelligence is incapable of absolute knowledge is one that has been slowly gaining ground as civilization has advanced. Each new ontological theory, from time to time propounded in lieu of previous ones shown to be untenable, has been followed by a new criticism leading to a new scepticism. All possible conceptions have been one by one tried and found wanting; and so the entire field of speculation has been gradually exhausted without positive result: the only result arrived

THE CREATION.

at being the negative one above stated—that the reality existing behind all appearances is, and must ever be, unknown. To this conclusion almost every thinker of note has subscribed. 'With the exception,' says Sir William Hamilton, 'of a few late Absolutist theorisers in Germany, this is, perhaps, the truth of all others most harmoniously re-echoed by every philosopher of every school.'"

We should therefore be very slow to conclude that our view of the universe, or of its creation, is more in accord with the reality than the Divine one is, even if the latter does appear in some respects ideal.

It appears from the above analysis that our knowledge is *composed of* impressions produced upon the mind by that which lies outside the mind. How is God's view of the Creation constituted, as we find it in Gen. i. ? Of two parts, (1) the plan, or rather the volition that certain things shall exist,—'Let there be Light,' 'Let there be a firmament,' etc. ; (2) the review, 'And God saw that it was good.'

The first of these parts does not find its parallel in our views of Nature, but an Inventor can perhaps form some idea of it. Merely remembering that it is the volition of the Author of *Being*, let us pass to the second part of the Divine view.

This we find is of the same nature as our knowledge, inasmuch as it is composed of impressions produced upon the mind.[1] Which set of impressions then is likely to be the truest, those produced on us, or those—if we may so speak—produced on God ? Without going into all the conditions necessary to a true impression, we see a most important one at the outset—the position of the observer.

---

[1] These statements about the mind, impressions, and the like, of God, may read like anthropomorphisms. Of course they must not be taken too literally ; but, in the sense here intended, they are, I think, warranted by what is revealed of the nature of God.

It should be a central position, where everything can be clearly seen, and valued according to its importance—not a one-cornered position, where things present a distorted appearance. The former is the Divine standpoint; the latter is our own. We can easily find an illustration of our liability to take a distorted view, by referring to the diagram on page 149. Situated as we will suppose ourselves to be at *e*, we may think, for instance, that *a* is not 'good,' because we take a relative view of the matter, and cannot take an absolute one. We look down when we should look up, from the starting point of Creation. Presently we will examine the respective merits of our view and the Divine view of certain things in Gen. i. First, however, let us notice one conclusion that seems to follow from the above metaphysical reasoning.

Since in all Perception, the Mind, discerning the position occupied by the exciting cause of its sensations, attributes to the external object those qualities which really are part of itself (though in their vivid form the Mind cannot of itself excite them); and since we cannot pass outside the region of these impressions, to know anything about what lies beyond them—does it not follow that, whatever other realities may exist, the Mind is a reality which far transcends every other reality that we can know? This seems to be a legitimate conclusion from the former position. This conclusion, indeed, opens wide questions which cannot be discussed here. But it is not the Idealist's creed; it leaves room for a like reality in minds other than our own; above all, for the greatest reality in the Mind of God. I should add, perhaps, to prevent misunderstanding, that it is here presented purely as derived from man's correspondence with Nature, not from his correspondence with God, as realized by the Christian. Lastly, does it not accord with the Scriptural doctrine which gives the spirit (the most real part of Mind) so important a place?

THE CREATION.

If then the Mind is so real, and if God is the author of Being, we should be very slow to attribute unreality to that which exists *as God sees*. It may be added that where, in Rom. iv. 17, it says, 'God who . . . calls the things which be not as being' (as another translation has it), we yet have Abraham's parentage asserted as a *reality* of a kind other than the fleshly one, namely, the spiritual.

We find therefore that the Divine view of Creation in its reviewing, or impression-receiving, character is, in its nature and from the position of the Observer, far more trustworthy than the human view; and that the apparent Divine Idealism, where it occurs, is entitled to profound respect.

Let us pass on then to consider the principles on which this Account of the Creation is drawn up. The first verse tells us that God created the heaven and the earth. The second verse proceeds immediately, almost abruptly, to deal with the earth; and we read no more about the heaven (except its mention in Gen. ii. 1); for the firmament, or expanse, which God called heaven (verse 8), and the 'firmament of the heaven' (verse 14) are clearly that which God made on the Second Day; not the heaven of verse 1. Having announced then these two things which make up the sum of what God created; the first of them, the heaven, is dismissed from the account as done with; and of the earth alone we have a detailed account. After the first verse, therefore, Gen. i. is devoted to a description of earthly things; and if there is any reference to other phenomena, they are consistently noticed only in their relation to the earth. Gen. i. 1 is a cosmogony; the rest is more properly a geogony.

But there are other reasons why the account should be confined to earthly things. (1) The 26th, 27th, and 28th verses tell us that the chief work of creation was man himself, who was not only given dominion over all the other things, but was even made in God's own image. (2) The Bible, and therefore Gen. i., was written for man's benefit. (3) It was meant to teach him religious truths only. It is therefore proper that the account should be devoted chiefly to man himself and his conditions of existence and environment; and, as man is an earthly creature, this limits the description to earthly things. From the religious point of view it is important for man to know his own origin—that God created him; his relation to the things around him—set over them by the will of God; and also their origin—created by God. Man, man's environment, and God, and the relations of these three with each other—these are *the* subjects of the chapter. And what a wealth of information this short chapter contains for man on these three subjects!

Since man and his earthly environment are *the* subjects of the chapter (with God and their relations to Him as just stated), not only is no account called for of the luminaries outside of their relations to the earth, but any other description of them would here be out of place. It is of no importance here what the sun, moon, and stars may be as *heavenly bodies*, or what their physical constitutions are. These things belong to astronomy, and the Bible has nothing to do with teaching astronomy. The one question here is, What are their effects on man and on the earth? From this position there are, as man sees when he looks up, two GREAT LIGHTS, which divide the day from the night, divide time into years, and furnish similar guidance; give light to the earth and its inhabitants, and produce the seasons; and there are other minor Lights, the stars. And as man looks upward, *where does he see* these Lights? He sees them set in the firmament of heaven above him, and accordingly that is where Genesis locates them. Such is an account of what

THE CREATION.

they are *to man,* where they are *to man,* and how they came to be thus, namely, by the will of God, who made them.

"Very good so far," it might be said, "and if one of the sun's potent effects on the earth—its attraction of gravitation—is omitted, the ultimate effects of even this are given, these being the years and the seasons. But this view of the luminaries is ideal, for it is confined to the *appearance,* whereas astronomy gives the reality which causes that appearance and those effects." Let us see.

First, it is well to notice *how real* things as described in Gen. i. are to man in general. It is only a small proportion of the human race to-day, the astronomically educated, who view things in some respects differently; and to *all mankind* down to about 400 years ago, as they appeared to the eye, so they were, *most real.* Even then were the argument raised that Gen. i. does not truly describe the effects on educated men to-day, it would still be right as a general application to man, this being but a small exception.

Not until we learn about other things behind the appearance, and by means of which this state of affairs has been brought about, does the appearance lose some of its reality. Then, as best we can, we form crude symbolic conceptions of a spherical earth on which we dwell, with empty space all round it, and the sun and stars as far larger bodies than the earth. For the most part, however, appearance is still too strong for us, and the original state of things retains most of its reality. When then we thus think away some of our original or natural conceptions, by what are they replaced? Merely by others which are based upon further *appearance* (as revealed by scientific investigation of the heavens), not upon the ultimate reality which underlies that appearance, for it is incognizable. Yet at each stage of our advancing knowledge we complacently regard our last-formed conception as that of *the reality.*

It appears then that our present conception of the region we inhabit is similar *in nature* to that of untutored man, both being *based upon appearance*. However natural, it is inconsistent, if we maintain that *the reality* accords with our present conceptions, simply because they are at present ultimate ones, and yet deny all reality to those original conceptions, which were likewise ultimate in their day. We need know more of Ontology before we can do this; and that is the lesson which Psychology has taught us, or ought to have taught us, as we saw before.

One reality has, however, continued throughout these changes in the appearance of the luminaries — a real effect has always been produced by these upon the human mind; which fact reminds us of the transcendent reality of Mind itself, already predicated. And not only have the effects produced on the mind of man, generally, been those taken account of in Genesis, but the different effects produced on the astronomer have not destroyed the original ones. To him, as to other men, the luminaries are still the *Great Lights* (whatever else they may be), which also divide the time and produce the seasons. Genesis therefore has recognized the abiding reality, the effect produced on the human mind; and, where that effect has varied, it has recognized those parts of it which have alone remained constant.

What physical science tells us, moreover, is confined to the *means* whereby these effects have been produced; for such is our knowledge about the heavenly bodies. Whence it appears that, after all, the Bible tells us about the reality, and science tells us about the means whereby that reality was produced.

But that is not all. Undue obloquy has fallen upon this passage of Scripture simply in consequence of the same name being applied to two different conceptions. When untutored man looks up and sees the Great Light of day, set as it seems to be in the firmament not far above the earth, he forms the conception of *a Light*, and he calls that Light 'the Sun.' When the astronomer, by various processes, perceives a huge *heavenly body* some 93 million miles beyond the firmament where the Light appears,[2] he forms the conception of a *heavenly body*, the great centre of the solar system, and he calls that heavenly body 'the Sun.' Here then are two totally different conceptions, two entirely different things, the Light in the aërial firmament, and the Heavenly Body some 93 million miles further away, and both these things are called 'the Sun.' The first thing is a real light, the second thing is a real heavenly body—both on a par, according to our common notions of reality; and both have been called by the same name, 'the Sun.' And this name originally appertained, not to the Heavenly Body, but to the Light. It is not, therefore, the Bible which is wrong if it calls that Light 'the Sun,' *for it is its own name*. It is astronomy that has taken the name of the Light and applied it to something else, to a later conception and different thing, the heavenly body. It had a right to do so, perhaps; but it is unjust to the Bible to charge it with such a misapplication where there is nothing of the kind.

Such then—in as far as this exegesis is correct—is the Divine view of the luminaries, considered in their relation to man. It is perfectly justified; and no one will say that the language of Gen. i. 14-19 is not well adapted to convey it to the human mind. But we must not forget the other side of the question—that the cursory sceptical reader sees in that language the notions of an ignorant age, and nothing more; the words of man, not the Word of God. A

[2] I have merely affirmed this distance between the Light and the heavenly body to distinguish clearly between the two conceptions. It would be most unjust to Genesis to say that it places the Light at this distance from the heavenly body. It only places the Light in the firmament, stating nothing about how far the firmament extends.

mere reference to the former portions of this work furnishes the complete answer to that objection. The passage was designed to teach all mankind these Divine views, but primarily, and most important, to teach them to people of an unscientific age ; and it was also produced by the agency of one of those people. Therefore these Divine Truths, which are the *Word of God*, are expressed in language generally adapted to all and specially adapted to the people of that age. If the account had been written to-day, the Truths would have been the same, the language somewhat different.

Here, and in some other places in the chapter, the language might be taken as describing the universe according to the notions of antiquity (see pp. 301, 302), and that is how the people of early times undoubtedly applied it, as they *could* only apply it. Yet the account nowhere *commits itself* to those views. The educated reader of to-day applies it with equal, or almost equal, facility to his own ideas of the Cosmos. Whilst, as a matter of fact, it describes neither the first nor the second, but is devoted to something higher and more important, namely, to teaching man God's thoughts about him and his environment and the creation of these.

I wonder if the reader has noticed one important respect in which the above remarks have done but meagre justice to Gen. i. 14-19. I did not notice the fact myself till after these were written, and I leave them as they were (with a slight alteration), for they show how the text is sometimes blamed for what is not even in it.

It has been shown above that the Bible has a perfect right to call the two Great Lights by their own original names, the Sun and the Moon. And in many places we read of the Sun and the Moon in the Bible. But here *these names are absent*. It has already been remarked that the opening chapters of the Bible are very important Scriptures, and special Divine care has been taken to ensure their efficiency. Later Scriptures are devoted to subjects different from those dealt with here, and the language used in them is chosen with a view to deliver their particular truths effectually, sometimes being defective if judged on other grounds. But Gen. i. is devoted to an *Account of the Creation*, and language which would pass without challenge elsewhere would be inadmissible here. The names Sun and Moon, which are used elsewhere, could not, as we have seen, have been objected to even here; yet, as if to make the very language as far as possible under the circumstances of its composition, unexceptionable, these names are omitted in the text. And that they are purposely omitted is clear from verse 16, where we have the name 'the stars.' Who, in writing the 16th verse, would have used such a sequence of words as these, "And God made *the two great lights;* the greater *light* to rule the day, and the lesser *light* to rule the night; the *stars* also," instead of using names of the same order, such as the sun, the moon, and the stars? A literary critic in the old times would surely have condemned such an inconsistency. But God, knowing all things, and not forgetting the needs of a subsequent and more enlightened age, has provided for those needs, by overruling the writer's choice of words, even in such a matter as this. We have but this one mention of the stars, which tells us simply that God made them. Verse 17 may be said to state that the stars, as lights, were set in the firmament; or it may not, though such is the implication.

We find then the account of the luminaries still further justified, inasmuch as it not only takes account simply of the Lights, stating that these were set in the firmament where man sees them, but it is careful also not to say anything about *the Sun* and *the Moon* which man, applying to-day to the *heavenly bodies*, might regard as incorrect.

We return to the first verse. The Hebrew word which

is translated 'heaven' does not, it appears, involve the conception of a spiritual heaven. Nor could we expect it, if that conception did not exist in Old Testament times. But we must not forget that the physical heaven was supposed in those days to be God's dwelling place; so that the *idea* which is expressed in Gen. i. 1 may, I think, be taken as including that important feature. Further on, in Gen. ix., x., and other places, where men and nations are enumerated, we find a deliberate practice of giving those last which are to be the subjects of future treatment, and those first about which nothing more is to be said. Probably, therefore, for two reasons Gen. i. 1 gives heaven first, earth second; namely, because as God's dwelling place heaven is the more important, and because nothing more is to be said about it in the chapter. We must, however, carefully note that Gen. i. 1 does not *commit itself* to any statement that the physical heaven is God's dwelling place. It merely tells us that God created the heaven, and gives us no further information on the subject. If the term 'the heaven' includes two distinct ideas fused together, or rather as yet unseparated, the physical heaven and God's dwelling place, the truth delivered in Gen. i. 1 may be, either that God created one, or the other (since the name 'heaven' is required to denote either of them), or both. A third reason for naming heaven first may be that it was created before the earth was.

What are the Days of Genesis i.? They are not ordinary 24-hour days. They are not successive and mutually-exclusive long periods, although they have a successive character, and embrace long periods; according to our thoughts, at least. Is it then a strange conception that is represented by these Days? No, it is a somewhat familiar one.

What is included in the term 'hour' in this passage :—

THE CREATION.

"The hour cometh, and now is, when the dead shall hear the voice of the Son of God; and they that hear shall live" (John v. 25)? The reference here is not to the resurrection of the body (as in verse 28), but to the passing from spiritual death to life which occurs at conversion. That 'hour,' therefore, has already lasted nearly 2000 years, whilst it has not embraced all that has occurred in the world during that period, but only those special events, the passing of certain persons from death to life. It had a beginning and will have an end, so that it has both longitudinal and lateral boundaries. It is a period possessing certain characteristics, and *its scope is confined to those characteristics*. Of such a nature are the Days of Genesis i., and in that sense we ourselves often use the term 'day.'

If, for instance, we use the expression 'Solomon's day,' we mean the period embraced by Solomon's life. We mean a period of many years, and we also mean a period not extending outside of the regal domain of a small kingdom, Israel. We may indeed say that certain events in distant Babylon occurred in Solomon's day; but that is, notwithstanding, a departure from the *essential feature of the conception*. We think of Solomon's life and surroundings; and these, or the period characterized by these, are what we really mean. For if we directed our thoughts to Greece and found that Homer lived at the same time as Solomon, we should speak of Homer's day and Solomon's day as two perfectly distinct times, in each case confining our thoughts to their respective lives, although from a purely chronological point of view these may have coincided.

Again, thinking of the state of civilized society, we say "This is a day of knowledge." Whereas, if we were occupied with the state of the negroes of Central Africa, or any other savages, we should have to say, "This is a day of ignorance." Confined to England it is a day of scepticism, a day of religion, a day of irreligion, a day of industrial progress, a day of peace, etc., according as we turn our attention to one subject or one section of the people. Yet all these distinct 'days' are synchronous.

Times out of number we find the term 'day' used in the Bible in this sense, more or less definitely. It is so used in Jer. l. 27, 'for their day is come, the time of their visitation'; in Zech. iv. 10, 'the day of small things'; in John viii. 56, 'Your father Abraham rejoiced to see my day'; in 2 Cor. vi. 2, 'now is the day of salvation'; in Deut. xxxi. 18, 'And I will surely hide my face in that day'; in Amos ii. 16, 'And he that is courageous among the mighty shall flee away naked in that day'; in John xiv. 20, 'In that day ye shall know that I am in my Father, and ye in me, and I in you'; in John xvi. 23, 'And in that day ye shall ask me nothing'; in John xvi. 26, 'In that day ye shall ask in my name.'

The conception of the Day of Genesis i. is brought before the mind more definitely by the use of the term 'day,' as applied to a human life, as in 'Solomon's day,' 'Homer's day,' than in the other cases before noticed. By this means, too, we may obtain an idea of the Six Days in their relation to each other. Thus if we take six persons' lives, such as Moses' day, Joshua's day, Samuel's day, Saul's day, David's day, and Solomon's day, we have six particular periods before the mind. They were successive periods, but not entirely successive. Each one was a later period than the one before it; some of them were entirely completed (from a chronological point of view) before others began, as were both Moses' and Joshua's day before Samuel's and the others. Several of them were contemporaneous, as Samuel's day, Saul's day, and David's day, during a certain part of each. Some of the events, too, of one of these were connected with some of the events of another, as with Saul and David. Yet, inasmuch as the essential feature of each conception is the period, events, surroundings, and characteristics, of the particular life, each of these 'days' is a period of itself, distinct from the others. Of this character, and thus related to each other, are the Days of Gen. i.

Dr. Reusch has given their character to some extent in these words (*Nature and the Bible*, Edinburgh, 1886, vol. i. p. 188) : " Taken as a whole, the six days correspond to the whole series of periods which elapsed between the first beginning of things and the creation of man ; but they do not mean six successive periods, but only six sides or phases of the creative activity of God; six principal heads under which the creating and forming acts of God can be brought." After discussing at length the other interpretations of the Six Days that have been entertained, he concludes this is the right one (pp. 363, 364). It is a mistake, however, to dismiss altogether (as the above diagnosis seems to do, though perhaps not intentionally) the *successive* character of the Six Days; for this clearly is one of their essential features, whilst it yields, after reaching a certain point, to other more important considerations.

These Days have been called 'ideal.' We have seen, however, that they do not express either a strange or an illegitimate conception, from our point of view. It remains to be shown that from God's point of view they need not be at all ideal, and that they seem ideal to us because we occupy a different standpoint.

The undue importance we attach to Time is one cause. We regulate our actions so much by our clocks and watches, and measure so many things in terms of the motions of these, that we have given Time an objective reality which it does not possess. It has only a sort of representative value like money, but more like a banking account where no actual coin passes; most convenient for measuring, for rendering expenditures of force, and what not, of one kind into those of other kinds, but not possessing *in itself* the properties attributed to it. It is so excellent a servant that we have made it our master. It is a conception which the mind has manufactured and then set over its own head.

Scripture is wiser than man; and not only here in Genesis i. is Time given a subordinate place, but it is very often treated so, sometimes quite disregarded, in God's thoughts as expressed in the Bible. Man thinks of the *dates* at which certain events occurred, or *the time* which they covered, according to his way of reckoning, as if these were the great realities. God takes account rather of the *events themselves*, and groups them together as He sees it suitable. Not, however, that man is altogether blind to the virtues of the latter system, for he frequently adopts it when it suits his convenience, notwithstanding the profound submission we all pay to the god Time.

Moreover, in arriving at his present geological knowledge, the arranging of the different formations in a chronological system has been of great assistance to man; and this has again tended to occupy his thoughts with the time aspect of the creation. But in Gen. i., as before remarked, the first thing of which we read in each instance of a creation is the formation of a certain plan in the mind of God. 'Let there be a firmament' is the first thing, and then follows, 'and God made the firmament.' We should say then, if we might so speak, that the Divine Mind was naturally occupied, not with the chronological sequence of the numerous events which occurred in the realizing of the plan, as revealed by science, but with the carrying out of the plan itself. Many other things may have occurred, incidentally connected with the carrying out of the Divine schemes; but it is not the business of Genesis i. to tell us about these. Its object is to tell us what God intended to do, and what He did. The Divine plans were duly realized, as we are told again and again in the quaint words of the old Hebrew writer, 'And God saw that it was good.' Biologists should remember what information Gen. i. is *meant to give,* if they find things in the animal-world which they think should have been referred to in this account of the Creation. I mean such things as predatory animals, parasites, struggle for life, etc.

We find very good reason, therefore, for concluding that the ideal character which we are disposed to attribute to these Six Days, results entirely from the standpoint from which we view them; and that from the Divine point of view they are probably not so ideal, but most real.

Lastly, seeing what Science tells us about the simultaneous and intermixed character of the work of Creation, we might perhaps with advantage pause and ask ourselves, What strictly chronological division of the work could have been made?

But, having thus recognized the true character of the Six Days, let us not seem to assert that there is anything in Genesis i. to indicate this. We have to thank Science for this information. As we shall see presently, there is a striking indication in the chapter that these Days were Divine Days, and not ordinary human ones; and, as the Bible is not meant to teach science, we conclude that that was quite sufficient information for it to give, without going into their character, as we are now able to do in the light of science. Moreover, six days of this kind are not readily united in the mind so as to form the idea of a week; whilst the Week is a most important feature of this account of the Creation. God has not only regarded the Creation as the work of several Days, but He has specially stated that there were *Six* of these Days, wherein He worked, and *One* wherein He ceased to work, or rested. The whole constituted the DIVINE WEEK, of which our week (or, to speak accurately, the Hebrew week) was the human copy. It was most important that the Hebrews should form such a conception of this Divine Week as would enable them, and cause them, to divide their time into the human weeks in imitation of it, and in obedience to the Divine commands. It mattered little, therefore, whether they thought of the Days accurately in their true character or not, whilst it mattered much that they should so think of them as to liken them to ordinary 24-hour days, and so adopt the human *week*. Therefore if they thought they were actually the same as earthly days, that mistake was a help, and not a hindrance, to the carrying out of this important Divine ordinance. No wonder, therefore, that they, and all the world after them, believed that these Six Days were earthly days till Science corrected the mistake.

Of course the Hebrew week did not come into existence suddenly in obedience to Divine command. The sacred character of the seventh day was as old as Accadian times; and so were the foundations of this Scripture, as we saw in the last chapter. There we saw that even before Hebrew times there had been a divinely-overruled development of Eastern theological sentiments and beliefs; and these were further developed and purified among the Hebrews. As there was even in the myth an ignorant worship of God, so, as we here see, this Divine command about the Sabbath was vaguely written in the human conscience, which regarded the seventh day as sacred, in Accadian times. It matters nothing at what point in the process it became strictly a Divine command and truly apprehended as such. Suffice it that eventually it became so.

It should perhaps be added that, although our week, with the observance of the first day as 'the Lord's day,' has superseded the old Hebrew week, it has come into existence through the latter; and the blessings of our weekly day of rest are due to this Divine Week of Genesis i., with the command about the Sabbath. The opponent of the Bible might remember this to advantage.

Another point should not be overlooked. The Apostle Peter writes, 'one day is with the Lord as a thousand years, and a thousand years as one day.' Therefore, notwithstanding the length of these periods of Creation, this Divine Week may well present to the mind of God much the same thing that the human week does to the mind of man. In that case, if the language of Genesis tends to make one regard the Divine Week as a human week, it presents God's conception of the Divine Week in the most suitable terms for human apprehension.

But we must not forget that this belief in the 24-hour duration of the Days of Creation presents a serious difficulty to an honest, well-educated mind to-day. It may have been well in ignorant times that all should thus interpret the words of Genesis i.; but it is not well that they should be so interpreted to-day. Sceptics may point to it, as they do, as the words of ignorance and therefore not the Word of God. God has not overlooked this. The indication that these Days were not the same as human ones, but were Divine Days, is given in this chapter. Since it was needful that the early Hebrews should recognize the days of Creation as human days, that so the human week might have Divine corroboration; and since it was imperative that the language of Scripture should convey Divine truths to its original recipients rather than be perfectly adjusted to the minds of later ages; how should we expect this Divine character of the Days to be expressed in Gen. i.? Certainly not in a conspicuous way. It could be done only in a hidden way. Hidden, that is, to the human writer, whose words were Divinely overruled so as to present and preserve this truth for readers of a later age.

The first indication that they were not ordinary days is that *three of the Divine Days had already elapsed before the human* 24-*hour day was brought into existence.* It may be added that this beginning of the human days on the 4th Divine Day is not purely ideal. As we shall see presently, the alternation of earthly day and night did not exist during the early parts of the Week of Creation.

Before we can discuss the second indication that the Six Days were Divine and not earthly ones, we must deal with the creation of Light. According to Genesis, Light was created on the First Day, but the two Great Lights were set in the firmament on the Fourth Day, a circumstance which has often been pointed out triumphantly as the proof of ignorance on the writer's part. There is, however, very evidently another side to that question, namely, Is it the sort of account which any man would have drawn up? Having the fact clearly before his mind, as expressed in the 14th to 19th verses, that the earthly light was produced by the two Great Lights, would any writer have stated, of his own free will, that Light itself was created three days before those Lights? In all probability, No.

If, however, we have here an account of God's own working in the process of Creation, what is the meaning of this statement about the creation of Light? According to verses 3, 4, 5: (1) 'God said, Let there be light; and there was light. And God saw the light, that it was good : (2) and God divided the light from the darkness. (3) And God called the light Day, and the darkness he called Night.' And according to verses 14, 15, 18: (1) ' God made the two great lights ' ' to give light upon the earth,' (2) ' to divide the light from the darkness,' (3) 'to divide the day from the night,' etc. I have changed the order in the second

THE CREATION. 213

passage so as to show the three-fold parallel. By comparing (1) with (1), (2) with (2), and (3) with (3), it will be seen that in both passages we have the production of Light, the dividing of the light from the darkness, and the dividing of the day from the night. *Does God do these three things twice?* and more especially, Does He create Light twice? Not the same Light, surely. Two different kinds of light must be referred to. It is clear that verses 14 to 19 relate to the light by which we see; for the Great Lights are made to 'give light upon *the earth*.' What other Light should there be, then? Surely, as God is giving an account of His own working, it is the Light by which He Himself sees, as He carries on that work. It has been well observed that Genesis i. gives Light as a creation of the First Day, so that God should not be represented as working three days in darkness. But would He not have been working all the Six Days in darkness if Light had not been created first? Would He work by the earthly light after it was made?
But did God really require any such light as this? We read in 1 John i. 5 that "God is light, and in Him is no darkness at all"—a truth, however, which was not known in earliest Hebrew times. The words of Gen. i. 3 conveyed the truth, though in a crude form, that God did not do the work of Creation in darkness, but in light, and also the principle that God does work in light. Presuming thoughtlessly that every one then knew what we know, we are liable to be occupied with the *form* in which a truth was conveyed, and to entirely overlook the important fact that that truth *was* conveyed by the words used, whilst only in a crude form could such truth then be communicated at all.

Clearly, this is the reason why Genesis gives the creation of Light on the First Day. Whence it has nothing to do with the earthly light, which was produced upon the Fourth Day. It is in no way connected with the luminaries. It is the Divine Light whereby the Divine Being works throughout the Six Divine Days.

We should not forget, however, that physical science is in favour of the theory that, before assuming its present form, the solar system existed as a *luminous* nebula.

Moreover, some have thought the *luminiferous ether*—presumably universal, all-saturating—may be the physical aspect of that light in which God dwells; and physical science could hardly object to that having been the first creation.

Of course we should not suppose these Divine Days to have consisted of alternations of light and darkness, like the earthly ones. If we suppose the First Day to have begun at the beginning of verse 3, verses 3, 4, and 5 may be taken as a figurative presentation of the Divine Day. For we have darkness followed by light as the *events* of the First Day, and then 'the evening and the morning' as *constituting* the First Day—a striking parallel. But this parallel does not appear in the other Days. We find, however, the enunciation of the First Day following close upon, and seemingly *connected with*, the work that had just been done. And this may be taken as defining the First Day as *the period wherein that work was done ;* so indicating the nature of these Divine Days. This seems a safer conclusion than the other. If it be said that this is not taking the words in their simple and apparent meaning, the answer is, as already said, that we have abundant reason to expect that God's thoughts, or rather some of them, would be presented figuratively in this place.

These words, 'evening and morning,' have been pointed out as inconsistent with the symbolic character of the Days. To which it has been well replied, that if the Days are figurative, so, consistently, are the evening and the morning. How important a place is given to Light in this account of the Creation ! since a whole Day seems devoted to the Divine light (though it is not quite clear to me that verse 1 precedes the First Day), and another whole Day to the Great Lights and the stars for giving light on the earth, etc.—apparently two whole Days out of the six.

It seems, then, that the object of verses 3, 4, and 5 is not only to convey the truth that God worked in the light, but *to present to us in figurative language the character of the Divine Days, as distinct from the earthly days.* We have seen the first indication of this in the fact that Three Divine Days elapsed before the earthly days existed. Here is the second indication.

Let us now see upon what principles this Account of the Creation is drawn up.

I. We have seen that, though not accurately representing the chronological order of the entire work, these Days are yet successive in character. Instead of presenting the progress *of Time* as determining the contents of each Day, they present rather the progress of *the work itself.* That work is portioned out into several natural grand divisions, and the order in which these followed each other is taken account of, though not rigidly adhered to throughout.

II. The *necessary* sequence is most carefully observed. Thus, Plants are not created before the ground whereon they grow. Animals are not created before their food—the plant. The Great Lights are not made before the Firmament in which they are to be set. And so on.

III. The Account is drawn up on the principle of Evolution. We find upward progress throughout, and particularly noticeable in the organic creation. It is a striking fact that we here find this truth, so fully realized in the Nineteenth Century, presented in the first chapter of the Bible.

Other things are observed, of which we may notice one or two presently; but obviously the account is drawn up on the above THREE PRINCIPLES. The first is not adhered to throughout; the second I think is; and perhaps the third also. Each of them is given the preference in those places where it is the most important and suitable of the three. In many cases they all lead to the same results, and there we may have the application of one, two, or all of them. These facts will be made clearer by the following analysis:—

1. HEAVEN.—Mentioned before the earth for one or more reasons, as already explained. Scripture does not say *this* is 'waste and void,' nor is any further information about it here necessary.

2. EARTH.—The subject now to be treated of. This is 'waste and void,' and has therefore to be reduced to order and completed.

First Day.
{ 3. LIGHT.—For God is not going to work in darkness. This is the Divine Light, not the earthly. Also Day and Night, or the division of light from darkness, must be given here, as forming the terms in which THE DAY is announced, before the term Day could be applied to the divisions of the work. This First Day also covers the period during which the work of verses 3, 4, and 5 (if not the previous ones also) was done, with which it is connected, so further defining the Divine Day. The 'evening and the morning' present the Day figuratively.

Second Day.
{ 4. THE FIRMAMENT OR EXPANSE.—Dividing the lower waters from the upper. First step in reducing the Earth to order. In this the Lights are to be set on the Fourth Day. It is also to be the habitation of the Fowls of the air on the Fifth Day—so preparing for both of these.

The Creation.

Third Day.

5. Division of the Earth into Land and Water.—Second step in reducing the Earth to order and completeness. The Water is to be the habitation of the sea-animals on the Fifth Day. The Land is to be the habitation of the plants, and, more important, the land-animals and Man on the Sixth Day.

6. Grass (or Sproutage), Herbs with Seed, and Trees bearing Fruit.—The first result of these is to clothe the land, and this finishes the Earth itself. The second result is that food is now provided for the coming inhabitants: green herbs for animals, herbs with seed and fruit for man, as stated in verses 29, 30. The mention of seed and fruit may also indicate provision for reproduction. The order in which these plants are named is *from lower to higher*.

Fourth Day.

7. The Lights.—To produce an earthly day and night (for the Divine Day is something different, and does not provide this), and other time-divisions; to produce the Seasons; and to give light upon the earth—all these being necessary for the coming inhabitants. They are set in the Firmament made on the Second Day. Everything is now ready for Animals and Man.

Fifth Day.

8. Inhabitants of the Water. — Lowest order of animals generally.

9. Inhabitants of the Air. —Intermediate order of animals generally.

Sixth Day.

10. Inhabitants of the Land (Animal).—Highest forms of animals generally. Not till now was all ready for Man.

11. Man.—The principal creation, made in God's image, to rule over all the other creatures. Completion of the work.

Seventh Day. } REST.

The following other features have been noticed by different commentators:—

The waters above the firmament constitute the clouds, and the rain which falls from these is necessary to the plants created the next Day.

The expression 'God saw that it was good,' implies the completion of the preceding portion of the work, the realization of the Divine plan. It does not, therefore, appear after the Second Day, the work of which was in a measure incomplete, whereas it appears twice on the Third Day. After the Second Day the Firmament still needed the Lights, and the lower waters needed dividing, whereas the Third Day comprised two portions of the work, each completed.

The earth, as first described, was both 'waste,' or 'without form,' and 'void.' The first of these two features had been completely removed by the first half of the Third Day. By then the earth was reduced to form, but was still 'void,' till life appeared thereon. Yet the appearing of the land and its producing vegetation are well placed on the same Day, as the land and its vegetation are so closely related to each other.

The works of the first three Days are respectively parallel to those of the last three. Thus—on the *first* Day the Divine light is created; on the *fourth* Day, the earthly light. On the *second* Day the lower waters are divided from the upper, and the aërial expanse or firmament formed; on the *fifth* Day the waters are inhabited by sea-animals, and the air by fowl. On the *third* Day the dry land appears, and the vegetation on it; on the *sixth* Day the land-animals and man are created.

In several respects the creation of man differs from that

of the animals. The waters and the earth are called upon to 'bring forth' the animals, but God creates man. He also announces His intention, 'Let us make man,' which He never does in other cases. Man's exercise of dominion is one feature wherein he is created in God's image. The animals, and all else, must be created before man, so that his kingdom may be all ready for his coming.

I may add that there is no 'evening and morning' to the Seventh Day; so that it did not end, like the others, so far as we are told; nor has it, therefore, the progressive character of the other Days. It has rest, hallowing, and blessing only.

When each portion of the work is reviewed the verdict is 'good'; when the whole is completed and reviewed together, it is 'very good.'

Such then—in as far as this exegesis and these comments present them correctly—are the Divine meaning and the Divine workmanship in the Genesis account of the Creation. Seeing these, and bearing in mind the sort of people for whom primarily, and through whose agency, it was produced, we may fearlessly encounter all that sceptics can urge against it. Let it be said that the narrative originated in Chaldean myth, and even that in its present form it clearly exhibits mythical features, the passage is none the less of Divine origin and replete with Divine truth. If it be urged that the writer represented to himself the Divine Being in human form, calling to the Light, to the Firmament, etc., to come forth into existence, and to the waters [3] and the earth to bring forth their respective animal

---

[3] Even here we have the testimony of Science that the sea was the cradle of the first animal population. Truly it "brought them forth," or "swarmed with" them (Gen. i. 20), though by a slower process.

populations, and believed that these and the other commands were instantly obeyed, and that the whole process was thus gone through in six ordinary days—we can admit all this. If this is myth, then Genesis i. is myth, but it is not *only* myth. An account of the Creation composed in such literature was well suited for bringing home its *Divine Truths* to the people of that age, as closely as their intellectual capacities would admit of it; whilst in all subsequent ages, when knowledge should be increased, not only a fuller apprehension of those Divine Truths, but others also, which had been hidden within it, were to be the portion of its believing and attentive readers.

Anthropomorphisms are there, but they are carefully veiled. We are struck with this when we compare Gen. i. with the following chapters, where they are conspicuous, but not out of place as they would be in this Account of the Creation. The Elohim of this chapter is the all-powerful Creator.

The crude knowledge and ideas of the age are also apparent; and, although they are turned to account and built together so skilfully, we cannot help noticing them, so that this Divine Account of the Creation is not a highly-finished one. It is as well for us to see these crudenesses; for otherwise we might mistake for God's thoughts that which is present merely through human imperfection.

Thus the classification of animals is :—water animals, animals of the air, land animals, with man last. Now, although in Gen. i. these sections of organic life are admirably connected, as we have seen, with their respective habitats, yet we need not conclude that on other grounds God prefers this classification to the one adopted by naturalists to-day. The inference is in the opposite direction. For Evolution is one of the principles on which the account is drawn up, but this classification of the animals does

THE CREATION. 221

not admit of more than a general application of that principle. The same applies to the plants. Possibly, therefore, if the chapter had been produced to-day it would contain such terms as Cryptogams and Phanerogams, Invertebrates and Vertebrates, or even the minor classifications; especially because with finer divisions the record could have been made to agree more closely with the actual progress of the work, as revealed by Geology. This is, undoubtedly, a small matter from a religious point of view; but, as the *progress of the work* is one of the principles applied, it would perhaps have been desirable to show that progress more completely. If this had no other virtue from a religious point of view, the account would, at least, have been better adjusted to the educated mind to-day; though we must never forget that what suits the learned does not usually suit the majority of the human race.

It is the largeness and crudeness of these divisions of the work that makes the account agree but generally, and not in detail, with the conclusions of science. As stated in a former place, some of the water-animals appeared early and others very late in the period of organic Creation; so that whilst, speaking generally, the water-animals were created first in the series, yet many of the air and land animals appeared before the inhabitants of the water were complete. So throughout. Reusch quotes the following passage from Pfaff:—

" If we look on the earthly creation as being *one* from the beginning of the earth up till now, as forming a *whole* in spite of all changes at different times, it is impossible to describe the events otherwise than is done in Genesis, or to suppose that they occurred in any other order. For in Genesis the separate kingdoms are contemplated separately and apart, without further reference to the changes in the history of each of them, and we are told how they successively made their appearance: the condition of chaos, the mass of waters, the formation of the land, after this the organic world, first the vegetable world, then the animal world represented at first only by inferior water animals, then by land animals, and finally the appearance of man, are represented as occurring in their true sequence, and these separate portions of the history of development are designated as days."

This necessary crudeness of human ideas affords a simple explanation of other differences relating to the earlier condition of the Earth. According to the belief of many geologists and astronomers, the Earth existed at first in a gaseous and then in a molten condition, before assuming its present form. In his work *Moses and Geology* (pages 69, 70) Dr. Kinns remarks:—

"And then, Figuier in *The World before the Deluge*, says, the metals, the chlorides, the sulphides, and even the silicates of alumina and lime, would exist in a gaseous form; also the enormous body of water constituting our oceans, seas, and rivers, would be in a vaporous condition; added to these, the component parts of air—nitrogen, oxygen, and carbonic acid—would swell the atmosphere to such an extent, *that it must have extended a thousand times farther into space than it does now.* Under these circumstances the different substances composing such an atmosphere would at first be ranged round the Earth in the order of their respective densities; that part of it nearest to the molten globe being formed of the heavier vapours. . . . . This order of superposition would not, however, be long preserved. In spite of their differences of densities, these atmospheric layers would become mixed by diffusion, also formidable storms and violent ebullitions would frequently confound these incandescent zones. As to the globe itself, without being so much agitated as its hot and stifling atmosphere, it would be no less subject to perpetual tempests occasioned by a thousand chemical actions which were taking place in its molten mass. In this manner would our globe circulate in space, carrying in its train the flaming streaks of its multiple atmosphere, unfitted as yet for living beings, *and impenetrable to the rays of the Sun*."

Also on page 73, as to the first formation of the universal sea, he writes:—

" Gradually these lurid flames would subside, and then the

water having given up its oxygen to these metals, they would become alkalies and earths. The hydrogen being set free, however, would again unite with the oxygen of the atmosphere, and, as a highly-heated vapour, would ascend to the top, where, coming into contact with the glacial regions of space, it would be condensed and fall again upon the Earth; but as time went on there would be no conflagration, for on coming into contact with the still heated rocks, the water would re-ascend as vapour. This might take place many times; but each time the earth would become cooler, for each time much heat would be withdrawn from the surface of the globe, and at last the waters would settle down and form a universal ocean, boiling and seething and assimilating all the soluble matters of very diverse natures, particularly the soda, potassa, ammonia, magnesia, and even the vitrified and agglomerated metals, which would be violently stirred and upheaved by the hot, thick, troubled water—a sort of witches' broth, wherein all the liquid and solid elements boil over the central furnace. . . ."

And on page 74, as to the formation of land :—

. . . . "in cooling, irregularities would appear on the surface, forming the earliest mountain-chains, valleys, rents, and ravines, according as the various parts of the surface might radiate heat in an unequal manner. Over these early mountains and ravines the boiling ocean would dash and the hot rain would fall, causing a disintegration of the rocks, which, after being suspended for a short time in the water, would be deposited at the bottom of the sea. In this manner, we have strong grounds for believing, the first stratified rocks were produced."

These extracts would have been clearer if I had space to give them in full, but they are sufficient for the present purpose. Comparing Gen. i. 1–10 with what Science, or scientific deductions (or speculations if the reader prefer), have to say about the earliest conditions of the earth, we find a general but not detailed agreement. First the earth is 'waste' or 'without form,' perhaps corresponding to the gaseous condition. But it appears as covered with waters; the expanse is formed in the midst of these waters, and then divides the lower from the upper. If Science is right we should say rather that the expanse was formed amidst the gases, and that their condensation into the waters below, with the clouds remaining thereafter floating above, left the expanse between the two.

Undoubtedly the old Hebrew idea, following the Babylonian, of the waters above the firmament, was that of an upper sea rather than clouds. But what did they know about the early conditions of the earth? *Nothing whatever.* Here therefore, as elsewhere, it appears that their crude ideas and beliefs were divinely overruled, so as to express approximately these facts about the first stages in the world's creation. Could aught but Divine knowledge have produced this account? Surely not. Accident will not account for it; and certainly the knowledge of those times will not do so. If, as we have seen, the Light mentioned in verse 3 is the Divine light, probably the darkness of verse 2 is the absence or negation of that Divine light. The earth itself would have been more luminous in its earliest condition than after it had cooled down. But we must not forget that light is *no light* before there are material eyes for it to act upon so as to produce vision. In a double sense, therefore, the earth was shrouded in darkness at that time.

This question fitly introduces another, which may have been present in the reader's mind from the first. It is the one *apparently great* disagreement of Genesis i. with Science, from a chronological point of view at least—the creation, or appointment, of the two Great Lights on the Fourth Day. The superficial reader says, "These two Lights are the Sun and Moon, and instead of their having come into existence so late as the Fourth Day or period, they existed as soon as the Earth itself did." Without going into the question whether or not the Hebrew word in verse 16 signifies an appointment to their special offices, and not their original creation; let us confine ourselves to the words of the text.

We have already seen that the passage only relates to, and mentions, *the Lights*, which appeared, or 'were set,' in the firmament on the Fourth Day ; that it neither mentions, nor has anything to do with, the *heavenly bodies*.

When did these Lights first make their appearance in the firmament to beings located on the earth ? The answer given by exegetes is related to parts of the foregoing extracts from Dr. Kinns' work, which is one reason why these are given here. The reader will have noticed in italics the words 'impenetrable to the rays of the Sun.' On pages 187 and 188 of his work, *Moses and Geology*, Dr. Kinns further says :—

"I have shown you before that both the Sun and Moon must have been created contemporaneously with the Earth, but that during the early ages of the world much of their light was hidden from our globe by the dense vapours which surrounded it; that, up to the time now under consideration, a similar climate existed all over the Earth ; and that, therefore, there were no seasons properly so called until after the Carboniferous period. When, however, the Sun blazed forth in all his glory, seasons commenced, as both the fauna and flora testify. There was probably also a continuous twilight from the dense and vaporous condition of the atmosphere, and here again Science and the Bible harmonise, for the Sun was not appointed 'to rule over the day and over the night, and to divide the light from darkness' until after this period, . . . the Sun became at this era not only the visible sign for distinguishing days and years, but also the efficient cause of seasons."

Dr. Reusch, however, says (*Nature and the Bible*, vol. i. pp. 346, 347) :—" Palæontologists will not admit that the sun first began to give light and warmth on the earth after the Carboniferous age, and that up to that time the earth was only warmed by its own heat, and was surrounded by such a thick atmosphere that the sun was quite hidden by it." So that it is safer, at any rate, not to try to make the parallel so complete as is done by some writers.

It does not here concern us to do so. We can see at once that the making of the Lights is well placed on the Fourth Day, just before the creation of the animals which were to see by their light. Lest, however, this arrangement should seem to be entirely ideal, it is well for us to see the general agreement of Science with Scripture on this matter :—The Bible first provides the Firmament (or expanse) on the Second Day, and then says about the Fourth Day, " And God said, Let there be *lights in the firmament of the heaven* . . . and God set them *in the firmament*, etc. : " Science says that in the first period there was no such aërial expanse between the earth and the clouds as there is now ; and that not until a later period would the Sun and Moon have appeared in this expanse (or in the sky) to an observer situated on the earth ; nor would the seasons have begun. Finally, it may be added that if there is any reference in Gen. i. to the *heavenly bodies themselves* it is in the very beginning, where " God created the heaven and the earth." ' Heaven ' may include these.

Of course a critic might object that light is required for the growth of plants ; that air, which is of vital importance to living creatures, is never mentioned as being created for that purpose ; and so on. But these and similar facts before noticed, show how the whole account is accommodated to the ideas of the time of its composition. Thus breath *within the body* seems to be inseparable from, if not identical with, life itself, according to the old Hebrew idea, but of outward material for that breath it takes no account. So again we find ' the fowl of the air '[4] in this very chapter, but the idea of '*gas*' nowhere, I believe, in Hebrew times. We need not wonder, therefore, if the waters are mentioned

[4] I believe, however, this should be translated ' fowl of the heaven,' or ' expanse.'

and not the gaseous condition of the earth, for the latter could not be literally expressed when the *idea* of gas did not exist.

Rather than occupy ourselves with such matters, we may perhaps with advantage notice what glaring defects might naturally have been present in the text, as they seem to have been during the shaping out of this Account of the Creation.

For instance, Genesis might have commenced with an account of the flood of the sea bringing forth the heavens and the earth, and the creation, or coming into existence, of the gods; as in the Babylonian creation-legend cited in the last chapter. But it opens with the stable and sublime announcement, 'In the beginning God created the heaven and the earth.' What a difference!

Here is another instance. In the sixth chapter of the Second Book of Esdras, the writer recapitulates, or reviews, the work of the Six Days of Creation. After going through the first Four Days and part of the Fifth (or perhaps all of it) he says (verse 49) :—

"Then didst thou ordain two living creatures, the one thou calledst Enoch, and the other Leviathan; and didst separate the one from the other; for the seventh part, namely, where the water was gathered together, might not hold them both. Unto Enoch thou gavest one part, which was dried up the third day, that he should dwell in the same part, wherein are a thousand hills: but unto Leviathan thou gavest the seventh part, namely, the moist; and hast kept him to be devoured of whom thou wilt, and when."

He then proceeds to the work of the Sixth Day, giving it approximately as in Genesis. In the Book of Enoch (lviii. 7) we read (in regard to the day of judgment) :—

"In that day shall be distributed (for food) two monsters; a female monster, whose name is Leviathan, dwelling in the depths of the sea, above the springs of waters; and a male (monster), whose name is Behemoth; which possesses, (moving) on his breast, the invisible wilderness. His name was Dendayen in the east of the garden, where the elect and the righteous will dwell; where he received (it) from my ancestor, who was man, from Adam the first of men, whom the Lord of spirits made. Then I asked of another angel to show me the power of those monsters, how they became separated on the same day, one (being) in the depths of the sea, and one in the desert."

Lastly, we find in the Book of Job long, and in some respects parallel, descriptions of Behemoth and Leviathan (Chap. xl. 15 to xli. 34). Comparing these three passages, it becomes evident that they relate to the same imaginary creatures of early Hebrew belief. And, seeing the general agreement of the work of the Six Days as related in 2 Esdras vi. with what is given in Gen. i., it seems clear that the account of the Creation which was current among the Hebrews in earlier times contained the creation of those two monsters. The Chaldean legend gives the first shaping, and this passage in 2 Esdras a more advanced but unfinished stage, of the Biblical Account of the Creation.

Now if Gen. i. affirmed the creation of these two monsters, or that of 'the *spirit* of the firmament' (as in 2 Esdras vi.) instead of 'the firmament,' there would be something to which the sceptic might point with due cause. In regard to this we must bear in mind the jealous care with which ancient 'sacred writings' have in many cases been preserved in their literal integrity.

These facts throw light on the passage in Job before mentioned. For, evidently, the early Hebrews believed in the existence of these two monsters; they believed God had created them; and these probably occupied a prominent place in their thoughts. Naturally, therefore, in the demonstration to Job of the greatness of God, as recorded by the Hebrew writer, these find a place in the subjects chosen.[5] There the mention of these two monsters, which

---

[5] Further remarks on this subject are made in Chap. iv., pp. 115-117.

would have been most out-of-place in an *Account of the Creation*, is perfectly admissible. In the Book of Job the pre-existing materials of Hebrew belief are taken up as a means to bring home to the people of that age certain *Divine truths*, such as the power and greatness of God. In Gen. i. an account of what God created is the substance of the chapter, and these two monsters were no part of that. If every Scripture were judged according to its efficiency in imparting its own special Divine truth, or truths, a host of difficulties would vanish out of sight.

Noticing then the *absence* of such real defects in Gen. i., in places where they might be expected, we shall be less likely to be unduly occupied with those crudenesses which are, for reasons so obvious, necessarily present. These may have some bearing on the non-reference to those biological phenomena which seem to disagree in character with this Account of the Creation. For, possibly, if the Account had been produced in a less crude age, some light would have been given on such matters. We have seen one other probable reason why there is no reference to them.

To sum up, briefly. Gen. i. gives *God's* views of the Creation. Whilst its truths are all, on that account, of the greatest importance to man, and higher than the facts of Science, we may yet safely assert that some of them are intrinsically more important than others. Thus the *fact* that God created all is clearly of more importance than the time, or order, in which He did so, or even than the particular principles on which He has drawn up this Account of the Creation. All such fundamental Truths are adequately and unequivocally expressed in this chapter, as elsewhere in the Bible. As regards the less important ones, no doubt many of them would have been expressed differently, and perhaps others would have been added, if the chapter had been produced in a more enlightened age. The general agreement of the chapter with the facts revealed by Science is such as can be accounted for only by Divine origin. Where it differs from Science, which is in matters of detail, this is due to two causes:—in some cases God's view of things differs from man's; in other cases the cumbersome ideas of the age when the account was composed were not suited to express the facts very accurately.

It is an admirable structure built out of rough materials. Because of this roughness it is not a highly-finished structure. The roughness of the materials is in places evident; but the skill of the Architect in fitting them together is everywhere more evident. In the words of the Hebrew writer, the structure of each part viewed separately is ' good': the edifice as a whole is ' very good.'

More especially when we consider its marvellous adjustment to readers *of all ages*, do we see how ' very good ' it is.

CHAPTER VIII.

HUMAN EVOLUTION AND THE FALL.

There are several theories respecting the Origin of Man.

(1) There is the old-fashioned belief that the clay was moulded into human form by the Hand of God, and transformed into man by a miraculous process. To those who hold this theory, it seems that a more natural process was unnecessary, that an intermediate animal stage would be opposed to the teaching of Scripture, and derogatory to the dignity of man. We have seen, however, in the first chapter of this work that this is a position which Science has overthrown.

(2) Others believe that man evolved from ape-like animals, belonging to a stock from which the anthropoid apes also arose. No Darwinian believes that man is descended from any existing form of ape; but all believe that man and the anthropoid apes sprang from one stock. Now Mr. Darwin and his followers have done little in the way of analyzing out the factors which could contribute to the evolution of so marvellous a result as man, though it must be allowed that they have been industrious in trying to make their general conclusion acceptable—the conclusion namely, that an ape-like animal evolved by natural and necessary processes, through stages uncontrolled in any special way by God, till at length arose the man. We have seen, also in the first chapter of this work, how untenable is any theory based so much on chance.

(3) Some authorities, such as Mr. A. R. Wallace, believe that man, as a physical organism—with body and brain—was evolved from simpler predecessors, but maintain that to account for the higher and most human characteristics it is necessary to postulate a special spiritual influx. If the view here to be maintained differs from that of Mr. Wallace, it differs in form rather than in substance.

To Mr. Wallace's views, some see the objection that they are a departure from the theory of natural evolution. In the first chapter (supplement) of this work we saw, however, that this 'natural evolution' theory proves to be an *un*natural one; because it is only in the lower parts of Nature that event demonstrably follows cause in a purely mechanical way, whereas in its higher parts we find that such mechanical sequences are often interfered with, and the course of things regulated by the Mind of Man; and, as a rational explanation of Nature requires that the whole of Nature should be taken into account, the most *natural* way of accounting for what exists is to postulate a personal, intelligent, and *active Creator*. We saw moreover that, rather than suppose that the process of Creation was designed and arranged once for all in the beginning and then set in motion like a wound-up clock, it is far more natural to conclude that the whole process was subjected to incessant supervision, planned out in general at the beginning, worked out in detail as it went on—that natural agencies did the work, or much of the work, under the control and direction of the Creator. If, therefore, we have to predicate spiritual influxes in order to account for the truly human qualities of man, these would not be an unnatural exception, but a process in part at least resembling the other processes, all being the work of an active Creator. But must we limit the spiritual influxes to the case of man? With the fact of Biogenesis before us, are we not obliged to affirm an influx of spirit, or at least of life, in order to account for the *lowest* forms of animal life? And, seeing the wide differences between the lower and the higher forms of animal life, the lower forms with no mind, the higher ones possessing the animal mind, is it not necessary, in order to account for all these forms of life, to predicate a whole series of influxes of spirit, or of mind, or of life?

From the fact that the higher forms have arisen by the common process of reproduction, which connected them, through millions of successive links, with their simpler ancestors, it may seem at first sight that the qualities of the higher were in some way present in the lower. But, in the first place, this inference is based on totally *insufficient data*, and, in the second place, the facts, as far as we *observe* them, testify that it is *false*. If indeed we compare any organism with its parent, we see that most of its qualities were possessed by that parent, and this tends to cause some confusion of thought. But when, taking links in the chain that are more widely separated, we compare the man with the higher animal, and the higher animal with the amœba, we see that the man possesses a host of qualities which the higher animal does not, and the higher animal possesses a host of qualities which the amœba does not. We not only see that these superior qualities are in no way present in the lower form in as far as it is amenable to observation—and it is only the aggregate of knowable parts of an organism that are properly included in our concept of it—but we also totally fail to conceive of any manner in which they *could be* present in it. But were not the germs of such qualities present? If the reader can represent to himself how the germs of æsthetic sentiments, or of abstract thoughts, *could be* present in the amœba, to him this proposition has a *meaning*. To my mind the attempt only shows that this whole assumption of the presence of the higher qualities in the lower forms of life, is an empty proposition, one whose terms may indeed be separately conceived, but which refuse to be *united* so as to convey any real meaning. It shows that of the *real genesis* of mental properties we know little or nothing, and if we know anything we derive that knowledge from subjective analysis, rather than from observation of external phenomena. The latter may tell us something about the conditions necessary to the development and workings of mind, such as the presence of a nervous system with its molecular motions; but of the essential nature of the genesis and growth of mind, such observations can reveal little or nothing. And it is with the substance of mind, especially of the human mind, that we have here to do. Whilst then Science has revealed that the animal was a basis necessary to the production of the man, we are compelled to believe that the higher human attributes are not of the same essence as those of the animal, and have not come from that source.

In the unthinking mind the association of the ideas, man, animal, and descent, produces thoughts of an essential relationship which does not in reality exist. There is the widest difference between this purely physical relation involved in the reproductive process—in this case involving, if not weakened by, myriads of links—and the psychical and social relationship involved in parentage and the family tie as known amongst ourselves. How largely our conception of relationship is composed of these psychical and social qualities is seen from the fact, that the child says of an unrelated person who takes the place of his parent, treating him as that parent should have done, "He is a father to me," "She is a mother to me." Or again, where two unrelated youths or men live together in mutual affection, it is said that they are like brothers. The failure to think of the purely physical aspect of the descent, or ascent, of man, *without associating these important psychical properties therewith*, leads to false ideas of relationship between man and the ape. The real genesis of the soul is not identical with that process.

The difference between the physical and the psychical aspect of parentage is strongly insisted on in Scripture. There we find that the only real relationship is the spiritual one.

In John viii. 37-44, the principle is expressed. Christ says, "I know that ye are Abraham's seed; yet ye seek to kill me, because my word hath not free course in you. I speak the things which I have seen with my Father; and ye also do the things which ye have heard from your father. They answered and said unto him, Our father is Abraham. Jesus saith unto them, *If ye were Abraham's children, ye would do the works of Abraham. . . Ye do the works of your father. . .* Ye are of your father the devil." Here clearly, while Christ admits the natural descent of those Jews, He maintains that it is nothing, the only *real* descent is the *spiritual one*. The only validity which the natural descent possesses is in virtue of the spiritual descent which is involved in it, which spiritual descent was here wanting. The principle is again expressed in Matt. xxiii. 29-31. "Ye say, If we had been in the days of our fathers, we should not have been partakers with them in the blood of the prophets. Wherefore *ye witness to yourselves, that ye are sons of them that slew the prophets.*" He knows their natural descent, but does not *on that account* charge them with such a parentage. He lays it to their account only on the ground of their own testimony and of their deeds (see also verses 32, 33). Again in Rom. iv. 16, 17, the Apostle Paul says, that before God Abraham is the father, not only of his natural descendants, the Jews, but *of all the faithful.* Can anything more clearly show that God knows where alone *real* inheritance lies? namely, not in the natural, but in the spiritual; not in the biological, but in the psychological. It is quite consistent with this that in its proper place and manner natural parentage is recognized—recognized because of what it involves. Natural descent in a general way involves, or is accessory to, spiritual descent; but where, as in the case of those Jews, and in the ascent of man, it does not involve it, there is no relationship in the real sense of the term.

But why is such prominence given to the ape-like progenitor? That was nothing more than *one* of the millions of links in the progressive chain of life. If it be selected in preference to previous forms because it was the last and most like man, it is on that account all the more worthy of honour. The naturalist divides the animal world into many classes, and the nearer any one of these resembles man, the higher it stands in the scale; the nearer it resembles inorganic matter the lower it stands. Yet *any* connexion of man with the highest form of animal life is offensive, whilst it is no dishonour to have come out of the lowest of the low—'the dust of the ground.'

This introduces us to another aspect of evolution. Descent furnishes nothing more than a series of *connecting links* between the successive forms of life in the upward chain; it has done none of the work of creation, or of evolution. We might, therefore, well lose sight of the individuality of the successive forms of life, and treat them as if they were successive states of one creature. If, therefore, in Gen. ii. 7, Jehovah-Elohim represents God, His hands (implied though not mentioned in the text) the forces of Nature —or if these forces are instruments in those hands—and His breathing the unseen connexion between God and His creature; then that which Science has revealed of the process of creation [1] is not essentially different from what is

---

[1] I do not limit the term 'creation' to the formation of something out of nothing. To me it means the bringing into being, by *any* process, through the will of God.

implied in the text.   If instead of many successive organisms in the evolution of life, as revealed by Science, there had been only *one* organism whose many successive states, identical with those of the many organisms that formed the chain, had followed each other rapidly *in this individual*; no one would demur to this method of creation as at variance with the teaching of Scripture ; and no one would be confused with false notions of relationship. And yet we here see that there is practically no difference between the two cases. The history of every individual human being presents approximately a miniature of such a continuous organism.

Let us remember, moreover, the difference between the Creation as described in Gen. i. and the account of it given by geology. In Gen. i. the creative acts, such as the separation of land and water, appear at first sight as if done by one stroke of the Creator's hand. From geology we know that these were slow processes. So here. Man is formed by the Creator of the dust of the ground. That is just what we learn from Evolution, whilst we find a very long process by which man was thus formed. Science tells us a good deal about that process as it appeared outwardly, but of the unseen part it can tell us nothing. What part of man's constitution was received from God, not being the outcome of organized physical substance; and the mysterious inner process of the formation of his being—these are matters on which Science can say nothing.

Some further suggestions on the question of influxes may be helpful. We might conceive that there was only one kind of influx, to which first the animal and afterwards the man was subjected. If we pour molten matter into a mould it solidifies into the shape of that mould : if we pour clear water into a muddy pool or a dirty vessel, it becomes dirty. So, if there were influxes of the formative substance of mind into organisms of many kinds, we should suppose that the structures of those organisms would cause it to assume their different *forms* of mind. And if we take the case of an influx into a partly developed organism; as clear water is made muddy, so we should expect this formative substance of mind to assume in some degree the *quality* of the pre-existing mind of that organism. Possibly, therefore, an influx of one kind would answer for all cases. But there may have been influxes of several kinds, and this seems the more likely of the two suppositions.

But, leaving the case of the animal, let us confine our attention to that of man. Here we have something more substantial to build on. For both Scripture and Christian experience testify to the fact that a spiritual influx of one kind *is known* to man—the influx of the Spirit which occurs at conversion, and also in after Christian life. Undoubtedly this is an influx of a higher kind than the one whereby man was made what he is; that, namely, which is implied in Gen. ii. 7 :—" Jehovah-Elohim formed man of the dust of the ground, and breathed into his nostrils the breath of life." But the latter is something which no development of an animal could ever produce; it is a life, a soul, received from God Himself.

We should, however, be on our guard against supposing such a spiritual influx to have occurred all at once, or even in large quantities at few times. Rather we should suppose it to have occurred in very small quantities at very many times, as fast only as the developing man was able to 'digest' it—perhaps so gradual as to seem like an absorption into man rather than an inflowing, of this formative substance of mind. This indeed brings us to another difficult question, the relation in which God stands to Nature, or to Matter. According to Joseph Le Conte, " Either God is far more closely related with Nature, and operates it in a more direct way than we have recently been accustomed to think, or else Nature operates itself and needs no God at all." Rejecting the latter view, he insists that we must believe in "a God *immanent*, a God resident *in* Nature, ... a God in whom in the most literal sense, not only we but all things have their being, in whom all things consist, through whom all things exist, and without whom there would be and could be nothing." After explaining these views more fully than can be done here, he proceeds to point out the difference between them and Idealism on the one hand, and Pantheism on the other.[2]   Mr. Herbert Spencer, rejecting the Christian conception of God, yet remarks:—"We are obliged to regard every phenomenon as a manifestation of some Power by which we are acted upon; though Omnipresence is unthinkable, yet, as experience discloses no bounds to the diffusion of phenomena, we are unable to think of limits to the presence of this Power. . ."[3]

If we very carefully guard against confusing the Personality of God with what we call Nature, or the Universe, distinguishing clearly between a God omnipresent in Nature and a God identical with it, His omnipresence in Matter differs little (from a theological point of view) from an omnipresence in space, except that it would seem to be the more rational assumption of the two. And if it be assumed that God is 'the unknown substratum,' the Supporter, of that which is manifested to us outwardly as matter, there is less liability to such a confusion as that of the Pantheist. God everywhere, is one of the doctrines of Scripture.

If such an omnipresence as this be assumed, those influxes which we have been discussing, or some of them, might well resolve themselves into a continuous absorption into the

[2] *Evolution and its Relation to Religious Thought*, pp. 279-285.
[3] *First Principles*, p. 99.

developing man, of the formative substance of mind, from Him "*in* whom we live and move and have our being" (Acts xvii. 28). And this may apply both to the evolution of the race and to that of every individual. Given (*a*) the inherent tendency of the physiological unit, or fertilized germ, to reproduce the parental form; and (*b*) this formative substance of mind in some way joined with what we call matter, whose future form normally is determined by the forces resident in that unit—will not these factors account for, or at least agree with, the phenomena which are manifested in the mental development of every individual? (The fact has been pointed out in Chapter I. that in the evolution of the race there was this difference, that the polarity, as we might call it, of the human germ did not exist. It was being made, that of each successive generation approaching nearer to it.)

But before adopting definite conclusions on this and some of the other matters touched on here, both a fuller investigation of these subjects than could be undertaken here, and much clearness of thought, are indispensable. It is not my purpose in this place to dogmatize on such matters, but only to suggest.

Leaving the question of influxes, there yet remains a testimony which no reasoning can overthrow, to the fact that there is no real relationship between the man and the animal—the testimony of the human consciousness. If there were any such community between the two, would not our forefathers have found it out, or at least suspected it, at some time or other, before the date when it seemed to be involved in the evolution theory? It is surely a striking fact that the instinct of humanity never pointed in that direction, but always in the opposite one. Mr. Darwin has remarked that it is only our natural prejudice, and that arrogance which made our forefathers declare that they were descended from demi-gods, which leads us to demur to the admission of such a relationship (*Descent of Man*, p. 25). *Whence this 'natural prejudice'?* a prejudice all the more striking when we remember that man has always observed and freely admitted certain points of resemblance between himself and the animal. It is the expression of that which is within man, of man's own essence, the human consciousness, which has always testified, and, resisting the voice of reason, still testifies, that the human soul is different in essence from the lower creation. Let us consider which of these opponents, Consciousness and Reason, we can most safely trust for guidance in this particular case.

Consciousness *versus* Reason.

In the first place, *nolens volens*, we must unreservedly allow Reason to conduct the argument; we must unhesitatingly accept the validity of the reasoning process; for if Consciousness, or Reason himself, or any one else, should show that that process is untrustworthy, the whole argument collapses at the outset.

But there is reasoning in the light and reasoning in the twilight. Arithmetical calculations performed in the light are presumed to be correct; but with those done in the twilight the figures are very liable to be misread; 3 may be taken for 5 or 8, 1 for 7, or a greater mistake may arise by overlooking a figure altogether. So, the reasoning process is wholly trustworthy, but in certain twilight cases, Reason is very liable to mistake his ciphers, and it is here that the blundering comes in.

In reading those sensations which answer to external phenomena, Reason is working in the light, or in the lightest place accessible to him. But in reading mental phenomena he is much more in the twilight; the ciphers are too close under his eye-lids to be distinctly seen; so that here he is far more liable to mistake 3 for 8, or 1 for 7. But Consciousness does not need such inversion of her eyes, here her reading is direct, immediate; it is not in fact a reading of herself, but an *expression* of herself.

Whence does Reason obtain his ciphers when he works out this community between man and the animal? There is only one source open; and that source is *Consciousness*. So he first *accepts* the testimony of Consciousness, bases his calculations wholly on the words of Consciousness, and thence arrives at the astounding conclusion that Consciousness is untrustworthy! meanwhile forgetting that *this* conclusion of his own, based as it is on Consciousness, falls with the fall of Consciousness! He has misread his ciphers. Seeing that the physical process of reproduction was in some way necessary to the genesis of the human soul, he has concluded that the two things are identical. Seeing that the animal was instrumental in the production of the man, he infers that the man is a modified form of the animal. Using the same name to denote things essentially different, he has mistaken the one for the other.

It may be objected to the above argument that the words of Consciousness on which Reason bases his calculation respecting the origin of man, are not *the same word* of Consciousness as that which denies the relationship with the animal; that the calculation is based on other deliverances of Consciousness, which are correct. But that is to say that there Reason accepts *unhesitatingly* the testimony of Consciousness (whence he must obtain all his ciphers) in hundreds, nay in *thousands* of cases (for the argument that proves evolution consists of a very long chain of links), an error in almost any one of which would prove fatal; and *thence* arrives at the conclusion that Consciousness is not trustworthy! His conclusion that she is not reliable is based on the undoubting assumption that, in thousands of cases at least, she is wholly reliable.

Throughout evolution Consciousness is always in advance of Reason: Reason follows after, and depends on Consciousness for all he has to say. Consciousness therefore is surely more reliable than Reason. The reasoning process is always mediate, often manifold mediate; but Consciousness is always *immediate*, she does not interpret or read; she is the *direct expression of that which* IS. The reasoning *process* is always valid, but in reading his ciphers he is in many cases most liable to err. When Consciousness seems to err, it proves on analysis that Reason has come to her aid, and it is he that has made the mistake. I do not see how Consciousness herself can ever err.

> " Trust in the Lord with all thine *heart*,
> And lean not upon thine own *understanding*."
> Prov. iii. 5.

That Reason does make such mistakes is well known. For instance, he asserts that (1) there must be, and (2) there cannot be, infinite space. (1) That matter must have a limit seems obvious; beyond that limit there can be no matter, we might proceed for ever, and never meet with a resisting substance. But (2) does not that imply that space itself is infinite? which is equally inconceivable. Reason has misread his ciphers. In trying to think of *nothing* beyond the matter, he has unwittingly brought that nothing into the category of entities, treating it in the second case as a *something*, which he calls space. It is this something which, it seems, must have a limit too. To assert, however, that matter must be finite, presupposes a measure which can be stretched thereon only so many times in succession. But as all measures are themselves relative, adopted merely for convenience, as we know of nothing to determine an absolute measure, it appears that, absolutely, there can be neither finity nor infinity. The idea seems to be fundamentally wrong.

Reason then, wholly trustworthy so far as the process goes, is so liable when in twilight to misread his ciphers, that in this important question of man's community with the animal, he is wholly untrustworthy as a guide. *So is he also in many psychological and theological questions, where he opposes the testimony of Consciousness and the testimony of the Word of God.*

As the simplest way of expressing myself I have had occasion to speak of man's descent from an animal, or ape-like progenitor; but let it be distinctly understood that the expression is not intended to involve anything further than what has been admitted in this discussion.

That there are similarities between some of the mental attributes of man and those of the animal, is a fact known to everybody; and it appears to follow therefrom that both are in part composed of the same formative mental substance. But I do not believe for a moment that the revelations of science in regard to the descent, or ascent, of man, establish *any closer connexion* between the man and the animal, than that to which observation testifies.

Moreover, since we can conceive of anything only in those terms which are furnished by our own consciousness, it is well to remember that we are very liable, in interpreting the animal mind, to attribute thereto qualities which exist only in our own.

For several reasons, therefore, I deny man's relationship with the animal. Science fails to give any real account of the genesis of the human soul. Several New Testament Scriptures teach that it is not identical with the physical process of reproduction. The human Consciousness, more reliable than Reason, is emphatic on the matter. Gen. ii.

HUMAN EVOLUTION AND THE FALL. 245

7, and other Scriptures, clearly teach that it was from God Himself that man received his being.

There is a wide difference between the subject of Gen. i. and that of Gen. ii. and subsequent chapters—a fact which should be distinctly borne in mind when examining these Scriptures. Gen. i. treats of the creation of the Earth, the Lights, the plants, the animals and man, etc. All, with such exceptions as noticed in the last chapter, are concepts familiar to the mind of man—physical things possessing their own conventional names. Gen. ii. and following chapters, on the contrary, deal with the moral history of the human race in the first ages, with man's relations with God—with spiritual things. It is true that Gen. i. does not consider Nature from the same point of view that physical science does, but rather from a spiritual standpoint, as we saw in the last chapter. The subsequent chapters of Genesis, however, have very little to do in any way with physical things. So that, as a general truth, we may say that Gen. i. treats of physical things and the following chapters of psychical things. Thus we are brought at once into the midst of unfamiliar concepts; or rather of things which, though fundamentally separate in themselves, are yet not commonly presented as separate to the mind of man—things of which he has formed, even to-day, but very vague concepts, and often not even any concepts at all.

Enough has been said in previous chapters as to the difficulty of expressing truths of this latter order—a difficulty which still existed in New Testament times; and which, working backwards from then, we find ever presenting itself as greater and greater. Here then in the very beginning of the knowledge of such truths we find that difficulty *at its greatest*. We saw that much later in Hebrew history there was need of such truths being presented by means of concrete pictures. How much more so, then, at the very beginning. *We cannot, in fact, see how such truths could possibly have been presented in any form other than in concrete pictures.*

Our analysis of Gen. i. further confirms us in this anticipation. There, naturally, we found those things with which the human mind is well acquainted, such as the earth, the sea, the animals, etc., called by their own familiar names. But when we passed from these to such things as the Divine divisions of the work of Creation, the Divine Light, etc., we found them presented for human apprehension in the likeness of natural days, natural light, etc. And, just as the Divine truths of Gen. ii., iii., are presented under the guise of a narrative, so were those of Gen. i. presented. We cannot very well deny, what there is no need to deny, that the writer of Gen. i. saw, in his own mind, the Creator going through the creative acts, calling things into existence, dividing the waters, etc., one after another for a period of six of our common days. Yet when we compare that chapter with what science has told us, we find that an almost infinite number of events, covering myriads of ages, are condensed, and thus as it were dramatically presented, in that short narrative. It will be a parallel case then, if we find the whole history of the human race in its relation to God, for many ages, in like manner condensed and presented, in the narrative of Gen. ii., iii.

Our own treatment of the latter story is still further significant. Whilst seemingly adhering to the *character* of this Scripture as a strictly historical record about material things, we have positively spiritualized some of it, and taken some of it as allegorical! The story mentions only a serpent, a real snake. This we have transformed, partly or wholly, into a spiritual being, Satan. The Divine Being is presented in the story as a man, or man-like being, throughout; for which, partly or wholly, we have substituted a spiritual God. (I speak here for myself, concluding that others have done likewise.) There has been no consistent adherence to either character in these two cases, sometimes the spiritual being and sometimes the physical one being before the mind, which has thus accommodated itself very conveniently, so as to make a compact between its own ideas and the details of the story. Convenient this indeed is, but *most inconsistent*. Seeing how the story itself relates *entirely* to material things, and how compact it is, it appears quite unallowable to allegorize some of the characters, leaving the others as the story gives them.

Let us make up our minds to accept the story as *what it is, an allegory altogether*.

And having done so, let us now examine it from other points of view. Comparing the passage with Gen. i., we find striking contrasts between the two. In Gen. i. we find, as noticed in the last chapter, a beautiful order preserved throughout its details. There nothing is created before its place is duly prepared to receive it. In Gen. ii. such necessity is utterly disregarded; for the man is made before the garden is planted; the serpent makes its appearance provided with human knowledge and a voice; and, after several other such inconsistencies and impossibilities, we find in the 4th chapter that the son of the first man finds a wife, and builds—not a house, or even a village, but—a *City!*

When, therefore, we find such inconsistencies in the story itself, need we wonder if it gives an order of Creation distinctly at variance with the one given in Gen. i.? Is the splendid order of Gen. i. to give place to a story of this character, or to be reconciled with it? Gen. i. deals admirably with its own proper subject, the Creation; this is meant to teach truths of a quite different nature. Surely God never intended them to present any detailed agreement. Gen. i. has given us the details and order of the Creation; if the language of Gen. ii. seems to contradict that order, it must not be set beside Gen. i., but examined in the light furnished by an investigation of its own particular province.

Comparing Gen. i. with the Chaldean legend of the Creation, and Gen. ii., iii. with the Chaldean Story of the Fall (as well as we can construct the latter out of the parts that remain in the Cuneiform inscriptions and ancient seals, together with the Persian myth which obviously grew out of it (pp. 173–178)), the narrative in Gen. ii., iii. seems to have undergone less change in Hebrew hands than that in Gen. i. It is probably more like the original myth.

In the light of Science, more especially of Evolution, the story of Gen. ii., iii. can have no basis as historical fact. It is swept away.

Now all these considerations point to two conclusions :— (1) that the story itself is an impossible old myth, (2) that the Divine meaning of the passage does not lie in its historical character as a narrative, but in those truths which are hidden within it.

The story is thus none the less a myth because the passage is Scripture; and the passage is none the less Divine because the story itself is myth.

It expresses, as before implied, in allegorical language, the early history of the human race in its relations with God. But *all* its truths are not conveyed allegorically, for there are certain features in the story which have other significance (see foot of p. 252).

Critics have pointed out as impossible, or inconsistent, many features in the story, such as the making and naming, in the manner related, of " *every* beast of the field and *every*

HUMAN EVOLUTION AND THE FALL. 249

fowl of the air;" the man's acquaintedness with family matters, and even future Eastern custom (Gen. ii. 24); the *Hebrew* names 'Isshah' and 'Havvah' which he gives his wife; the *increasing* of the woman's travail, whereas she had then borne no children; the supposed change in the condition of the Earth's soil; the connection of the four rivers with each other, etc. Also the anthropomorphisms of the Story, such as the *planting* of the Garden, and *driving* out the man; the bringing the animals to the man; preparing the skins; and the self-communings of Gen. ii. 18, iii. 22, etc.

I have already remarked how our thoughts have run to and fro between the Divine Being as presented in the story and a Spiritual God, and between the Devil and the snake, so destroying in many respects the simple meaning of the beautiful old story. I have little doubt that, if we could read the story in its original simplicity, we should discern many significant and not unimportant features in its details, especially in the beautiful (although man-like) character of the Divine Being. For this reason it would have been desirable to try to trace out the simple story as it was read by the Hebrew of old; but its *historical* character and details have become so sacred in people's eyes that, no matter what the reader may believe, his *feelings* would most likely take offence at some of the things which would have to be said, and thus more harm than good would be done.

The following extracts from so old a writer as Josephus are of special interest (*Antiquities of the Jews*, Book I. Chapter 1):—

"Now the garden was watered by one river, which ran round about the whole earth, and was parted into four parts. And Phison, which denotes a multitude, running into India, makes its exit into the sea, and is by the Greeks called Ganges. Euphrates also, as well as Tigris, goes down into the Red Sea. Now the name Euphrates, or Phrath, denotes either a dispersion, or a flower : by Tigris, or Diglath, is signified what is swift, with narrowness; and Geon runs through Egypt, and denotes what arises from the East, which the Greeks call Nile.

"God therefore commanded that Adam and his wife should eat of all the rest of the plants, but to abstain from the tree of knowledge; and foretold to them, that, if they touched it, it would prove their destruction. But while *all the living creatures had one language*, at that time, the serpent, which then lived together with Adam and his wife, showed an envious disposition, at his supposal of their living happily, and in obedience to the commands of God; and imagining, that, when they disobeyed them, they would fall into calamities, he persuaded the woman, out of a malicious intention, to taste of the tree of knowledge. . . . But when God came into the garden, Adam, who was wont before to come and converse with him, being conscious of his wicked behaviour, went out of the way. *This behaviour surprised God;* and he asked what was the cause of this his procedure. . . . *He also deprived the serpent of speech*, out of indignation at his malicious disposition towards Adam. Besides this, he inserted poison under his tongue, and made him an enemy to men; and suggested to them that they should direct their strokes against his head, that being the place wherein lay his mischievous designs towards men, and it being easiest to take vengeance on him that way; and when he had deprived him of *the use of his feet, he made him to go rolling all along, and dragging himself upon the ground.*"

Do not the passages in italics in the above extract show that, in bringing our own conceptions and beliefs to the narrative, we have destroyed the real meaning of the sentences, *i.e.* the meaning which the Hebrew writer attached to his words? Truly we have believed in the historical character of the *substance* of the story (or of one something like it), but of *many of its details* we have not done so at all.

We have believed that we believed it all; we have really believed it but in part. Could we possibly represent to ourselves an omniscient spiritual God bringing,—*bringing*—the animals to Adam *to see what he will call them?* or addressing a snake, or even Satan, in these words :—" upon thy belly shalt thou go, and dust shalt thou eat all the days of thy life"? Surely, as above stated, we have not read the *real story*, but only an approximation to it.

Many of these details, so impossible, and some of them out of place, in the story regarded as a story, we shall see to be both possible and possessing important signification, when the true meaning of the passage is apprehended.

There is a great difference between the Elohim of Gen. i. and the Jahveh-Elohim of Gen. ii., iii. The first creates all things, and lastly man in his own image, whom he makes lord of all. Nearer to man than this he does not come. The second enters into relations with man, and shows a desire for his friendship. Elohim is all-powerful, and whatever anthropomorphisms there are in that chapter, are indefinite and inconspicuous. But Jahveh-Elohim is like a supernaturally-powerful man.

Before endeavouring to compare this passage of Scripture with what is known of pre-historic man, it will be best to make a few general remarks applying to the whole of Gen. i.-xi. Although some of them have already been applied to Gen. i., they are more conveniently given here, and they relate more especially to Gen. ii.-xi. It has already been stated that much of the contents of these chapters is of symbolic character, presenting the moral history of primitive man, by means of narratives about individuals, and concrete pictures. In searching for the full Divine signification of these passages, we may very safely lay down the following principles :—

I. Since for some 3000 years they have been almost invariably regarded by their readers as purely historical, we may be certain that the most important part of the Divine meaning is such as would be taken in by readers in the act of reading them as historical fact. For whether they are regarded as historical or not is, undoubtedly, of no importance, provided that God's meaning is apprehended; and mankind have not been left much in the dark as to this all this time. As remarked in Chapter V. of this work, if the Divine truth of any passage is not the same as that which the words express in their literal meaning, we may be sure that that Divine truth is of a nature similar to that which the words do convey.

II. The object of these Scriptures is not to give a scientific account of the early history of the world and man, but to teach certain Divine truths about them; especially to impart moral truths. But, as these truths relate very largely to primitive man, there must be considerable agreement between the Divine record and the teachings of Science. As the latter were unknown when these Scriptures were written, we shall expect such of them as Scripture does give, to be hidden, and not clearly expressed. We shall expect the Scriptures to be so constructed as to give prominence to the more important moral truths, whilst showing in a less conspicuous way their historical application to primitive man.

III. On account of their psychical nature and the absence of psychological language and ideas in those days, those spiritual truths are expressed by means of narratives and concrete pictures; therefore they must be expressed crudely, and in some cases only approximately.

IV. For the above reasons we shall not expect any passage to contain a complete representation of any portion or event of primitive history; nor that any passage will be entirely devoted to the giving of such a representation. Consistently with the marvellous economy of Scripture, we should rather expect to find the narratives packed with as many truths as possible. Therefore we may have truths of different kinds intermixed :—historical facts (such as the creative acts of Gen. i.), what we may call historical spiritual

HUMAN EVOLUTION AND THE FALL. 253

facts (such as that God made woman out of man), expressions of what is in God's heart (as manifested in the character of Jahveh-Elohim), general moral principles—in fact truths of all orders.

V. It is quite possible that certain sentences are nothing more than necessary links connecting the important parts of the narratives. Some parts contain primitive notions which have passed away (as that of the serpent eating dust for food); these may have important symbolic significations, as some of them certainly have, or they may be merely such necessary connecting links.

VI. Those truths in these chapters which are specially referred to in the New Testament are probably amongst the most important. But we must not forget that the writers of the New Testament necessarily read these chapters according to the light and ideas of their own age. If, through the light of Science, we are able to arrive more precisely at the Divine truths of Genesis, the writers of the New Testament could not do this in their times. They apprehended those spiritual truths whilst reading the old narratives simply as historical fact, as their predecessors had done; and therefore we must not expect to find in their words those truths expressed apart from the details of the old narratives. As it is in the old Scriptures so we may expect it to be in the New.

A few remarks are here necessary respecting the human race in the very earliest times. Gen. i. gives the beast of the earth as the last but one, and man as the last, of the things which God created,—an order which is strikingly in accord with the testimony of Geology. According to Gen. ii., iii., and Acts xvii. 26, God 'made of one (or one blood, A. V.) every nation of men for to dwell on all the face of the earth.' The question whether the human race came of one stock, or of more than one, has been freely discussed; and, although some writers have held the latter theory, the evidence in favour of one common origin so preponderates that modern zoologists take this view. Darwin maintains it; O. Peschel adduces powerful arguments in its support in his work on the *Races of Man;* E. B. Tylor writes (*Anthropology*, 1881, p. 6), "We may accept the theory of the unity of mankind as best agreeing with ordinary experience and scientific research." Of course this does not mean that all men descended from a single *pair*.

From this it may be inferred that the race at first occupied some particular region, from which it spread to other parts. From the necessities of the case it follows that that region had a warm climate; and there are other reasons for assuming it to have been somewhere in the equatorial regions of the Old World. Southern Asia, Central Africa, land then occupying the site of the present Indian Ocean, have been pointed out as covering the most likely spots.

There, we must assume, the human intelligence had begun to develop. It is unlikely that, before men began to separate, their intelligence was equal to that of the lowest races of the present day. They must have lived on the natural fruits of the earth, chiefly if not entirely, which in such regions grow wild in abundance. They must have lived in the open air, without dwellings and without clothing. We know, moreover, that in the lower races there is much less difference between the man and the woman, both physically and psychically, than in the higher; and since, in the very beginning, there would be practically no difference of the latter kind, and much less of the former kind than there is now, these must have gradually developed during that and all later periods. As intelligence increased, individual differences made their appearance, and the need, or desire, for communicating ideas, led to the beginnings of speech. As to marriage, evidence can be gathered only from the various races of man as they exist in the present day. Among all races marriage is customary, though in some cases it is said not to be a life-tie, and in others polygamy and polyandry prevail. On this subject O. Peschel writes (*Races of Man*, p. 229), "The hypothesis that at a remote age marriage was unknown to the human race is hardly credible. Even among animals we sometimes find a strict pairing, that is to say, among monkeys, predatory animals, ungulates, ruminants, and among songbirds, chickens, and birds of prey. Darwin has also disputed the probability of a community of wives among prehistoric man.... The Veddahs of Ceylon, whom we should expect to find most primitive, have a beautiful proverb that death alone can part man and wife." And he adds other arguments to the same effect.

Professor Drummond has described the Central African of to-day as half animal, half child. Perhaps, as the reader has thought of beings much nearer the animal, while perusing the above remarks, his lips have curled uncomfortably. (Mr. Darwin would have replied with the cutting remark that this act betrays his own origin.) But this should not be lost sight of—that the fault lies with ourselves if we are inclined to disgust. It is the result of intruding our own feelings, which belong to our present mental and social state, upon another domain in which they are irrelevant. The first condition may have been pure and good, though not refined, and it existed at a time when *nothing in advance of it had come into being*. The different parts of that region of life were mutually adjusted, as the different parts of our own environment are adjusted to each other, and we to them. There was nothing *essentially* offensive in the first, the offence merely arising in *our* minds through associating two things (our mental constitution and that of primeval man) which are essentially distinct. We should think of these things with the intellect only, if we must think at all. It is much to be regretted that in our position it is impossible to form a correct estimate of those first human beings. It would be possible, if one could divest one's self entirely of knowledge of good and evil, of all experiences of man—if, not being a man, not ever having seen or conceived of one, having watched the upward progress of life through its lower forms, one should then look upon the beings just referred to. Then would they possess their true dignity in the spectator's eyes. The misfortune is that our standpoint is at the wrong end of the line: we look down when we should be looking up.[4] But the wrong becomes most apparent when it is remembered that he who despises them despises those through whom he himself has come into being. Where would he be but for his predecessors? It is better not to look down on the work of God's hands, but rather to reflect how we ourselves have been "fearfully and wonderfully made."

As the race spread to other regions they came gradually under very different conditions of life; conditions which, in the course of ages, produced the existing differences between the various races. The natural fruits of the earth no longer sufficing for food, hunting and fishing were resorted to. The skins of the animals also afforded clothing. The taming of certain wild animals was followed, in course of time, by the practice of keeping numbers of those kinds which were useful for food, etc., and the systematic breeding of them. Similar to this beginning of the *pastoral* life was that of *agriculture*, the wild plants yielding food

---

[4] There is, however, another view of the matter, which fuller reflection brings. For when we consider man, the end to which all antecedent steps were tending, we are better able to recognize the dignity of those steps.

HUMAN EVOLUTION AND THE FALL. 257

having suggested the idea of planting and harvesting the same. Gradually, too, the useful arts were discovered, and civilization and social organization grew up among the higher races.

But that the course of the human race has not been altogether an *upward* progress, appears from the following remarks, with which Mr. Wallace closes his work on *The Malay Archipelago*.

" We most of us believe that we, the higher races, have progressed and are progressing. If so, there must be some state of perfection, some ultimate goal, which we may never reach, but to which all true progress must bring us nearer. What is this ideally perfect social state towards which mankind ever has been, and still is tending? Our best thinkers maintain, that it is a state of individual freedom and self-government, rendered possible by the equal development and just balance of the intellectual, moral, and physical parts of our nature,—a state in which we shall each be so perfectly fitted for a social existence, by knowing what is right, and at the same time feeling an irresistible impulse to do what we know to be right, that all laws and all punishments shall be unnecessary. In such a state every man would have a sufficiently well-balanced intellectual organization, to understand the moral law in all its details, and would require no other motive but the free impulses of his own nature to obey that law. Now it is very remarkable, that among people in a very low stage of civilization, we find some approach to such a perfect social state. I have lived with communities of savages in South America and in the East, who have no laws or law courts but the public opinion of the village freely expressed. Each man scrupulously respects the rights of his fellow, and any infraction of those rights rarely or never takes place. In such a community, all are nearly equal. There are none of those wide distinctions of education and ignorance, wealth and poverty, master and servant, which are the product of our civilization; there is none of that widespread division of labour, which, while it increases wealth, produces also conflicting interests: there is not that severe competition and struggle for existence, or for wealth, which the dense population of civilized countries inevitably creates. All incitements to great crimes are thus wanting, and petty ones are repressed, partly by the influence of public opinion, but chiefly by that natural sense of justice and of his neighbour's right, which seems to be, in some degree, inherent in every race of man. Now although we have progressed vastly beyond the savage state in intellectual

S

achievements, we have not advanced equally in morals . . . it is not too much to say that the mass of our populations have not at all advanced beyond the savage code of morals, and have in many cases sunk below it. A deficient morality is the great blot of modern civilization, and the greatest hindrance to true progress. . . . Our mastery over the forces of nature has led to a rapid growth of population and a vast accumulation of wealth, but these have brought with them such an amount of poverty and crime, and have fostered the growth of so much sordid feeling and so many fierce passions, that it may well be questioned, whether the mental and moral, status of our population has not on the average been lowered, and whether the evil has not overbalanced the good. . . . Until there is a more general recognition of this failure of our civilization . . . we shall never, as regards the whole community, attain to any real or important superiority over the better class of savages. This is the lesson I have been taught by my observations of uncivilized man."

The upward progress of the higher races has, in fact, been accompanied with a degeneration, as the upward progress of the lower races was accompanied with degeneration into heartless cruelty and other vices. The former have grown in *corruption* in ways quite unknown to the latter, which have grown rather in *violence*, though this has been abated in cases, as we see here.

We have now to compare Gen. ii., iii. with the early history and conditions of the human race, and to see how those Scriptures apply.

Speaking generally we may say that 'the man' of Gen. ii., iii., represents *the race*, and the history of the man represents the history of the race.

But let us distinctly understand that this Scripture is not intended merely to give a history of the race. Its object is a very different one, namely, to teach certain important truths. The chief of these truths are :—That God made man first, and woman of man; and ordained that, the two being one, man and woman should in all ages be united in matrimony as a life-tie : that God made man, of the earth earthy, yet with a life of relationship with God; and that man was intended for life and other divine blessings, and not for death: that He placed the first of the race where labour was unnecessary, and fruit for food was to be had for the taking; but that sin came in, which passed unto all mankind, and consequently the whole race forfeited the right to life and other blessings; and the race—or its first representative at least— was condemned to a life of toil. These are manifestly the leading truths contained in the passage itself, and in subsequent Scriptures relating to it; and therefore the object *par excellence* of these two chapters was to teach man such truths, whilst they contain others also. For this reason, and others already given, we shall not expect to find an exact parallel with the history of the race, following certain hard and fast lines throughout; but rather an arrangement such as would not fail to convey these truths to simple readers, while those with which we have now to do will be less conspicuous. Yet I think that the parallel is on the whole unmistakable, the story agreeing with the history of the race in a manner that could only be the result of design.

There are, moreover, several instances in which the words of Gen. ii., iii. have been *commonly understood to apply to man and woman generally*, and not merely to the first pair: so that this exegesis is not altogether new. These instances will be noticed as we come to them. And, since the object of the passage is to teach truths about man, truths relating to the human race, which includes primitive men, it is natural that it should relate both to the race and to its earliest representatives. At the end of this chapter we shall remark on some of the cases where the words relate to the race generally; others will be touched on as we come to them; but these Scriptures will now be considered chiefly in their application to primitive man.

As in Gen. i. the events of vast ages are presented as those of a day, so here the history of the human race for long periods is covered by apparently short episodes in the narrative. And as the divisions in Gen i. are in some cases arbitrary, so here necessarily are they still more so. Of this we have seen an instance in Gen. ii. 7, where the communication of life to man which (taking into account all that the human soul is) must be regarded as a gradual work, extending from the beginning onwards to recent times, seems from the narrative to have been the work of a moment. Obviously such truths must have been presented in that way, or not at all; and we shall find similar instances. Yet the chronological order is given, generally, as we shall see.

I prefer to read 'the man' instead of 'Adam' in the text, because 'Adam' is merely a Hebrew name for man, and in the Revised Authorized Version it is translated 'the man.'

First it is necessary to remove a very common error. Many of us have arrived at the conclusion that the first man was a highly endowed being, superior to any of his successors, and that the Garden of Eden was a paradise little, if anything, short of heavenly. Whence these notions?[1]

We have not derived them from Gen. ii., iii., for there is no such account of things there. They have come partly, perhaps, from inferences too hastily drawn from the language of Gen. ii., iii., but also from another source. For when we turn to the Persian, Hindu, and other legends of the Fall, which were cited in the sixth chapter of this work, we find glowing descriptions of Paradise. As we saw in the sixth chapter, the Genesis story and these legends had a common origin; and, as the tradition of the Fall was handed down to posterity in the Eastern nations, Hebrews included, that feature of the story never died out; and, although the language of Genesis is different, no doubt the Hebrews, as they read this Scripture in later ages, brought their own ideas to it, read it in the light of those ideas, and taught their children that such was the teaching of Scripture, just as is sometimes done amongst ourselves. So, further, the belief was passed down to us through the same hands that preserved the Bible itself. But, although we thus trace this belief to its origin, it has been magnified into greater error amongst ourselves through the work of the poet Milton. Deriving his ideas from the same source originally, he so enlarged upon them in Paradise Lost, as to impress the English mind with the belief that the Bible teaches much which exists only in his poem.

For we do not find these glowing descriptions in Genesis. We read of *a garden where grows every tree that is pleasant to the sight and good for food, a (naked) man and his wife who live there, and whose business it is to dress and keep it.* But we find also God's presence there, and the Tree of Life; on the other hand the serpent is there, and the Tree of Knowledge of Good and Evil. From Gen. iii. 19, 22, it appears that the man is not *in possession of* any life other than an earthly and temporal one—so the words 'till thou return unto the ground, etc.,' and 'lest he put forth his hand and take also of the tree of life, and eat, and live for ever,' seem at least to imply. One might further infer from the expression '*multiply* thy sorrow' (or pain), that the man and woman also know pain.

It seems a medley. Some of the trees are natural, others supernatural. The man and woman, and the animals are natural; God and the serpent, although presented in material form, are beings possessing supernatural powers. Man is there, in relation with God, blessed, and, if we connect him with Gen. i., made in God's image; yet he is the uncivilized man; subject to death, yet with a right to life.

All these things do not apply to the same scene. There is the double environment of man, the natural world and the spiritual world. There is the human race in general, with God's purposes concerning it; and there is the earliest representative of the race—primeval man.

Let us now pursue the part which relates to the latter. What truth there is in the notion of Paradise we shall see later on.

Some of the language is not far removed from that which would describe the conditions of life of the human race in earliest times. For it is in a garden, without a dwelling, in a state of nature, that the first man lives, without toil, on the fruit which Nature provides. Not, of course, that the fruits on which primeval man lived were like the best cultivated fruits to which we are accustomed; for these are the result of long cultivation and careful selection. But probably if they had been such as these, man would have died. We must here correct the ever-recurring mistake of judging things from our own point of view. The excellence of *those* fruits consisted in their suitability to the men of those days. *To us* such fruits would be anything but good for food; but that primeval man, before his dispersion over the earth, existed under suitable conditions of life, with his environment adjusted to himself, I think we may safely say. In the open air, amongst the wild fruit-trees of a tropical climate, without clothing, without labour, as we must conclude, lived primeval man.

The Bible does not teach that the first man was acquainted with the useful arts and knowledge, for not before the 4th chapter of Genesis do we read of such things. Except in one or two particulars which seem at first to imply otherwise, but are really *necessary for presenting other important features*, the man appears as a child of nature; and, notwithstanding our thoughts of him as a superior man in Paradise, we have gathered more or less of that impression.

HUMAN EVOLUTION AND THE FALL.

Taking leave somewhat of common sense, we may have thought the *natural* conditions of life would be very pleasant; but, if we could have tried the experiment, it would probably have changed our ideas of this imagined Paradise. Common sense affirms that upon the Earth such a life would suit only the child of Nature, unacquainted with civilization and its ways. And such, as Science tells us, was primeval man.

The change from this free life, which suited the men who lived it, to that of toil for the necessaries of life, especially the toils of early agriculture, was a punishment for sin.

To us it may seem that the hardships of the hunter's life were far worse than the toils of agriculture. But, though these were probably a part of the punishment, the sayings of hunting tribes to-day lead us to modify these views. The following remarks are made by O. Peschel (*Races of Man*, pp. 153, 154):—

". . . The so-called savage prefers a life of freedom to all the advantages and conveniences of civilization. The difficulty of accustoming hunting tribes to a sedentary life, is not that they are incapable of living in our way, but that they choose to live in their own way. . . . 'White fellows work, not black fellows; black fellow gentleman,' say the Australians. When the English and Dutch colonists settled on the Eastern shores of the United States, a native was here and there observed watching from an elevation how the farmer followed his plough, not in order to learn his secret, but first to gaze in wonder, and then to turn away in pity. . . . The Red Indians of North America imagine the next world to be a continuation of the present existence. The Great Spirit, as they hope, will transplant them to regions abounding in game. . . . The life of the uncivilized man appears to him so full of enjoyment that he can think of another life only as an enhancement of the same. . . . We must therefore conclude . . . that the so-called savage prefers to renounce existence rather than undergo the burdens of civilization . . . Freedom is enjoyed only by the Botocudo, the Australian, or the Eskimo."

When, therefore, we remember that Gen. ii., iii. treat of primeval man's environment and conditions of life, not as they would affect us, but as they *affected him*, which is obviously the real question, we find that it gives a true report of his earliest history—the first natural, out-of-door, non-laborious life, and subsequent change,[5] not so much to the hunting life as to the toils of agriculture, and more especially the toils of early agriculture. We shall notice the other judgments as we proceed; and we shall also see why certain features of the narrative, from which have been gathered some false impressions as to the high endowments of the first man, *are necessarily present* in the passage.

And where does Scripture say the Garden was? In Eden, watered by a river which, in its lower course, separated into the Nile, the Euphrates, the Tigris, and the Indus (or perhaps the Ganges). Such an account of the river seems reconcilable only with defective geographical knowledge on the writer's part. It seems to have been a common belief in early times that certain of the known rivers were different parts of the course of the same river; and that is probably the idea here. But is not this ignorance made use of by God to embody another truth in the passage? If we try to find any connexion, either between one and another of these rivers, or between them and a planted garden, such as we have imagined the Garden of Eden, we utterly fail. But when, tracing these rivers on the map, we find that North-Eastern Africa, South-Western Asia, and the middle of Southern Asia, are the regions which they occupy; and when we compare these with the regions already named as covering the most likely spots for the first home of the human race, the agreement is striking. Surely here we have an intimation that the Garden was no small, supernaturally-prepared garden, but a natural garden

---

[5] But this is only one of the truths which Gen. iii. teaches as to the Fall of Man. The most important of them will be discussed at the end of this chapter.

of wild fruit trees, covering considerable regions; and probably a further intimation that these regions were somewhere in that part of the world—a general indication as to what portion of the earth's surface was inhabited by primeval man.

We have already noticed that the order of creation in Gen. ii. differs from that in Gen. i. It also differs from the order revealed by Science. For according to the story the man is made first, then the plants, (or rather those of the Garden only,) and lastly the animals. The narrative gives the impression that the Garden and the animals are *both made specially for man* (the Garden for his dwelling-place, the animals for their society, such as it is). I believe the above order of creation is given in the narrative in order to convey this truth. This is not expressed in Gen. i., where the plant-world and the animal-world are given a place of their own in the scheme of creation, whilst subject to man who has dominion over all. Thus the two accounts supplement each other, the two together giving us God's two-fold object in creating these things. We shall soon have to notice other significant features in the passage relating to the animals. First let us see how some of the details of the story, especially when taken in the sequence given, symbolize certain phases in human evolution.

Throughout the earlier part of the story, up to the end of the second chapter, 'the man' is the only existing human being: it is only in the latter half that we have the man and woman together, after the woman has been made out of the man's rib. I have already remarked on the gradual evolution of sexual difference in *homo*, which is greater in the higher than in the lower races to-day; and which we may treat as very little in the very beginning. The psychical difference was then very small,[6] and the physical dif-

---

[6] To prevent misapprehension, it is perhaps better to state that

ference much less than now. The psychical difference chiefly concerns us here. That is the great distinction between the sexes, and that is the one of which Scripture takes account. How well chosen are the words of Gen. i., which draw this distinction in man's case, in contrast with the animal. To the inhabitants of the water and of the air God says, "Be fruitful and multiply," as He also says to man in verse 28. But nowhere does the text say of the animals that God *made them male and female.* This is the grand distinction that applies to man, as the other also does with which it is connected in verse 27—that they are made in God's image. (That the expression, 'male and female' animals, is used in the story of the Flood, does not at all affect this matter. For that is not an *account of the Creation,* and the words were quite necessary to convey the desired meaning in that case.) Therefore we may say that in 'the man' of the first part of the story is symbolized the human being of the earliest age, before the psychical differentiation of the sexes. *It is man as the general type of the Race that is made first.*

I do not mean for a moment that there ever existed completely human and at the same time completely asexual beings; but that throughout evolution the human attributes were at all times in advance of the womanly attributes. As applied to the complete human beings, the above is only relatively true—as the males and females of the lower races to-day are more alike than those of the higher races, the higher womanly attributes not having made their appearance in the women, so at a far distant day the sexes were much more alike, few or none of the truly womanly attributes having made their appearance in the females.

here and throughout this argument I ignore those emotions which existed in the animal. Such lower activities may be of importance to the biologist, but we have here to do with that only which is purely human.

Scripture does not confine itself to distinctions between individuals; it takes account of spiritual distinctions existing within the same individual. And here the truth inculcated is, that the essentially human attribute was evolved first, and then differentiated into the manlike and the womanly, the latter being the one wherein the greatest differentiation was involved. Not that all the human attributes were first evolved, or that what we may call the essentially human attribute was fully evolved before the womanly began to appear, but that serially the human took the lead. Denoting the human attributes, or the component parts of the human attribute, by a, b, $c-z$, and the womanly by 1, 2, 3—26, a preceded 1, b preceded 2; and so on. Perhaps the reader will object that female qualities existed in the animal before there were any human qualities. Doubtless the female *animal* qualities did, but not the female human, *i.e.* the womanly. If he still object, let him fully define the term 'womanly,' and he will have to call it first that which is human (the genus), then that species of the human which is characteristic of the woman. Of course I do not mean that *femaleness* was made out of *maleness*—the two are opposite poles—but, as we might express it, that the mental substance which was made female in the woman was the same substance as that of which the mind or soul of the man was composed.

To have been explicit and accurate, many parts of this chapter should have been analyzed as above, and even more closely. If the reader fails to apprehend me in such cases, he is requested to read those parts in the light of this explanation, which I could not repeat at every stage. These Scriptures treat of human *qualities* rather than of human beings.

As men and women thus come into existence in course of time, in lieu of the pre-existing beings of inferior order, they unite in natural marriage. The men do not necessarily say *with their lips* the words of Gen. ii. 23, 24, but they act in accordance therewith. If we turn for a moment to Rom. x. 13, 'Whosoever shall call upon the name of the Lord shall be saved,' we find another instance where the language of the heart is meant: for no one could suppose that the mere utterance of the words would avail in that case.'[7] So, obviously in this case (Gen. ii. 23, 24); the acting upon the natural emotion implanted by God in primeval man, is here indicated by the words which, according to the story, the man speaks concerning the woman.

In Gen. ii. there is no marriage ceremony; the transaction is thus parallel to this natural marriage.

How beautifully does Scripture differ from human compositions in its account of these things. Often in the latter the words used excite offensive or erroneous thoughts; whereas the offensiveness really arises through our cumbersome way of thinking. Our thoughts are based upon space-divisions and time-divisions, because these enter so largely into the formation of our concepts; and we cannot help regarding them as the essential dividing-lines between things, even when we think of psychical phenomena, as we do here. But God sees more clearly; and Scripture teaches accordingly, that the fundamental dividing-lines are different from these, being those of the spirit. This we might know to be the case with spiritual matters, such as these; yet we are constantly repeating the mistake, when thinking of such subjects. Is it any wonder then that in early Hebrew times we find these unseen spiritual divisions, which cannot even now be accurately expressed in words, approximately expressed by means of familiar forms of thought? Is it not wonderful how that primitive language is arranged so as to

---

[7] Not that the stress should be laid on the 'calling,' but rather on the *whosoever*, in this text, as appears from verse 12.

exclude offensive and false impressions, whilst conveying all that is needful? Such facts as these tend to convince us that, in spite of all the crudenesses and inaccuracies which Science shows to exist in these old stories, he who simply believes them just as they stand, *comes nearer to the greater truths and has fewer seriously erroneous beliefs*, after all, than he who believes only what he learns from Science.

There is difficulty when treating of some subjects, with all the rich language of to-day before us, to use words which shall convey the desired meaning *and nothing more*. How much more in old times. So from this text (Gen. ii. 23, 24) one perhaps infers that the man could speak untaught, or had prophetic knowledge of family relations ; and therefore one supposes that he was created in a highly-endowed condition—all these being merely contingent implications of the language, which is used for the *one object* of conveying special truths about the original psychical unity, the formation thereout of the two sexes, and thence the Divine ordinance of the marriage-tie. We find that, (1) the language is well suited to convey these *most important truths;* (2) it is so well chosen as to avoid inculcating those errors which anthropologists are liable to make ; whilst (3) it inevitably tends to produce certain mistaken beliefs in scientific matters, which harm nobody. So it is in this passage, and so it is in others in the early chapters of Genesis. Yet if one carefully compared Scripture with Scripture, these unimportant mistakes would in many cases be eliminated by the process.

Let us turn our thoughts from the sexual differences as manifested outwardly to the sight, and confine them to the mental qualities which constitute the inner self, the psychical being, that which is conscious, and which is the real individual; so that we may see how real is the truth taught in Gen. ii. 21-24 about the formation of woman.

In the story, the woman's body is formed out of the man's rib; the result of which proceeding is that there are two beings, (1) the man minus the rib, (2) the woman made out of the rib; both, therefore, somewhat different from the pre-existing man of Gen. ii. 7-20, and both made out of him. Approximately so it appeared in the evolution of the sexes; the man and the woman of the later age apparently developing out of the less sexually-differentiated human being (psychically considered) of the earlier age. This primordial human being—the type of the race in earliest time—would thus correspond to 'the man' of Gen. ii. 7-20, which God first makes; and the man and woman which were in course of time developed, as the sexes became more psychically-differentiated, would correspond to the man and woman of Gen. ii. 24 to iii. 24. But although this represents in part the historical aspect of the matter, it is not sufficient. Though we speak here of only the strictly human qualities, there never was an asexual human being; and, as already stated, the process of reproduction is not equivalent to the real genesis of the human soul. Only by turning our thoughts from human beings to human *qualities* can we arrive at the essential constitution of man and woman, and realize the deeper truth expressed in Gen. ii. 21-24—the hidden process of the formation of the soul of woman out of the soul of man,[8] the production of that psychical relation between the sexes, to the existence of which the human consciousness testifies, but which it cannot explain. This, and kindred historical spiritual facts, may seem to us of

---

[8] If the evolutionist's sense of precision is offended at the use of the term 'man' in Gen. ii., he may be reminded that it serves better to express this relationship than a more general term equivalent to human being would do; even presuming that the Hebrew language contained such a term at that early age.

less importance than the details of a narrative, when weighed in the balance of Truth; but, if our perceptions were duly qualified, I doubt not we should see that they are the deepest, the truest, the most real, of all historical fact.[9]

Thus is "the woman of the man" (1 Cor. xi. 12). Thus we see how "He which made them from the beginning made them male and female, and said, For this cause shall a man . . . . cleave to his wife; and the twain shall become one flesh" (Matt. xix. 4, 5). How admirably is this psychological fact of creation conveyed in the old story of the rib! Could the dullest person, in believing it as historical fact, possibly fail to perceive its Scriptural signification? Believing in, and thinking of, the physical fact, he inevitably believes in the more real, and only important, psychical fact. The other view of the matter, as seen outwardly in the light of Evolution, does not adequately convey the truth to our minds. It tells us nothing of that hidden process of the formation of the soul of woman out of the soul of man, of the psychical relations of the sexes, of the definite hand of God in this work, whilst avoiding offensive and erroneous thoughts; all of which are so well conveyed by the deep sleep, the taking out of the rib, and the formation of the woman. For those who can believe the old story simply as it stands, it is far the best.

We must now return a little to the passage relating to the animals (Gen. ii. 18-21); the main features of which are:— (1) that they are made as companions for the man (vv. 18, 19);[10] (2) that they are formed out of the ground, as the man was,

[9] Has not the idealist who believes that states of consciousness are the only things that exist, gone somewhere near, but missed, this doctrine, so often insisted on in Scripture, that spiritual activities are the transcendent realities? "God is a Spirit," or "God is spirit" (Margin, R. A. V., John iv. 24).

[10] This seems the simple implication of the words; and so several exegetes, at least, have explained the passage.

but do not, like him, receive their breath of life direct from the Creator; (3) that the Creator brings them to the man to see what he will call them, and that, in his naming them we have the first act of intelligence, the first speech, recorded of the man; and (4) that they do not prove altogether satisfactory companions (v. 20), so that something better—something worthy—is eventually provided in the woman.

We need not further discuss the second of these matters. But in the first and fourth I think the upward progress of the race in its very beginning is indicated. That the animals are made for the man's companions seems to place him on a level with them, to imply a community between the two, which holds only for a time, till he rises superior to it, requires something better, and his need is met by the making of the woman. Have we not here implied that primeval men were first of a low order, nearer to the animal, and that, rising above it, in sexual intercourse they attained to a suitable social life in a higher state ? [11]

The third feature seems still more significant. One of the first things which primitive man would notice, as his intelligence developed, would probably be the difference between men and animals; and the latter, on account of their motions and life, would be the first things to excite his curiosity and interest. What then so natural as to imitate their cries; and when desiring to communicate thoughts about them—perhaps to warn each other of approaching danger—to repeat the animal's cry to indicate the animal? as we do to-day when we speak of the cuckoo. Professor Whitney states that to this onomatopoetic principle in the first steps of language-making, he has been led to assign a higher and higher efficiency the more he has studied the subject.[12] Surely these first-fruits of the human intellect, these first beginnings of speech, are implied by this part of the passage about the animals.

But why this interest on the Maker's part *to see what the man will call* these animals and birds ? Clearly it is not the question *what* men will call them, so much as the all-important fact that *they begin to call them anything.* Parents take special interest in the first prattlings of a first-born child. Is not this something like it on the Creator's part ? After watching the slow upward progress of this, the greatest work of His hands, through untold ages, is it not natural that He

---

[11] On this, and some of the other conclusions which follow, the reader will form his own judgment. They are not of much importance to the main argument.

[12] Preface to *Language and the Study of Language*, 1884.

should take such interest in the first poor beginnings of human speech?

Nothing is said about the man's nakedness in the first part of the story; not till after he has a wife do we read that they were both naked. Nakedness only becomes nakedness when human mind and sexual difference come into existence.

Upon the subject of nudity in existing races, O. Peschel says (*Races of Man*, 1876, p. 171):—

"The more familiar we have become with foreign customs by means of thorough research, the more frequently have we found that nudity is not incompatible with modesty, and, above all, that in different nations modesty enjoins the veiling, now of one, now of another portion of the body." (After giving numerous instances he continues, p. 173) "Thus habit and custom decide what is permissible and what is offensive" . . . (and, p. 176) ". . . as we have shown, chastity and morality are quite independent of the absence or vividness of sexual modesty" . . . A dark skin, to a white man's eye at least, does much to remove the impression of nakedness.

If, therefore, we are inclined to think that the nudity of a whole community must have been a very different matter from that of a pair, as in Gen. iii., these facts will serve to correct that impression.

The forbidden fruit.—A distinction is made in Gen. ii. 9, between the Trees of Life and Knowledge and the other trees; and more strikingly in Gen. ii. 16, 17, iii. 2, 3, where they are represented as not being trees of the garden. "Of *every tree of the garden* thou mayest freely eat; but of the tree of the knowledge of good and evil, thou shalt not eat of it." Here is one reason why we should not regard them as natural trees.

But, seeing the allegorical character of the whole passage, seeing the difficulties of adhering here, as elsewhere, to its apparent meaning, and seeing how such difficulties disappear when a rational interpretation is applied, the sooner we dismiss the old idea the better. The same applies to the colloquy between the woman and the serpent, whether we take the latter as a snake or as Satan in some way personified in one. The same applies also to the command not to eat of the Tree. Transfer the whole scene to the region of mind and conscience, and the interpretation is obvious.

It is foreign to the purpose of this work to discuss fully the details of the sinful act; nor can we know exactly what occurred. The words of Gen. iii. 6 have been regarded as embodying 'the lust of the flesh, the lust of the eye, and the pride of life.' At any rate the passage seems to imply carnal desire for indulgence of some kind, the unseen tempter urging the heart to yield, the instinct of conscience warning that the act was wrong, and the yielding to the temptation; followed by the acquisition of such a knowledge of right and wrong as was not possessed before. We cannot think so easily of these occurrences in the case of many as in that of one, nor can we conceive so readily of what passed in the hearts and minds as of the events of the simple old narrative. He who simply believes these will not accurately represent to himself what occurred, but he will be impressed with the most important facts, as nearly as he needs, and probably as nearly as he can, apprehend them. It is clear that the sin was brought about by the devil, and that woman was in some way foremost therein.

These events may seem to presuppose a knowledge on the part of man greater than he could have possessed at this early stage; because they must have preceded his spread over the earth, though not necessarily over a considerable portion of its warmer parts; because the spreading process must have been very slow; and because by the time he inhabited Europe his condition was very rude, as shown by the earliest flint implements which he used in these regions. His intelligence, however, during the mammoth period seems to be shown by his sketchings and carvings. Tylor remarks that these have been done with so artistic a touch that some have supposed them modern forgeries; but (he says) "they are admitted to be genuine, while forgeries which have really been done to palm off on collectors are just wanting in the peculiar skill with which the savages who lived among the reindeer and mammoths knew how to catch their forms and attitudes."[13] It must be remembered, too, that we are not now speaking of the very earliest of the race, which are the subject of Gen. ii., but of those who lived after the beginnings of speech and the psychical differentiation of the sexes, *i.e.* when intelligence was more developed. Yet here we must beware of attributing an intellectual knowledge of God, which, as we have seen, did not exist till Hebrew times; perhaps there were not even those earliest crude ideas of the Deity which were discussed in Chap. IV. Neither could man have had, at that time, a thoroughly clear and rational distinguishing of right from wrong, or a knowledge of the true nature of sin. But these were not necessary. In many branches of knowledge an intuitive perception of truths long precedes a rational one; and this is pre-eminently true in regard to spiritual or moral truths.[14] It is, therefore, quite possible that primitive man

---

[13] *Anthropology*, 1881, p. 301.
[14] Rom. i. 19-22, 28, presents a similar difficulty, and has a

had a feeling, an intuitive perception, that the deed was wrong. He had a conscience, and in this we see the command of God, which was disregarded. Such was the beginning of conscious wrong-doing; which increased continually, as related in the following chapters of Genesis, and as our knowledge of the human race tends to show it must have done. Moreover, we should not too quickly assume that the events to which this passage relates occurred all at once; some of the details may have long preceded others.

Gen. iii. 7-10.—The first consequence of the deed is that the man and woman discover their nakedness, and therefore sew fig-leaves together and make themselves aprons (or girdles, margin). It hardly needs saying that this represents primitive man's beginnings to clothe himself. "The simplest form of dress," says O. Peschel, "consists of leaves or twigs stuck into a girdle" (*Races of Man*, p. 177). "Leaves, also," says Tylor, "are made into aprons or skirts which clothe various rude tribes" (*Anthropology*, p. 245).

The second consequence of the deed is that they fear their Maker. In other words, primitive man had a bad conscience. We must not here, and in the passing of judgment on the several offenders, suppose any interview, with spoken words (unless possibly in the case of the Enemy). The words of the text relate to the judgments which God determined in His own mind to inflict, and which are necessarily represented as spoken personally to the offenders, in character with the whole passage.

The judgment passed on the serpent.—It is hardly necessary to say here that this relates to the devil. We have allegorized that part of the story, and learnt the deep significance of the words, "it shall bruise thy head." The serpent's seed also represents the wicked section of the human race, whilst the woman's seed also signifies the righteous. But the purely allegorical character of this passage is more clearly seen when we remember that these were not at all regarded as the meanings of the words in early times. It was *the snake itself* that had done the wicked deed, that was condemned to go on its

---

similar explanation. We know, though we are apt to forget, that 'the world' did not possess a full intellectual knowledge of God till after apostolic times. But from history and mythology we know that men had vague ideas of the Deity—a kind of intuitive knowlege of God—and a perception of right and wrong. The truth expressed in this passage seems to be, that in these things there was the beginning of a revelation, which was withdrawn because men preferred sin and darkness to goodness and light. Scripture ever deals with the underlying reality, the heart's emotions.

belly (instead of on feet as before), that was to eat dust for food—an Eastern belief which, Kalisch says, arose from the fact that the serpent can subsist on very little food; or it may have been due to the way in which some serpents feel about the ground with their forked tongues—and that was to be at enmity with mankind. In some parts of the East the extirpation of serpents was regarded as a religious duty. The snake naturally bites the heel of man, who in return crushes its head.

It is well to see how the true significance of this passage has been known only in later times, through the light of subsequent knowledge; how, the very existence of the Devil being unknown in early times, men were taught as near an approximation to the facts as they could then grasp, by means of the character of the common serpent as they conceived it. We see that it was but an approximation in the first place; that, when fuller knowledge made it possible, people saw more of the real significance of the words; that, after the Atoning Sacrifice, they saw the hidden meaning of another part of the passage (the bruising of the serpent's head), of which no one had an idea before. How parallel is this to the interpretation of the other parts of Gen. ii., iii. insisted on here, and which could be known only by the light of Science, in these days; long after the completion of the Bible, so that we should not expect the full explanation there.

The reader may object that more than one meaning has sometimes been attributed to the same paragraph, or perhaps even to the same words. But this is not new to exegesis. We have noticed one instance where the words are known to have a double application:—the seed of the woman denoting, (1) Christ Himself, who destroyed the devil's power, (2) the righteous section of mankind, who are subject to the enmity of the wicked. Such is the wonderful economy of Scripture, as we all know;[15] such the wisdom wherewith it has been put together by its Divine Author. Greater wisdom than that of the serpent is manifested in this "old Hebrew myth" of Gen. ii., iii. Jesus said to the disciples, "I beheld Satan as lightning fall from heaven" (Luke x. 18). The devil is seen to be cast out of heaven into the earth in Rev. xii. 7–10, and lower still in Rev. xx. 3, 10. Some of these things are doubtless symbolized in the words of Gen. iii. 14, relating to the degradation of the serpent.

But why have these and other passages in the story a double

---

[15] Of course these arguments are not meant to appeal to those who do not believe in this economy, or even in the divine origin of the Bible.

application? Because, as already remarked, they do not relate to specific human beings so much as to the *underlying spirit* which they manifest; a spirit which may continue for ages, being outwardly expressed in different human beings at different times. They have really one application, but under two (or more) forms. The excellence of these old Scriptures consists in their wonderful power of imparting their truths to readers of all ages. If, therefore, in the light of science we see that they apply to primeval man in general, and not to individuals, such as Adam, or Cain, or Noah, this interpretation is not a totally different one, as it may at first appear, but one *essentially* the same as that which it replaces. The change is in form, not in substance. The seemingly double interpretation is a single one, after all.

It may appear to the reader that such an economy in these early Scriptures is inconsistent with the statement made in a former place, that the writers were not automata, but wrote naturally. If so, let me remind him of the conclusions of Chap. VI., in regard to the antecedent leading of traditional beliefs, to which the writers gave expression when they wrote. Their work being divinely guided, by this and other means, they thus used language in their writings which was packed with some significations above their own knowledge and comprehension. The writers of the Bible were something like instruments in the hand of a Divine Writer. In New Testament times they were like the well-finished pen; but in earliest times more like a blunt pencil, so that the lines in the beginning of Genesis are necessarily thick and crude. Exhibiting the imperfections of the instrument, these compositions are none the less the work of the Divine Author. To some readers it will seem, perhaps, that certain interpretations here suggested are rather far removed from the language of the text. But those believers who have carefully compared Gen. i. with the revelations of Science, and have discerned how, disagreeing on the surface, it presents a wonderful general agreement underneath, must see that the cases are very parallel. Finding such a richness in Gen. i., we should naturally expect to find the like in Gen. ii., iii.; the subjects of all three chapters being so important.

"*Unto the woman he said, I will greatly multiply thy sorrow (or pain) and thy conception; in sorrow (or pain) thou shalt bring forth children. . . .*"—How could her conception and its pain be *multiplied* if such things did not yet exist? For it appears from Gen. iv. 1 that she as yet had no children. According to the true interpretation of the passage, however, there is no such difficulty. For child-bearing was known to the women of that age, and was increased, in their own case or in that of their successors; the text relates to the history of woman, not merely to that of individual women. Bishop Colenso, in the same paragraph [16] where he denies that the pain of childbirth has been increased, says (inconsistently, as it appears to me, at least in the light of Evolution), "In tropical countries, indeed, the birth of a child seems often to be attended with little more pain and disturbance than the birth of a beast." If this be true of the woman of tropical countries —more like than others as we suppose her to be to primeval woman—we need only compare her with the woman of the higher races, to see that the punishment has been literally fulfilled. There appears to have been a gradual increase in the pain from the beginning.

This text, then, possesses three significant features:—
(1) the mention of pain, or sorrow, as already in existence;
(2) the mention of child-bearing as already having occurred;
(3) the inflicted increase of the child-bearing and its pain.
The first of these is quite irreconcilable with the character of the *earthly Paradise* which the Bible does not teach, but is erroneously supposed to teach. The second is so at variance with the other part of the narrative, that one is led to think the words must have been altered, or specially overruled, so as to make them agree with the actual fact of history, which is really indicated by the passage. The third cannot well be applied to an individual woman, but appears to be confirmed when applied to the race. As to this, it will probably be replied that everybody knows it applies to the race. This is what Bishop Colenso denied, at least, as if it were common belief. Here, then, we see that this exegesis is but an extension of principles which have long been applied in part.

And thy desire shall be to thy husband, and he shall rule over thee.—As the inflicted toil had special reference to early times, so, apparently, had this judgment on woman. Among the more barbarous people to-day the husband generally exercises over the wife the rights of a proprietor. In the East there is a subjection of the wife to the husband which is unknown amongst us, and this has been usual from earliest times. Professor Delitzsch has remarked that this condition of woman has been bettered, first, through the religion of Revelation. Here, again, we apply the words to the race rather than to the first woman.

The ground cursed, and the man turned out of the garden and condemned to a life of toil.—We cannot suppose that there has been any change for the worse in the soil of the earth generally. There may have been such a change, however, in the particular

---

[16] *Bishop Colenso on the Pentateuch*, p. 337.

region which man first inhabited. But that is not the important question. Here is a judgment *passed on man;* it suffices that *he* underwent the change indicated, from the non-laborious life on the natural fruits of the earth, to the toiling life necessary for obtaining food. We can understand that men of early times would gather that impression most readily in believing that the ground had undergone a change,[17] and that, therefore, the language of the text takes that form, whilst it seems to imply also that, as associated with man, the ground was in a sense regarded as cursed. It has already been remarked that the toils of early agriculture seem to be specially indicated in this passage. In Gen. viii. 21, 22 we read, "And Jahveh said in his heart, I will not again curse the ground any more for man's sake. . . . While the earth remaineth, seedtime and harvest, and cold and heat, and summer and winter, and day and night, shall not cease." Of Noah Lamech says (Gen. v. 29), "This same shall comfort us for our work and for the toil of our hands, because of the ground which Jahveh hath cursed." The latter remark has been said to mean that Noah was looked upon as an improver in the means of agriculture. There can be no doubt that in early times the labour of tilling the ground was much greater than in the present day, because of the want of proper appliances. Here, therefore, in the reduced labour of agriculture, and in other ways—such as the procuring of a living by other means, which a large portion of the community do, when division of labour comes in with the growth of society—we have a mitigation of the burden on man, which is, doubtless, the Sciptural meaning of the passage above quoted, Gen. viii. 21, 22. It is of no consequence whether the judgment was brought by a cursing of the ground, and a withdrawing of that curse, or by any other means. Suffice it that there was such a judgment passed, and afterwards mitigated. Nor is that all; for it would probably be a mistake to apply it exclusively to agricultural labour. It is more reasonable to apply it to all the toils of human life, remembering that to the people amongst whom this Scripture was produced these would be most effectually represented by the toils of agriculture, to which they were accustomed.

[17] In the absence of a fuller discussion of the subject than I have space for, it is not unlikely that some readers—confining their thoughts to other aspects of evolution, and judging of primeval man's environment too much by its unsuitability to our own constitution (as no one can well avoid doing)—will not see the above change in man's conditions in the light in which it is presented. How, then, in crude times, when nothing was known of man's early history, could this truth be so well conveyed in few words as in the language of the text?

We have yet to consider how primeval man was turned out of his original place of dwelling. The extremely remote period at which the event occurred, leaves ample room for those geological changes which take so long. A subsidence of the land may have expelled man from that region, if, as some suppose, it was on the site of the present Indian Ocean. Or climatic changes may have converted it into a desert, or less fruitful region. This would accord literally with the cursing of the ground. Another effectual agent, if it took effect so early, was the increase of population, resulting from the judgment passed upon woman. With however slow an increase, some of the people must, sooner or later, have moved to other regions to procure food. Thus, without resisting the testimony of Science, we find that, in *the effects produced on man*, those Scriptures were fulfilled; and it also appears that in the expulsion from the 'garden,' if not also in naturally-produced deterioration in the soil, the words have almost a literal application.

There would be the greatest difficulty, here as elsewhere, in applying these events to the history of an individual man. He might indeed be turned out of the garden; but to change his whole mode of life, from the garden-life to the agricultural one, would be a very different thing. The difficulty as to his need of knowledge might be got over, no doubt, by predicating of him an original possession of all knowledge. This, however, would be of no use without the means of applying it; and if the reader will try to get through a few hours of his ordinary occupation with the use of nothing but his hands, it may suggest a few thoughts on this subject which did not occur to him before. To maintain the traditionary interpretation of this Scripture one must predicate an original supernatural knowledge, and a host of other similar impossibilities; which it may be allowable to do, but not to say that such is the teaching of Scripture. Here, therefore, we see that another group of grave difficulties, standing in the way of the traditionary reading of the text, disappear completely when we compare it with the facts of anthropology, and when we follow the exegesis already confirmed—namely, that of applying to the race what the text applies to the first man.

It will be more convenient to discuss the question how the threat of death was carried out, at the end of the present series of observations.

And the man called his wife's name Eve (margin, Havvah, *i.e.* Living or Life), *because she was the mother of all living.*—How could this be if she had as yet borne no children? It appears that the man himself gives her the name (meaning "living") for the reason assigned; as in the previous case (Gen. ii. 23) he had called her 'Isshah' because she was taken out of 'Ish.' What man would, in writing a story, put in such contradictions as this? We have seen, however, that primitive woman had borne children, and thus these words are in order when applied to the race—to primitive woman. *Parentage is here first recognized, namely, after men and women are evolved, who unite in marriage, and also after the first sin.* Thus the human race are born of woman; and they are children of sinful parents.

It is not without significance that all mankind down to this period are summed up in *one*, and presented under the likeness of one. It is natural to us, seeing only the physical aspect, to regard the human race down to that period as consisting of many. God, seeing the psychical aspect, and doubtless the most real, regards it as *one*. If we consider the mental condition of the individuals, we shall see, (1) that they possessed, in the beginning especially, very little mind—one man to-day would equal a great number of them in this respect; (2) that mental differences in individuals of the same sex did not come into existence till after the psychical difference between man and woman did—which agrees with the course of things in Gen. ii., iii., iv., where we have first one man, then man and woman, and lastly individual men and women; (3) that, until such differences existed, individuality could not count for much; (4) that, as one spirit sometimes pervades large bodies of people (as in the case of a body of soldiers fighting for a common cause, in the prevalence of a fashion, etc.), there may have been a spiritual unity in the race at that time which has never existed since. These are probably reasons, additional to those already given, why the race is presented under the likeness of an individual in these chapters.

And Jahveh-Elohim made for Adam and for his wife coats of skins and clothed them.—As we have seen, it is at the hunting stage in human progress that people clothe themselves with skins. Pastoral tribes also clothe themselves thus. In the narrative, this clothing of the man and woman seems to take place before the complete expulsion from the garden, though not till after the judgments are passed on them, and may have begun to take effect. The chief feature in verses 22-24 seems to be man's being shut out from the Tree of Life, rather than the change in his conditions of life. In the history of the race the hunting stage came before the toils of agriculture, but after the primeval state of man. People may still live partly on the natural fruits of the earth after adopting the hunting life. Familiarity with this passage has blinded us to the fact that, as a part of the narrative, it appears somewhat extraordinary. Why should the man and woman, so lately, if not still, in such conditions of life that clothing was not necessary, be now covered with anything so rude as the skins of animals? Should we not naturally expect that their Maker would have clothed them with an apparel fit for civilized people, such as cloth? Some have supposed the passage to imply that bloodshed was necessary for the covering of the sinner, but this seems rather far-fetched. Whilst ill-fitted to the narrative, the passage so agrees with that stage in the history of man when such clothing was adopted, that there can be little doubt as to its meaning. Judging from the Persian version, cited in Chap. VI. of this work, it seems likely that in earlier forms of the legend the man and woman *clothed themselves* with skins, which would agree with man's own efforts to better a fallen condition. It is as provided by their Maker that this clothing seems so unsuitable. Yet how significant is this feature in the Scripture version. God did not make His creatures and then leave them destitute; the clothing was of God's providing, and, as Science tells us, it was suited to primitive men. Not till after the adoption of skins, which man finds ready for use, does he begin to use the better kinds of apparel. Plaiting and the first forms of weaving require more ingenuity, and the presence of suitable materials. It appears that spindle-wheels were used by the people of the "kitchen-middens" of Denmark, and bone needles by the more ancient "cave men." Clothing therefore dates from a very early age.

And Jahveh-Elohim said, Behold, the man is become as one of us to know good and evil.—No doubt there was an increase of evil *pari passu* with the progress of man. This appears to have been the course of things also wherever savage tribes have developed a considerable civilization of their own. This growth of evil in more advanced nations is illustrated in the extract from Mr. Wallace's *Malay Archipelago*, already given. It is distinctly traceable in the early history of the world, as given in Gen. iii. to vi., and it seems to be the universal course in the history of man.

This brings us to the end of the 3rd chapter, and of this wonderful 'Story of the Fall.' It is well known that the 4th chapter exhibits the progress of evil, and that of civilization, in early times. Yet here, as in the Scriptures just considered, there is not accuracy of detail, or of chronological sequence, the respective passages being devoted also, and more especially, to the inculcation of moral truths. Thus we have a general outline of the history of the human race from the very beginning up to its civilized stage, the 4th chapter continuing what the 2nd and 3rd had begun.

Birth of Cain and Abel: Abel a shepherd, Cain a tiller of

the ground.—Higher than the Hunting life are the Pastoral life and the Agricultural life, and in a general way the three succeeded in this order. But as men spread over the earth, and adopted lives suiting their respective habitats and habits, all these occupations were pursued by different tribes at the same time, as they are to-day. The brothers Cain and Abel might be taken to represent the agricultural and pastoral peoples respectively. But this application is open to some doubt, as we shall see further on. It should be remembered that, as these chapters give the progress and general course of the human race, Scripture notices here only its more advanced sections. It does not imply that people of the inferior grades of earlier civilization no longer existed on the earth; it is merely occupied with the higher ones, as representing the race.

Cain's offering unacceptable because of sin: he slays Abel, and is utterly rejected.—We may here sketch a *Dispensational outline.* Notwithstanding the Fall, men still continued to hold the position of being *God's people* on the Earth. Not until the world is found full of sin do they lose that important right. A portion of the human race are here rejected on that account, as symbolized in Cain (as the wicked man, not as the agriculturist). Seth, however, and his descendants continue to occupy the former position (see Gen. iv. 25, v. 1, 3, etc.); they fill the foreground—in the 5th chapter—and are *the* people, till the Flood; whereas Cain and his descendants are the outcast wanderers. Thus at that time the world is regarded as God's world, the true seed (including the sons and daughters in each generation of chapter v.) constituting the world, and the wicked being in the minority—as regards position before God, at least, if not in numbers also—a condition of things the reverse of that which now is, when God's people are but a selected few. This lasts until Gen. vi., when the whole world becomes full of iniquity, and is rejected at the Flood.[18]

[18] Of course this does not mean that man's position before God then was the same as that of His people in the world to-day; but that until Gen. vi. they have a recognized position before God, though only, it may be, on the ground of sacrifice. Seeing how Cain is the outcast; how Seth is put in Abel's position; how Gen. v. goes on to give the family of the man whom God created in His own likeness and blessed, with Seth the first link, and the other sons and daughters included in each generation; it does not appear that the true seed occupy the position of *a remnant* in God's sight—until Gen. vi., when Noah alone is found righteous.

'Cain,' says the Apostle John (1 Jno. iii. 12), 'was of the evil one; his works were evil, and his brother's righteous.' In this episode, then, we seem to have the first fulfilment of the curse spoken to the serpent—the enmity between the seed of the serpent and that of the woman. The woman indeed says of Cain, 'I have gotten a man with the help of Jahveh,' but in Gen. iv. 25 that has been cancelled; Abel is the seed of the woman, not Cain. Here, too, in this murder, is a great advance in sin on the part of man, beyond anything before mentioned.

Cain builds a city, his descendants progress in the useful arts, and invent music. Lamech's homicide and song.—Further strides in civilization, here noticed only on the part of the rejected portion of mankind. The fact that Lamech sings about his act of slaying a man, seems to indicate a heart hardened in iniquity—a worse state of things than anything preceding it in the Scripture record. The attentive reader of the Bible will notice a strange feature in this chapter. Cain, condemned to be a fugitive and a wanderer, goes and settles down in a city, and his descendants prosper in like manner. The fact of his building a *city*, so irreconcilable with his being only one generation from Adam, fits into its place, presenting no difficulty, when these Scriptures are applied to the race. The other fact is explicable when we see that these Scriptures give what I have called a "dispensational outline," indicating the position of man *in God's sight*. Cain is to be shut out from God's face (verse 14), *before God* he is as a wanderer. That he takes little notice of this, and prospers in the world, accords with the general course of the world, which makes itself comfortable, and has its pleasures (as the music in this case) away from God, and in an already condemned position.

Of course we are not to suppose that that portion of mankind which is symbolized by the descendants of Seth, lived separate from the other portion (descendants of Cain), or that they did not also progress in civilization. No doubt people were mixed up then, as now, when Scripture still makes divisions between people which are equally fundamental—not regional, but spiritual divisions—the people of God and those who are of the world. The righteous Noah, it may be remembered, is as far advanced in the useful arts as the rest of men, in chapter vi. At the same time, he and Lamech both appear as agriculturists in chapter v. 29; perhaps implying that they, and the other descendants of Seth, accept the position to which man was condemned, instead of ignoring God's judgment, as Cain and his descendants had done. Cain is not refused in the first place on account of his being an agriculturist, but because of sin (Gen. iv. 7); and also because his offering was inappropriate (Heb. xi. 4).

Then began men to call upon the name of Jahveh (at the time of the birth of Enosh, the son of Seth).—This is one of those passages which cannot possibly be taken literally. According to Exod. vi. 2, 3, the name of Jahveh was unknown till ages after this, namely, in Hebrew times; and in a former chapter of this work we have seen the truth which Exod. vi. 2, 3 conveys. According to the letter of this same chapter of Genesis, too, Cain and Abel had already made offerings to Jehovah; and, *as commonly understood*, the first man had had direct dealings with Jehovah-Elohim in the Garden. It is well known that the name Jehovah often has the scriptural signification of God in relationship, or covenant, with man. We may take the meaning nearly as in our translation, 'then began men to call upon the name of the Lord,' or of the Deity—in other words, it was at this period that men began to have definite religious sentiments, those first crude conceptions and worship of the Deity, which were discussed in a former chapter of this work. And it seems probable that the name 'Jehovah' being used rather than 'Elohim,' further signifies primitive men's approaches to the Deity by offering sacrifice; which, although done in much ignorance, was the only ground on which God could have dealings with man.

The birth of Enosh, the son of Seth, is not presented in the Bible as very long subsequent to the offerings of Cain and Abel; so that, if we avoid drawing hard and fast lines, the latter event might be taken as occurring within the *general period* referred to in this verse. Religious emotions, as we have seen, did not spring up in a day, but were a slow growth. Until Hebrew times the worship of the Deity, although on the right track, was performed in darkness. But there is another reason why the passage about the offerings of Cain and Abel should be placed thus early in Gen. iv. In the third chapter we have been told about the fall of man, and sin has passed upon the whole race, excluding them from God's presence. It was important, therefore, that there should be given *in this early place* an intimation of the truth, that only upon certain ground could God thereafter accept man—the ground of sacrifice. Cain thinks that *of himself* he can produce something acceptable to God; he offers the fruit of his own labour. The same belief holds to-day—that man can work his own way up to God. Abel, on the contrary, has perceived that nothing but a sacrifice will be acceptable. After the incoming of sin God can have to do with and accept man only on the ground of the Atonement, which is here foreshadowed in the offering made by Abel. We need not suppose that, at so early a period, any man could have fully apprehended this truth; though, by the widespread custom of offering sacrifices to the Deity in early times, we see that God had begun to lead men's thoughts in the right direction. Here, as in other early Scriptures, it was important that *God's* thoughts and principles should be expressed; and for expressing them suitably in those times, such narratives were necessary. It was much more important that such truths should be expressed in the early Scriptures, than that these should agree precisely with the progress of human knowledge and civilization.

It has been remarked by critics that Jabal, the descendant of Cain after several generations, is said to have been 'the father of such as dwell in tents and have cattle,' although Abel had been a shepherd long before, according to the narrative. But it appears that this account of Abel was necessary for the expression of the important truth just referred to. This may have been the sole reason why Cain and Abel appear as an agriculturist and a shepherd; or the passage may have the additional application already suggested. At any rate we have, evidently, in this chapter only general indications of the early progress of mankind. The details do not all agree accurately with each other, nor with what Science teaches about man. Yet in a general way the progress is clearly indicated, whilst the teaching of more important truths takes the precedence.

I have remarked that the letter of this verse, Gen. iv. 26, cannot be reconciled with certain passages in the Story of the Garden, where the man seems to have direct intercourse with Jahveh-Elohim, if the letter of these is also maintained. Probably it is chiefly from these latter passages that people have inferred the superior endowments and conditions of life of the first of mankind. But the presence of these admits of the same simple explanation as that which I have given in other cases. The important truth which they do convey is God's deep interest in, and sympathy for, His creatures, and His presence among them, though unseen and unknown, in those days before sin intervened. And if we ask how this truth could be conveyed to readers in early times, I think we shall see there was no other way than by those features in the narrative which give the impression of a more conscious intercourse between God and man. We should also remember that the needs of the soul can be met, and are largely met, to-day, without conscious contact with God. May there not have been some such influx, real though unknown to man, in primeval days?

Some have too hastily inferred that, before social life and civilization produced better things, primitive men must have been utterly barbarous and devoid of good qualities. Refinement we cannot affirm of them; but facts tend to show that the former conclusion is wrong. We have seen, in the extract from Mr. Wallace's *Malay Archipelago*, that everything is not due to high civilization, but that savages can live together in a peaceful and comfortable way. The following extract may be added from Tylor's *Anthropology* (p. 406):—

"Under favourable circumstances, where food is not too scarce nor war too wasting, the life of low barbaric races may be in its rude way good and happy. In the West Indian Islands, where Columbus first landed, lived tribes who have been called the most gentle and benevolent of the human race. Schomburgk, the traveller, who knew the warlike Caribs well in their home life, draws a paradise-like picture of their ways, where they have not been corrupted by the vices of the white men; he saw among them peace and cheerfulness and simple family affection, unvarnished friendship, and gratitude not less true for not being spoken in sounding words; the civilized world, he says, has not to teach them morality, for though they do not talk about it, they live in it. At the other side of the world, in New Guinea, Kops, the Dutch explorer, gives much the same account of the Papuans of Dory...." (He gives several other like instances, but adds) "Of course these accounts of Caribs and Papuans show them on the friendly side, while those who have fought with them call them monsters of ferocity and treachery. But cruelty and cunning in war seem to them right and praiseworthy; and what we are here looking at is their home peace-life. It is clear that low barbarians may live among themselves under a fairly high moral standard, and this is the more instructive because it shows what may be called natural morality."

Professor Drummond's description of the Central African may also be cited as an instance of savage life which is not bad, but of primitive innocence and simplicity in its way.

These facts prove that *everything* good is not due to civilization and culture; but rather that whatsoever is good in man is of God's implanting, which civilization and culture have merely aided to develop, the good and the evil having grown and increased side by side, like the tares and the wheat. They show that before such growth of evil there may have been a better condition of things. Even in civilization it is well known that many tribes have retrograded.

We conclude, then, that this passage, 'Then began men to

call upon the name of Jahveh,' relates to the earliest theological sentiments in man, and that it is perhaps given as a corrective of certain erroneous impressions one is liable to gather from some parts of the Story of the Garden and that of Cain and Abel, which are placed there for expressing other truths.

In concluding this subject, perhaps it should be added that the foregoing outline makes no pretence to show the exact chronological order in which the historical truths of Gen. ii.-iv. should be applied to the history of primitive man. Such a task would be neither profitable nor possible.

To many readers the absence of a complete chronological parallel between these two series, will perhaps seem a grave objection to the whole of the foregoing interpretation of those Scriptures. But it is obvious the latter do apply, chiefly at least, to the early history of man. For if not, to what *do* they apply?

Gen. v.—The ten long-lived Patriarchs.—It may help us here to turn for a moment to the epistles to the angels of the Seven Churches in Rev. i. 20-iii. 22, and ask what are meant by these angels? Not what are commonly understood as angels, surely, for they are subject to human failings; nor can we say that they are men. We regard each of them as the ruling spirit, or representative, of the particular church which bears its name. Somewhat of the same character are these patriarchs of Gen. v. Their lives cover long periods, and we may say that each of them represents the age in which he lives; not necessarily giving any particular character to that age, as the aforesaid angels of the churches give to theirs, but like them only in representing it. Thus, as each one lives a long time, we gather the impression of a very long period in the aggregate,—the period between the creation of man and the event represented by the Flood. There cannot be any special meaning attaching to the exact figures given as the life of each patriarch; for the existing versions of the Old Testament differ considerably in respect of these; and the Septuagint Version, which was in general use in New Testament times, makes Methuselah live till fourteen years after the Deluge. Several successive ages in human history, covering a very long period in the whole, are all, therefore, that we gather from their long lives.

It should be particularly noted that these patriarchs and their sons and daughters are presented as the family of the man who was created in God's own likeness and blessed; so that they are thus distinctly recognized as God's people. The rejected Cainites having been disposed of in the preceding chapter, these, who are *the* people of the earth, and represent the human race, are the subject of Scripture treatment through the long ages till the Flood. Other features of the chapter are:—that it is the *seventh* in the line who walks with God, and is taken by God; that, with this exception, all of them are said to have died; that, whilst only one of them is named in each generation, the 'sons and daughters' are of the same standing, through descent.   Lastly, it presents a genealogy, and one through which the descent of Jesus is traced back to God in Luke iii. If it seem that such a genealogy must lose its reality if we cease to regard these as historical men, living their respective ages, we shall do well to recall what we have already seen as to the Scriptural principle of descent (see page 235). It is not the natural descent from the man Abraham that is important; it is not Abraham *as a man* that is important as a progenitor, but the *spirit manifested by him*, and the possessor of that spirit is the only real descendant in God's sight. At the same time, the natural genealogy serves well to represent the spiritual genealogy. This genealogy presents a chain connecting (1) God's people, the Jews, and (2) Jesus, with the man created in God's image, who is called the son of God. It may further be remarked that the first link mentioned in the chain (Luke iii. 23), Joseph, was only the *reputed* father of Jesus.

These considerations show us how significant is the fact that Abraham, the first man and father of the Hebrews, manifests faith so conspicuous in his life; because his descendants thus come, through their natural descent, to be regarded as the children of the faithful man and of his faith, and are thus stamped as God's people, the children of (the spirit of) faith.

We now come to the important question, How, in the light of Evolution, is it true that sin and death passed upon all men through the sin of the first man? Believers in the historical character of the Story of the Fall have been puzzled as to how the threat in Gen. ii. 17 was fulfilled, since the man did not die on the day he ate the fruit, in the manner to be expected. Some, referring to the passage where it is said that 1000 years is with the Lord as one day, have argued that he did not live quite 1000 years. Others, taking the marginal reading, 'dying thou shalt die,' have thought that he began to die at the time of his transgression. Others have regarded the death as a loss of fellowship with God. Others again, have thought that the punishment affected the manner of his dying, rather than the fact of his natural death. The difficulty, therefore, is not a new one.

If, however, the foregoing conclusions as to the true meaning of the Story of the Fall be correct, it is evident that a somewhat different explanation must be the true one. It must be an explanation that agrees with the fact that through the sin of the first man, or men, sin and death passed upon all the race; one that agrees with the facts of Science; and one that agrees with the characteristic features of the Story in Gen. ii., iii. We have already remarked that parts of Gen. iii. have generally been interpreted as applying, not only to the first individuals, but also to the race; and this exegesis, so fully confirmed before, we shall find applicable here.

In the next place the question naturally arises, Is the life in question an eternal earthly life, or an eternal life elsewhere, which should have followed the earthly life? We shall get a sufficient answer to this question by considering a very striking fact relating to the Believer in Christ. Scripture distinctly states that he *has* eternal life, that he shall never die, that he is already passed from death to life. Yet he is subject to bodily death, just as other men ; Scripture takes it for granted that he is ; which event it regards as a " falling asleep." Here, therefore, the life which the Believer has hereafter is a continuation of the life conferred on him at his conversion; it is *one life*, which begins then and never ceases. Applying this to the matter under consideration, we may dismiss the question as to what sort of life is meant, as of no consequence, and entirely out of place. As, with the Believer the two kinds of life, here and hereafter, constitute *one life ;* (the bodily death not having been annulled because he has this life, and not being regarded as death;) so here, all that we should go so far as to predicate is *life itself*, never mind of what order, or orders. Either an eternal earthly life, or a life beginning on earth and lasting for ever under different conditions after bodily death, would equally satisfy the requirements of the case. Both analogy and Science would, however, decide in favour of the latter.

Now let us observe a peculiar feature in the narrative. Not only does the man not die directly after eating the forbidden fruit, but it is *taken for granted* that the day will come when he will " return to the ground." In addition to this, Gen. iii. 22 distinctly expresses that he was not in possession of eternal life. The Tree of Life had been placed where he could have eaten of it, but he had not done so; he was driven out of the garden lest he should eat of it. So far then as the details of the Story go, the man did not lose his own earthly life, either immediately or eventually, through his eating of the fruit; neither did he lose his own eternal life, for he never actually had it. But what *he did lose was the power or right to obtain the eternal life which had been intended for him.*

Science says that the lifetimes of the first of the human race were of limited duration; and that the human body is not, and never has been, so constituted as to admit of an eternal life in it. (As to a post-earthly life of primeval man, Science can say nothing. We know that the human mind has been a gradual growth, the men of each age possessing more of it than their predecessors; but, knowing so little about the soul apart from the body, we know nothing about the souls of primeval men.)

The New Testament says that, for the Believer, God has made another provision to make his life eternal.

Putting all these facts together, we arrive at the conclusion, that God had intended eternal life (of some kind) for man; that the first representatives of the race were not probably in possession of more than the earthly life, and so could not lose it for themselves; but through their sin—which passed upon their successors, who sinned in their turn—the whole human race forfeited the eternal life which God had intended for them. Rom. v. 12 states that "death passed unto all men, for that all sinned." They do not simply inherit death, but they receive the sinful nature, they sin themselves, and therefore merit death.

We conclude then that the Tree of Life placed in the Garden, and the threat of death in Gen. ii. 17, represent God's purposes concerning the whole human race; whereas the act of eating of the Tree of Knowledge symbolizes the sin of the first representatives of the race. *First man stood at the head, holding the responsible position of determining the destinies of the race: first man sinned, and so death to the race followed.* Thus "through one man sin entered into the world, and death through sin; and so death passed unto all men, for that all sinned" (Rom. v. 12). If this present a difficulty in seeming to predicate the sin of many, and not of one, let us recall our former conclusions as to the mental condition of the many (page 281). Moreover, the sin may have begun with one individual. It may also be remembered that, though Rom. v. 12 says 'one man,' the narrative in Genesis says one woman first and then one man.

Of course it does not follow that the life which God had intended for the race involved all that the Believer possesses in Christ. It could have been an eternal not-earthly life without that; perhaps a very different one. As things are, no one who is born into the world inherits eternal life; it is only the few who believe in Christ now that get it. But for sin, those who come into the world would have life as their natural possession. Thus has death passed unto all men.

Before leaving this subject it may be well to make a few remarks as to the moral condition of primeval man. Considering the manner of his development, with the 'struggle for life' which Evolution supposes him and his progenitors to have passed through, it may appear that he was originally and essentially of evil nature. But that does not follow.

We may learn something of the structure of the human mind indirectly, which goes to show that, as the mind nhabits the body, so does spirit inhabit the structure of mind. As Scripture teaches, and as Christians experience, they themselves are complex creatures. Within the Believer now dwells the Spirit of God, where formerly dwelt and ruled the spirit of evil. The spirit of evil is not entirely removed from within him, but whilst he 'walks in the spirit' it does not act, its former place is occupied by the Spirit of God, which guides his actions and emotions. Yet, notwithstanding this change of the ruling spirit within him, a great part of his mental system remains unchanged. His intellect remains almost entirely so, for he thinks by the same process and in the same manner as before ; on most subjects at least ; and where there is a change, it is in the product of thought, and not in the process of thought. The same applies largely to his emotions. Be his original disposition dull or lively, so it continues after. His tastes, bodily and mental, continue ; as, for instance, if he have a taste for music, or study. His natural affections continue ; and so throughout. *These things*, formerly defiled, are consecrated, as he lives for God, and not, as before, to please himself ; but we can clearly see that in themselves they constitute a portion of the whole mind which is equally distinct from the Spirit of God and the spirit of evil. We have no evidence, perhaps, that they can exist apart from both of these, without any such ruling spirit ; but here is evidence that they do exist apart from each in its turn, and hence they are not, in their own constitution, identical with either. To give them a name, we may say that they constitute *the human mental structure*, within which may dwell the ruling spirit (good or bad), somewhat in the same way that the mind inhabits the body.

In the Scriptures which treat of these subjects (as Gal. ii. 20, and others), we find divisions which run deeper than those which divide man from man, and individuality is even predicated of the indwelling spirit. In 1 John iii. 9, for instance, it is stated that whosoever is begotten of God does not, and cannot, sin ; which is not true of the man as a whole, but is true of the Spirit of God within him.

We may look yet closer. Anger as manifested in man is evil, but as manifested in God it is not. Clearly then there may be such a sentiment as anger in other beings (theoretically at least) which does not contain the evil element—the two even here are distinct. What we see in the animal we do not regard as sin ; because, perhaps, the animal does not possess reason ; but, whilst it appears in some cases as if it were of the same essential nature as the sinful anger of man, we cannot say whether it is so or not. The principle of evil may be a distinct element, which is present in man and not in the animal. Thus it is quite possible that primeval man was rough and coarse, but at the same time had not the evil principle within him.

As to the origin of evil, Scripture is silent. But it distinctly teaches that the Devil is a being distinct from man ; he is the source of evil ; he is the 'god of this world.' Christian experience says the same. Scripture teaches, too, that God overrules the devil's actions to work out His own ends. It may occur to us that such was also the case before historic times, namely, in the evolution of life ; but there is nothing in Scripture to substantiate this.

If it be assumed that primeval man had the evil principle within him, the following facts should be borne in mind. The difference between conscious and unconscious sin is great. A child may do many things very displeasing to his parents, and yet in all sincerity hold up his head before them, so long as he does not *know* that he is doing wrong. If after that he persist, the case is totally different. " Until the law sin was in the world : but sin is not imputed when there is no law " (Rom. v. 13)—law of conscience in the case of primeval man (see also verse 14). ' Sin ' has been called the tree, of which ' sins ' are the fruit ; and in this sense these terms are used, sometimes at least, in the Bible. ' Sin ' thus relates to something deeper and more fundamental than sinful acts—to the essential nature of emotions, the root, the substance, the evil principle, as I have elsewhere called it.

The assumption of such an unknown impurity in primeval man, seems at first sight to imply that God created man sinful; which will seem inconceivable to some who will hold at the same time that He created Satan, who is essentially sin. As regards this, those divisions must be borne in mind to which we have just been referring, which run deeper than the divisions between individuals. It would then appear that what God created was *the mental structure of man*, which, as we have just seen, is not essentially evil ; not that He created the evil which dwelt within it. Regarding this mental structure as the man, we should thus see that all that God created was good, as described in Gen. i.

Finally, let us turn again to the matchless Old Parable, so that Scripture may be our guide. Is there a double character in the nakedness of the man, since the consciousness of this makes him feel unfit for his Maker's presence, and makes him perceive his bodily nakedness ? Do the words, " Who told thee that thou wast naked ? " imply that he was naked in the worst sense before, and knew it not? Why is the Tree of which he eats not called 'the Tree of Evil,' but the 'Tree of *Knowledge* of Good and Evil'?

In the next place it should be remarked that an external agency is distinctly suggested in the episode of the sinful deed. The act is brought about by the devil. In the New Testament, too, attention is called to the fact that the woman was beguiled by the serpent in his craftiness (2 Cor. xi. 3). In another place it says that Adam was not beguiled, as the woman was (1 Tim. ii. 14).[19] In the sinful deed, not only was forbidden knowledge acquired, but certain desires also were indulged. "When the woman saw that the tree was good for food, and that it was a delight to the eyes, and that the tree was to be desired to make one wise, she took of the fruit thereof, and did eat; and she gave also unto her husband with her, and he did eat."

He who believes that God works by magic, and not by a natural process, may perhaps take it upon himself to say that primeval man, as we have here considered him, would have been, mentally, a product unworthy of God. I have lately seen it remarked that the earth 'without form and void' could not have been, for this reason, created in that state, but must have lapsed into it. But as the first step in the process which, by the end of Gen. i., leaves everything in order, there is nothing unworthy of God. So is it also with man.

It may again be objected—if we view things from our own one-cornered position, forgetting that the absolute, not the relative, is the true standpoint—Is this the man of Genesis i., who is made in God's image? If we look *down* on him from where we stand, we may think not. But if

---

[19] These references are, however, made in behalf of the subjects under treatment, rather as taking the moral lesson from the Old Testament passage, than as adding to, or explaining it.

we look at him from the bottom and beginning of the scale we say, Yes, in part. From the time he began to assume the human form he began to take God's image, and in every step of his progress he has assumed it more and more, from that day to this (albeit and excepting his moral regress). Gen. i., as already stated, gives the general view—man as the general type of the human race; not primeval man. So, doubtless, in another aspect than the one we have chiefly considered here, does Gen. ii., iii. Finally, it may be asked, if we must have man in God's *perfect* image, where in past or present is he to be found ? I can only think of ONE, who might have been found in Palestine some 2000 years ago.

Hitherto, with some exceptions, we have considered Gen. ii., iii., only in its application to primitive man. Now we have to do with its application to the human race as a whole, and God's purposes concerning it.[20] We have touched upon the latter in the foregoing remarks about the Tree of Life.

It may help us to an apprehension of the truth if we look at a somewhat similar case. A rich man, possessor of large estates and princely wealth, has a son and heir. As yet the heir is but a youth : the time is not yet come that he should enter upon his possession. But his father is disappointed in him ; he utterly disgraces himself, and consequently he is disinherited. Say, reader, Does he really lose all these things, or is it a purely ideal affair? Yet perhaps "unreal" was the mental comment, on perusal

---

[20] Here it is well to note why there is the double application, and that it resolves itself, for the most part, into a single one. For the passage gives—and has always been more or less understood to give—the history of *man*, and the judgments passed on him for sin, the spiritual history of the human race; and the spiritual history of primeval men is a part of this whole.

of the foregoing statements as to how man lost *the Life* which was intended for him.

Let us return to the Garden of Eden, charged, as much as possible, with the belief that 'the things which are not seen' are not ideal, but most real. Let us draw a picture of the whole scene, embracing both the physical environment of man, the natural world, and also the spiritual environment, the spiritual world. It may help us to conceive the natural world as in the centre of the spiritual world—the natural garden as within the spiritual garden—whilst that which belongs to the spiritual has free access to the natural, but not quite *vice versa*. In the natural garden are the fruit-trees of the earth: in the spiritual garden are the fruit-trees of the spiritual world, including the Tree of Life. God is in the spiritual garden, having access, as we said, to the natural garden. Satan and the Tree of Knowledge are also there. In the midst of all this, in the natural garden, God, the owner of all, has placed man. Not an individual man; not primeval man—we have done with that side of the question—but *the human race*. Without making it quite a hard and fast line, we may say that the natural garden includes what man has, the spiritual garden what he is to have. There God has placed man, with purposes of life and blessing for him. If this be Paradise, somewhat such as this is the Paradise of Genesis.[21]

But sin comes in, and man is disinherited. He is shut out from the Tree of Life, from the fruit-trees of the spiritual garden; he is never to taste of them. He is thrust out of the spiritual garden; and, if it help us to think of it so, we may say that the natural garden is thrust out too.

[21] The word 'Paradise' is not in Genesis.

CHAPTER IX.

THE FLOOD.

ONE of the greatest of the difficulties raised by the text of Scripture is the Story of the Flood.

He who reads the account in Genesis in the light of his own conception of the Earth's shape, very naturally understands it to assert that the surface of this huge spherical Earth on which we dwell, was once entirely covered with water some six miles deep. We shall see, however, that that conclusion is drawn too hastily. The impossibility of maintaining such a belief is so manifest that Evolutionist and Anti-evolutionist, Opponent of Scripture and Defender of Scripture, are alike agreed that, never since the Earth has been inhabited by man, has it been subjected to a universal deluge. A few of the facts which enforce the latter conclusion may be given here.

Vast physical changes, entailing an entire re-constitution of the Earth, would probably have been necessary. Upon this subject Dr. Kinns writes (*Moses and Geology*, 1889, p. 398) :—

... "The water could not have covered the whole globe and all its mountains without a very large quantity being created specially for the purpose; for if all the water existing in the oceans, seas, rivers, and atmosphere, was deposited upon the globe, and equally divided over its surface, such a universal sea would only be about two and a half miles in depth. And *thirty* times as much would have been required to have formed a casing of water that would have covered over all the mountains of the world; and then a most stupendous miracle would have been necessary to get rid of this enormous extra quantity of water, amounting to more than a thousand millions of *cubic miles.*

... "If the whole globe had been so encased with water, science would have discovered a confirmation of it, whereas there is everything in the infallible Book of Nature to contradict such a supposition."

There are mountain craters of older date than the first men, composed of loose materials, which would have been swept away by such a flood, and they bear no marks of any disturbance of the kind.

The world may be divided into zoological provinces. Numerous species of animals are, and always have been, confined to those regions which they now inhabit. If anyone supposes that pairs of these animals traversed the Earth to the place where the Ark was, and back to their original habitats afterwards, he must conclude that many of them crossed several thousands of miles of *ocean* in the journey! He is brought face to face with many other such absurdities, if he attempts to reconcile the details of the narrative with their necessary implications. In the light of anthropology it is impossible to hold that the lower races of man are descended from a fully-developed and highly-civilized man, such as Noah. It is known from the Egyptian monuments that some of the distinguishing physical characteristics of the different races were in existence 4000 years ago, *i.e.* within two or three hundred years of the date commonly assigned to the Flood; whereas there is every reason to believe that vast ages were required for such a differentiation of mankind. There is also the best evidence that Egypt existed as a developed kingdom more than a thousand years before that date.

We are thus forced to the conclusion that whatever deluge of waters there was, must have been confined to a certain low-lying region; that the lower races of man could not have been destroyed by it, unless it occurred at a very early period, long before civilized times; and that but a very small proportion of the species of animals could have been preserved in the manner related.

The superficial reader of his Bible, surprised and perhaps shocked at these plain statements, will be not less surprised to hear that he himself has never really believed all the details of the story. He has only believed that he believed them. For, as explained in Chapter VI., the account in Genesis is composed of parts of two different versions of the story, pieced together; and in places where there is a duplicate account of the same events, these are sometimes mutually contradictory.

Thus from internal evidence, as well as from external evidence, it is undeniable that *some* of the story cannot be historical fact. After all that we have seen in foregoing parts of this work, however, we are not surprised or alarmed at these facts. It is merely one more instance in which God has made use of a crude primitive literary composition, embodying the beliefs of an early age, to convey important truth to the minds of men.

First, let us try to read the ideas entertained by the Hebrew writers of the story. We shall then be in a better position to consider for what purpose it is placed in the Bible.

The following is an outline of the ideas held by the nations of antiquity in general, and by the Hebrews in particular, respecting the structure of the Universe.

The Earth was not supposed to be spherical, but a flat surface. The Babylonians, and the Hebrews after them, believed that it had been originally drawn together out of the waters of a vast abyss of ocean, upon which it afterwards rested. "This dark infernal lake (says the author of the

Chaldean Account of Genesis, p. 69) was shut in by gigantic gates and strong fastenings, which prevented the floods from overwhelming the world." The celestial vault (composed of material substance) was supported by the Earth, by means of pillars. Above this vault, in heaven, (or fixed in it) were the luminaries (supposed to be insignificant in size). There dwelt the gods, the luminaries being in some cases regarded as gods, or as the visible manifestations of gods dwelling in them. With the Hebrews, of course *God* dwelt there, and the stars were often regarded as angels. In earliest Hebrew times an ocean of waters was supposed to be situated in this upper region, out of which came the rain when the doors or "windows of heaven" were opened for the purpose. Of course these beliefs varied amongst different people and at different times.

These notions explain how the men of Babel thought they could build a tower that would reach to heaven; also the language of Exod. xx. 4, "any form that is in heaven above, or that is in the earth beneath, or that is *in the water under the earth;*" also the language of David in 2 Sam. xxii. 8, and of Job in Job xxvi. 11, as heaven was supposed to be supported by the earth. (In verse 7, however, of the last-named chapter, we find a change in the notion about the lower waters, since it is said that "he hangeth the earth upon nothing.") Other facts might be given which illustrate these beliefs.

It is important to see that these notions lie at the very foundations of this old Story of the Flood. We read them clearly in Gen. vii. 11, "on the same day were all the *fountains of the great deep broken up,* and the *windows of heaven were opened.*" In Gen. viii. 2 we have the same again. Water rising from the ocean below, and water coming down from the ocean above, were supposed to have raised the level of the waters on which the earth rested, so as to completely cover it. Such is the event described, and there is *no such idea* as the flooding of the vast surface of a spherical earth.

Thus he who reads the account, thinking of the latter phenomenon, is reading *a story totally different* from the one which was in the minds of its writers.

These views explain another feature of the story. The account represents, not only that the men and animals were killed, but also that the Earth itself was destroyed. In Gen. vi. 13 we read, "I will destroy them with the earth"; and more plainly in Gen. ix. 12, "neither shall there any more be a flood to destroy the earth." Such an earth as the old notions represented, drawn together out of the waters, existing in and resting on them, would naturally be regarded as utterly destroyed by such a rise of those waters, out of which it was supposed to have received its very being.

It is not represented that the animals were destroyed merely as a necessary consequence of the Flood, but that the judgment was designedly extended to them. Gen. vi. 7, 8 :— "And Jahveh said, I will blot out man whom I have created from the face of the ground; *both man, and beast, and creeping thing, and fowl of the air;* for it repenteth me that I have made them. But Noah found grace in the eyes of Jahveh." Here, too, and in Gen. viii. 21, the Divine anger, vexation, and acceptance of the sacrifice, are represented as like the emotions of a man—"And Jahveh smelled the sweet savour; and Jahveh said in his heart, I will not again curse the ground any more for man's sake, etc." Though these are conceived of after human thoughts, the passages yet express important truths. It is better to see that the story is of the same primitive character throughout, for we shall then be more likely to arrive at true conclusions as to the Divine meaning which lies beneath it.

Again, Gen. vi. 1-5 is a strange passage. 'Sons of God'

was a Hebrew name for angels. No doubt the idea was that of gods, or god-like beings, in early times; and it was believed that some such denizens of heaven had joined themselves in marriage to the daughters of men, producing giants as offspring.

The event seems to be closely connected with, in fact to produce, the wickedness of man, for which the Flood was sent. Comparing the passage with Jude 6, 7; 2 Peter ii. 4; 1 Peter iii. 19, 20; also Job i. 6, 7; we seem to have indicated here the work of evil spirits in the hearts of men.

Critics have not failed to remark on the utter impossibility of the existence of such a numerous and motley group of animals in a place like the Ark, of the coming of the animals to Noah, etc. And until *forced* by Science to abandon our former position, we have, with more zeal than knowledge, endeavoured to make possible the impossible old story, by predicating a host of miracles. The fact, however, that in the narrative all is supposed to be accomplished by natural means, should have taught us better. It is our cumbersome way of treating all parts of the wonderful Book of God alike, that leads to such mistakes—mistakes harmless enough, perhaps, so far as we are concerned; but too well calculated to bring the Bible into contempt with those who see these *apparent* defects, but do not *know* its wonderful and divine character.

But here we are *compelled* to own that this composition belongs essentially to a primitive and ignorant age. The word 'ignorant' is not, however, a good one to use in this case. If we use it, we do so much as the child of ten does who calls the child of seven 'ignorant.' For, with all our knowledge, we ourselves are but children, only we are rather older children than our predecessors of three or four thousand years ago. If they needed something simple and 'ignorant' to teach them the rudiments of the knowledge of God, we too require some things simple, and others very symbolic, to teach us Divine truths somewhat more advanced. Let us take a salutary lesson from this; and, seeing how well it is that each portion of Scripture is expressed in the language and ideas of its own age, we need not hesitate to admit that this old Story of the Flood was primordially adjusted to, and intended for, our juniors in knowledge.

It has been remarked, not at all in defence of Scripture, that it is not easy to account for the widespread belief in a Flood. Some writers have attributed it to the presence of marine shells in the geological formations, and to magnified accounts of local floods. If we do not suppose that all people till Hebrew times were left entirely without Divine light, it seems very likely that some such traditions as the above were so overruled as to lead men's beliefs near to spiritual truth of a similar nature. Exegetes generally adopt the belief that there was a partial Deluge, which is the subject of this portion of Scripture, and the traditions of other nations are adduced as corroborating Scripture. It is quite possible that there was such a flooding of a large low-lying region, or the subsidence of an island home, with destruction of the inhabitants. The unsatisfactory part of this explanation is that, with the facts of Science before us, we could not suppose the flood to have destroyed all the race, unless it occurred before the spreading of man over the earth, and therefore before there was such an evolution of sin and of civilization as we find associated with the event in the Bible. But it is not necessary to abandon that view of the matter. Whilst it is not the explanation brought forward here, the passage may have that as part of its meaning.

For, in accordance with the principles maintained on pp. 251-253, we must not expect a complete parallel between the old narrative and any one event. The passage is long, consists of four chapters, and possesses several different features; each of which features may have a special signification, distinct from the others. Such an economy of Scripture is consistent with the principles maintained in the second chapter of this work; with the exegesis adopted in the two preceding chapters; and with the experience of divinely-taught students, who often read the *mind of God* in these old Scriptures as in a parable, whilst, however, still retaining belief in their historical character.

We shall find, then, without going into minor details, three special significations attaching to different parts or features of the narrative, whilst the parallels between these applications and the corresponding parts of the narrative are not complete in all particulars. If the old story has succeeded in imparting these truths, or even an approximation to them where they involve unfamiliar concepts, we can see that it has answered its purpose.

It may help us if we take a somewhat parallel case. It has already been remarked that the Book of Revelation, treating of unfamiliar subjects, necessarily uses symbols very largely. If any one searches in the Book of Revelation for any complete agreement of the symbolic language with the facts of history, he reads his Bible in vain. But if he compare its pages with the *spirit manifested* in certain pages of history, present and past, also carefully observing and comparing with each other the characteristic features of these Scriptures, he will find much. Let us take a case. Students of Rev. ii., iii. have noticed striking parallels between the descriptions of the Seven Churches, and the successive phases of the Church's history from Apostolic times to our own. But there is not complete agreement. Very likely the members of those original seven churches in Asia in like manner found that these epistles corresponded but partially with the facts which they observed. It is natural to conclude that Rev. ii., iii. was intended partly to apply to those seven churches, and in other respects to be prophetic of the general history of the Church. Now it was as impossible to express the truths of Gen. vi.-ix. literally, in early times, as the truths of Revelation in later times.

First let us consider the ethnological parallel. In the story death passes upon all men except one family. Of the parent of that family come three sons who people the whole Earth. What have we in a general ethnological classification of mankind in historical times and to-day? Anthropologists do not all make the same divisions in minor respects; but they agree in the main divisions of mankind, which is all that is important, at least to us here. A classification commonly adopted gives three main divisions:—the Ethiopian, the Mongolian, and the Caucasian or Mediterranean. The first two of these divisions comprise all the lower races, and the third, the Caucasian, are lords of the earth.[1] This Caucasian Race consists of *three branches*:—(1) the Hamite, represented chiefly by the ancient Egyptians, who were the first to make great progress in civilization and culture, far beyond any existing elsewhere in the world at that time; (2) the Semite, represented chiefly by the Babylonians and Assyrians, who improved upon the older Egyptian; (3) the Indo-European, represented by Greece and Rome in the old world, and by modern European nations to-day. To what extent these three branches are related by family ties does not concern us much, as we do not look for a strict parallel;[2] suffice it that their likeness is such that they have been classed as one race. But compared with these three, or this three-branched race, all

---

[1] Peschel divides mankind into seven classes:—the Caucasian, and six others which comprise all the lower races.

[2] For reasons already given, and because the simple ideas in Genesis are quite inadequate to express the existing relations between races, or the facts of ethnology generally.

the races included in the other two divisions are of small account. Some of these excel in numbers, and there are many grades in their civilization and culture; but (notwithstanding certain partial exceptions, as the Chinese), speaking generally it may be said that they have been subjected to the death of stagnation and inferior conditions of life; whereas this Caucasian Race has had the progress, the civilization, the light, the culture, the intellect, the power—practically the earth is theirs—and, last but not least, the BOOK is theirs. In that day, far back in the ages past, when the rest of mankind stood almost still, this Foremost Race began, and have ever since continued, their marvellous career of progress. In a sense then, and a real one, they alone retained *the Life*.

These blessings, this lordship of the Earth, seem to be implied in the words, "and God blessed Noah and his sons, and said unto them, Be fruitful and multiply and replenish the earth" (Gen. ix. 1), also in the 8th and 9th verses of the same chapter. And the agreement is closer still. For the list of nations who peopled the Earth after the Flood, as given in Gen. x., consists of members of this Mediterranean Race.[3]

Hamite and Semite have, however, in the last few thousand years fallen into the rear. TRULY GOD HAS ENLARGED JAPHET (Gen. ix. 27), since now the Indo-European is far before the other two.

According to the story, "the Earth was corrupt before God, and the Earth was filled with violence" (Gen. vi. 11). Doubtless corruption has increased since that time; and probably that aspect has more to do with the other applications of the passage, to be considered presently. For, as before remarked, corruption is not a characteristic of the lower races so much as violence is. Perhaps, too, in the

[3] There may be an insignificant exception or two; I am not sure.

ages that have passed since, their manners have been softened; and if so this feature of the passage may have more special meaning than we can now learn anything about from observation of men to-day. Violence in Cain; wanton violence in Lamech; finally the Earth filled with violence—this is an important feature of the brief outline in Gen. iv., vi.

The application of Canaan's curse to the Negro is open to doubt. The Negro belongs to one of the lower races; and if, on account of his dark colour, place of abode, and position of slavery, he be considered as identified with Ham, we yet fail to connect him in any way with the Canaanite, with which the name Canaan seems to agree. The God-honoured position of the Hebrews seems to be twice implied :—(1) In the words "Jahveh, the God of Shem," (2) in the words "God (enlarge Japhet), and let him dwell in the tents of Shem"; which seems best understood to mean that God, not Japhet, was to dwell in the tents of Shem; as He may be said to have done in Hebrew history. This relationship of God with the Hebrews brings us to the second application of this passage about the Flood.

First, however, let us recall one fact which impressed us in the third chapter of this work. After seeing how God had bestowed upon all mankind the necessary preparation of mind for comprehending those Divine truths which He first taught the Hebrew, we saw, notwithstanding, that the special blessing of receiving those truths has hitherto been almost confined to the higher race of man. Does not the foregoing ethnological application of this Scripture about the Flood give the explanation of that fact? This does not imply, of course, that such a judgment on the lower races would shut out every individual from these blessings; but that exclusion from them was part of this general judgment, passed on those races long ago.

One most important feature in this Scripture is the universality of the judgment. "The end of all flesh is come before me. . . . I will destroy them with the earth" (Gen. vi. 13). Obviously, it is of little consequence whether the physical earth was covered with water or not. The all-important thing is universal judgment on the *world of men* for its sin. Let us consider for a moment how we use the term "the world," and how it is used in the New Testament. We do not always refer to the physical earth when we use the word. It is often used to denote Society. If a person goes to an uninhabited or little-inhabited region, he is said to go out of the world. If a person, while remaining in the same place, withdraws from society, he is said to withdraw from the world. The converted man who gives up his old associations and manner of life, is said to give up the world. In the New Testament we find a somewhat similar signification. "If ye were of the world, the world would love its own; but because ye are not of the world, but I chose you out of the world, therefore the world hateth you" (John xv. 19). ". . they are not of the world, even as I am not of the world; I pray not that thou shouldest take them out of the world . . ." (John xvii. 14, 15). "God so loved the world . . ." (John iii. 16). So, many times, in the first Epistle of John.

In most of the above cases we see that "the world" has no reference to the physical earth, but denotes the world of men *regarded as one whole*. And it is to this world of men, *taken as one whole*, that the judgment recorded in this passage about the Flood in one sense relates. We need but reflect that there were not, probably, in existence any such mature idea and corresponding expression as this in earliest Hebrew times, and we shall see that the language used in Genesis was suitable and necessary for representing it. The idea is embodied in the account in Genesis, as becomes more apparent when we compare Scripture with Scripture.

I have used the term 'dispensational' to denote the course of things *as God sees them*. This is the meaning here, inasmuch as this world (of men) held, before the Flood, the important position of *God's recognized people on the earth* (see p. 283), but was never allowed that position afterwards.

Let us turn again to Revelation. The words in the epistle to the church in Sardis (Rev. iii. 5), "I will in no wise blot his name out of the book of life," have puzzled some, seeing that a saving faith secures eternal life. We need but refer, however, to the beginning of this epistle to the church in Sardis (Rev. iii. 1), to see that the Speaker had just blotted the name of Sardis out of his 'book of life,' in the words " thou hast a name that thou livest, and thou art dead." The faithful individual in Sardis was to escape this general blotting out from the book of life. Here it is a judgment of works, and seems to have no reference to eternal life in Christ.

If, then, we should attribute special meaning to two expressions in this passage in Genesis, we should find a striking parallel to the passage just referred to. "The end of all flesh is come *before me*" (Gen. vi. 13). "I will *blot out* (marginal Hebrew reading) man whom I have created from the face of the ground " (Gen. vi. 7). *Before God* the world ceases to exist; it is blotted out of His book. We have seen that in Gen. v. the inhabitants of the earth are distinctly recognized as God's people. Also the words in Gen. vi. 3, "My spirit shall not rule (or abide) in man for ever (marginal reading) . . . yet shall his days be 120 years," seem to have a like import. It now remains to be shown that the world is never allowed that place after the Flood.

In Deut. xiv. 2 we read concerning Israel, " And Jehovah

hath chosen thee to be a peculiar people unto himself, out of all peoples that are upon the face of the earth." We have the same thing in Exod. xix. 5, and Ps. cxxxv. 4; also in Amos iii. 1, 2, "O children of Israel . . . *you only have I known* of all the families of the earth; therefore I will visit upon you all your iniquities" (since 'whom the Lord loveth he chasteneth,'[4] whereas because of their sins 'cometh the *wrath of God* upon the sons of disobedience'[5]). This clearly shows that God does not acknowledge *the world* as His people, but Israel only (at that time).

When we read Gen. ix. alone, we gather the impression that Noah's descendants were to have all that before belonged to the ante-diluvian world. But on reading the Bible through we find that God never again associates His name with the world after its rejection at the Flood; afterwards He has to do with Israel alone. We have seen, moreover, that that part of Gen ix. appears to relate to those earthly blessings which have been conferred on the three-branched Mediterranean race, raising them so far above the rejected lower races; so appertaining only to the ethnological application of this Scripture passage about the Flood.

The only place where we again find the world the subject of Scripture treatment in this part of the Bible, is the 11th chapter of Genesis. There we read of 'the whole earth' being of one speech, trying to make themselves a name and a position, by building a city, and a tower *whose top should reach to heaven*, lest they should be scattered abroad upon the face of the whole earth (Gen. xi. 4). But does this passage imply a rejection of the post-diluvian world similar to that of the first world? It appears rather to imply an attempt on the part of man to make a position *to which he had no*

[4] Heb. xii. 6. [5] Eph. v. 6.

right before God, and that therefore his efforts are defeated. He seeks a heavenly position, whereas God will allow him no such position, or relations with Himself. On the contrary God Himself gives Israel its position. In Gen. xii. 1, 2 we read, "Now Jehovah said unto Abram, Get thee out of thy country . . . and I will make of thee a great nation, and I will bless thee, and make thy name great." But as to the position before God of the people of the earth after the Flood—the world—this has changed; it no longer figures in Scripture as God's people; it has come to an end in His sight. He never again recognizes the world of men as His own world. It has no such place before God; He has blotted it out of the book of life.

In subsequent Scripture history, other nations are noticed only where they come in contact with Israel. In another position, however, 'the world' is referred to in the New Testament; but that is not *God's world;* it is an evil world with which He has nothing to do but to judge it. In John iii. 17 it is a lost world which the Son of God comes to save. Now He saves, and has relations with, individuals only (the 'whosoever' of verse 16). I suppose the world itself will be saved in that sense in *millenial* days.

But is this not an ideal judgment? Not altogether ideal, seeing how people now wonder why certain things are allowed to be, or why they are, in the world; which is sometimes called God's world. The Divine *ideal* is apt to be followed by what man considers real. Similarly there are many things which people cannot understand, which they might find explained in the Scripture, and in its principles. This does not mean that God has nothing whatever to do with the present course of things. In 1 Tim. iv. 10 it is said that "the living God is the Saviour," or, as another translation gives it, " preserver, of all men."

Still these two applications of this passage about the

Flood do not seem to fully satisfy its language. The dreadful judgment of which we there read, as poured out on all men for their iniquity, seems to imply something more; and, considering all the circumstances of the case, I think we shall not be wrong in assuming that what the lake of fire is in the present world's eschatology, the flood of waters was in that of the old world.

That so very little knowledge is exhibited throughout the Old Testament as to anything after bodily death, is sufficient reason why such a judgment should be expressed in language limited to the present life. All that we know about the fiery judgment on the wicked is necessarily conceived in terms relating to natural fire, though we do not suppose it to be that; and if we trace the growth of that knowledge, we find links connecting it with certain Old Testament passages where it is first foreshadowed—such passages as Mal. iv. 1, Zeph. iii. 8, Joel ii. 30, 31; which use language expressing physical things, but may not improbably relate to this judgment on the soul. In 2 Peter iii. 5-7, which uses the language of the Old Testament, we find the judgment on the old world connected with that on the present world:—" . . . there were heavens from of old, and an earth compacted out of water and amidst water, by the word of God; by which means *the world that then was*, being overflowed *with water*, perished; but the *heavens that now are, and the earth*, by the same word have been stored up *for fire*, being reserved against the day of judgment, and destruction of ungodly men." Here, undoubtedly, the language refers throughout to physical things, and if it be held that its application must be limited to these, I do not wish to insist on something different.

Not before the New Testament do we read of judgment by fire as relating to the soul. The language of Rev. xx. 11-15 may be taken as applying to all the wicked who have ever lived on the earth, or as having nothing to do with the ante-diluvian world. The lake of fire is twice said to be—as regards man—the second death (Rev. xx. 14, xxi. 8). A little reflexion will show that this second death, the lake of fire, may well have its parallel in the old world in a 'second death' by water; in both cases these terms being the most appropriate to convey an idea of the reality. Both, moreover, are additional judgments, not included in the loss of eternal life, which, as we saw in the last chapter, passed on the human race in consequence of the first sin. The lake of fire is a special judgment for man's iniquity, as we are taught in the New Testament; and the Flood was a special judgment for iniquity, as we are told in Genesis. But rather than dogmatize on any of these matters, I would, having laid these points before the reader, leave him to form his own judgment.

But it should be added that we must be slow to assume, as to these three applications of the passage about the Flood, that the events occurred simultaneously, or were subject to any arbitrary time-division. Bearing in mind the groupings of the works of creation which constitute the Days of Gen. i., the use of the term 'hour' in John v. 25, and other considerations before named, we see that the divisions here may be of a nature more fundamental than mere arbitrary point of time.

The Tower of Babel and the confusion of tongues.—It has already been remarked that the letter of this passage cannot be reconciled with known scientific fact. There never was a time when all the inhabitants of the Earth thus dwelt together, building cities, and speaking one language. We have also seen in the sixth chapter of this work, that the story itself originated in Chaldea, like the others already discussed. But when we remember that, here as elsewhere, not the letter but the *spirit* of the passage is alone important, difficulty vanishes.

We have recently had occasion to notice one aspect of the

passage (p. 312). In that aspect of course we do not suppose that the 'men of Babel' understood the significance of that figure in God's sight. Now, however, we have to treat of their own thoughts and deeds. This much is clear, that there was human self-exaltation, apparently with a spirit of opposition to, or setting themselves above, the Deity. There could be all this without a knowledge of the oneness of God, as afterwards revealed to the Hebrews; for we find much the same thing in Nebuchadnezzar. Dan. iv. 29, 30, represents him as walking in his palace and saying, 'Is not this great Babylon, which I have built for the royal dwelling-place, by the might of my power, and for the glory of my majesty?' As we read in Dan. iii., he makes an image and sets it above all the gods, in that he commands everyone to worship it. Again 2 Thess. ii. 3, 4 states that one is yet to come who 'opposeth and exalteth himself against all that is called God, or that is worshipped; so that he sitteth in the temple of God, setting himself forth as God.' Such is the kind of spirit that was first manifested in the people represented by the men of Babel. That spirit may not have been common to all the people then on the earth; suffice it that such were those who represented the head and greatness of the world. In such a case a difference arising in the language (which may have been a gradual process) may well have had to do with the separation of the people, and of the power they constituted. But the more important feature doubtless is, that their greatness was levelled, in judgment for their pride and self-exaltation. The confusion of tongues seems also to have a Scriptural connexion with the opposite course of things which we find in Acts ii. 1–4.

This passage, and the subsequent genealogy of Abram from the God-honoured Shem, bring us to the end of that portion of the Bible which treats of events before the beginning of Hebrew times, and is thus altogether prehistorical.

General Summary.

Two revelations have come from God to man—the Bible, and the Book of Nature which Science undertakes to read. Modern Science has revealed certain apparent discrepancies between these two books, the first result of which has been a resisting of Science by theologians. Astronomy and Geology, both at first resisted, maintained their ground and were finally accepted by all. The Theory of Evolution, which now occupies the contested position, is in like manner being recognized on all hands. The concurrent testimony of many independent sciences in favour of the Evolution Theory is overwhelming; but this is true only of the general fact of Evolution. Common sense and logical science testify that the forces of Nature must be but instruments in the hands of a Creator, to whose will the whole is to be attributed. This conclusion receives further confirmation from the present position of the Evolution Theory, inasmuch as nearly all men of science are agreed as to the *fact* of evolution, whilst there is great diversity of opinion in regard to the factors in the process. When we interpret Nature we should take account of the *whole* of Nature, and at its head we find Man, whose mind, will, and ways regulate the course of many things. It is therefore quite natural to assume that God in like manner takes an active part in the course of events (both in the world of men and in nature outside of man), not miraculously opposing the forces of Nature, but regulating them at the source, controlling and directing them in a natural way, as He chooses. But it does not follow from this that every minor event is the result of special Design, some of these being merely contingent results of the more important processes.

Whatever be the precise relation of God to Nature, we should naturally expect that His control of natural agencies would be an action of the Unseen upon the Seen. Even the mind of man is invisible. Observation of the physiological processes concerned in the voluntary motion of a human limb, can never reveal the volition which was its unseen cause; every motion appears to be the necessary result of some visible cause. Similarly in Nature—without entertaining any pantheistic notions—we might expect the mind of God to be invisible; and consequently those who build their philosophy wholly on what they can see, would inevitably be brought to such conclusions as that of 'natural evolution'—the universe must appear to them as a vast system of machinery. Some believe in 'natural evolution' as God's appointed means of carrying out His purposes; but, though this theory is not necessarily opposed to the doctrines of Scripture, the foregoing conclusion is much preferable, much more natural.

To the believer in Scripture, Evolution presents at first sight graver difficulties than either Astronomy or Geology does; but, as this work undertakes to show, the antithesis is only apparent, not real; whilst there are satisfactory reasons why the language of Genesis should be such as it is. It is a fatal mistake to resist the truth of Evolution on religious grounds. Scepticism, so much increased of late years, is confirmed by such a course.

The notion is prevalent that meaning is inherent in language, and that language can exist without having first been made. But the fact is that all meaning lies within the *mind*, that ideas are formed first, and language comes into existence only as it is required for communicating those ideas. All language is nothing more than a system of symbols, whose only office is to call up the mental states. Therefore there is no common language unless there is community of ideas. Strictly speaking, everyone has a peculiar language of his own; and, as minds differ much, these peculiar languages differ, and ever must differ, considerably. Therefore there could be no Bible quite suited to every reader; its language could only be such as to call up as close an approximation as possible to the desired ideas, in the widely-different minds of all mankind. For this reason many different kinds of literature are adopted in the Bible. It was not prepared specially for ourselves, or any other class of people.

In this case the meaning, the *Word of God*, is part of the Mind of God, which has to be communicated to the mind of man, the language of Scripture being nothing more than a series of symbols designed and arranged for this purpose. It is no part of the Bible's mission to teach science, which man can acquire by his own efforts. Its object is to teach spiritual truth only. Of all kinds of knowledge this spiritual truth is the most difficult to impart to man; it differs in nature from ordinary knowledge, and it is of many kinds. Since, therefore, the object of the Bible is to teach truths of this higher order, and of various kinds, to minds of all classes, its excellence must essentially consist in its suitability for this purpose.

The universal course of things is a natural and gradual one, as we find it manifested throughout Nature and also in the spiritual work of God in the hearts of men—two departments which fill the whole region accessible to observation. The only reason for departure from this natural and gradual process would be that of special necessity, or as a special proof of God's action. This natural course of things held therefore in Hebrew history, miracle being the special exception. It was, above all, necessary that the spiritual work of God amongst the Hebrews, which was connected with the writing of the Bible, should be natural and thorough. There miracle would have done harm.

The conclusions of this work are based on this fact—that the normal course of God's actions is natural: He does not usually work by miraculous interference.

When two things have to work together, they must fit into each other in their working parts, a state of affairs which can be produced only by evolution. Therefore a complete Bible could not be delivered to man all at once. Its delivery necessarily involves a gradual process of adaptation, Scripture and the mind of man being moulded by each other, little by little. The two must grow up together. This is in some measure true also of the relation between the mind of man and the mind of God.

But two things cannot grow up together in mutual adjustment without being first placed in contact. Therefore man is brought sufficiently near to God to produce contact; which consists in man's knowledge of general truths about God, such as civilized nations have. Thus a channel is formed along which deeper divine knowledge can flow, as it does flow in the Christian's case, so that his mind grows together with God's mind in a closer way.

But this general knowledge about God could not be imparted to man without a pre-existing basis: man must have some conceptions of a Deity before he could comprehend those truths. The conception of gods constituted such a basis; it arose largely through the effects produced on primitive men by physical phenomena. This was very different in its own *origin* from corrupt idolatry, into which it was afterwards degraded; at first it was ignorance and mis-directed reverence (though the worshippers themselves may not have been free from evil). As the Athenians ignorantly worshipped *the unknown God* (Acts xvii. 23), so with more sincerity was this worship of superior Powers an ignorant form of worship of the true God. There is no doubt that God's Hand was in it, guiding the development of the conception of the god, preparatory for the knowledge of God Himself. He prepared that basis amongst all peoples on the earth, purified and developed that conception amongst the Hebrews into the true conception of God, teaching them a full knowledge of Himself, and then commissioned them to instruct the already-prepared heathens.

Scripture was delivered little by little to the Hebrews, and, as they passed through great social changes and gradually progressed in knowledge, its literature differs much. It was necessary that the writers of Scripture should be like the people, and should express themselves in the literature of the day, in order to reach the popular mind. The result of their writings was to increase divine knowledge in the people, and that in its turn produced other writers fit to receive further revelation from God—a process which was repeated again and again. This growth of the people in divine knowledge was quite as important as the writing of the Bible; neither could proceed without the other.

We might therefore expect much ethically defective language in the early parts of the Bible; but, as it was intended for the use of enlightened people in after ages, every serious defect of language has been removed, and the minor ones which remain are cancelled by later Scriptures, written in fuller light. Miraculous inspiration of the writers would not have been at all effective: not only would great miracles have been required for this, but it would have impeded, instead of furthering, the progress of truth. Defective knowledge, whether spiritual or scientific, on the part of the writers of Scripture, may be freely admitted.

Before we can form a true judgment of the Scriptures

we must know the work which they had first to do, and we can know this only by inquiring into the condition of the Hebrews at different periods. It is specially important to know what their condition and knowledge of spiritual truth were in the very earliest times. The characters of Rahab, Jael, and others, clearly show that they were then in a crude social state, so that they required a long training in the principles of the Law before they were fit to learn the Grace of God. The Hebrew upon whom such teaching had taken most effect, was the fittest subject to learn something of God's merciful character, and hence to write Psalms. At a later date, the one who had been instructed and softened by the Psalms and the historical records of God's dealings with Israel, was fitted to learn more from God, and then to write such truths as are expressed in the Prophetical Books. The latter further prepared the way for the teachings of Christ.

Moses had not perfect knowledge of God, but was none the less effective as a spiritual power among the early Hebrews. In those days spiritual truths could enter the mind only when associated with ideas of material things; neither the abstract ideas, nor the language that expresses them, having yet come into existence. Consequently, there is strong reason to suppose that portions of the Books of the Law are the expressions of traditionary beliefs, which were so guided by God as to embody spiritual truths, and present them in a form such that Hebrew readers could most readily apprehend them. The *man* Moses is of little moment, the principles of the Law are the Word of God. These principles, and the active part taken by God in fostering their growth, and in the people's history at that time—He being present among them, and watching over them—are the important realities, which the language of those Books is well suited to impress upon the reader. In some cases, therefore, Moses may be merely the figure under which such truths are presented. Biblical criticism reveals facts relating to date of composition of parts of the Books of the Law in their present form, and also some other facts, which tend to lead us to this conclusion. The method of inculcating spiritual truths by means of narratives, such as we find in the beginning of the Old Testament, is suited to readers in the present day, as well as to early Hebrew readers.

The Hebrews were originally Polytheists, possessing no more knowledge, or even conception of the nature, of God, than the other early nations had. Jephthah evidently regarded Jehovah in the same light as Chemosh the god of the Ammonites; he also positively believed that He delighted in human sacrifices! We saw before that there must be the conception of the god before there could be that of the God; and examination of certain Scripture passages (such as this one about Jephthah) reveals the fact that God first introduced Himself to the Hebrews in the name, and under the likeness, of one of their gods, Jahveh. That conception was the raw material, which required to be slowly developed, purified, and modified, till the true nature of God, who was still called Jahveh or Jehovah, was made known. The Hebrews first thought of the Deity vaguely as the Elohim; then as Jahveh, one of the Elohim; eventually (under both names) as God such as He is. But full knowledge of God was not necessary for a considerable attainment of spiritual truth, or for saintliness of character; so that we find such qualities in Moses and David, and faith in the Patriarchs.

All the theological systems of other nations completely failed when tested, because they were human; but the testing of the Hebrew theology was the means of proving its Divine origin. It alone stood the test, and the power that was within it caused it to take deeper root and flourish more and more.

It was absolutely necessary that the Hebrews, and mankind after them, should understand the principle of the great Atoning Sacrifice. It was indispensable that the Hebrew mind should be gradually prepared for this; the preparation was accomplished by means of the ancient sacrificial ritual. In the Law we find the germs of other important truths which were not fully understood before the coming of Christ. Thus we see the important part which was played by such ceremonies.

It was also necessary that at the time when Christ came the Jews should be expecting such a Person. Otherwise He would, humanly speaking, have had no followers. Such prophecies of His coming as there are in the Old Testament Scriptures, were not sufficient for this purpose; also they were written hundreds of years before. To produce this expectant attitude was the work of the Book of Enoch.

It was equally necessary that Jewish thought should be occupied with the unseen world, and the subject of Eschatology; because otherwise the teachings of Christ could not have been understood and appreciated. To develop such thoughts amongst the Jews was also the work of the Book of Enoch. Whilst this Book is not a work of the same class as the Scriptures, it nevertheless contains spiritual truth. It served as a preparation for better things to follow.

There is no Scriptural authority for asserting that the writers of Scripture were habitually endowed with knowledge in advance of their times, or with knowledge which their minds had not been prepared to receive. None of us can apprehend new truths of a nature totally strange to us; we must have some pre-existing ideas of a similar kind. We accordingly do not find that the writers of Scripture were habitually inspired in a miraculous manner, or that they were the subjects of unlimited revelation ; but we find evidence that they were duly prepared by natural means for the work which they had to do. In the Old Testament there are many passages which seem at first sight to be merely historical, but which we know possess a typical, prophetic, or other special signification. In many of these cases it is certain that the human writers did not understand the special import which God attached to their words. Moreover, we find that passages written by different hands fit into each other and form wholes, in a manner which shows that their writings were controlled and directed by the unseen Hand of God. Much of the wonderful economy of the early Old Testament Scriptures is due to this process, the writers of that age having had little spiritual knowledge of their own.

Early writers could not have more than approximate perceptions of spiritual truths, and their writings could not directly express more than they apprehended. In the course of ages those approximate perceptions approached nearer and nearer to the ultimate truths, and *pari passu* there was evolved language suitable for the expression of those clearer thoughts. For this reason spiritual truths could be conveyed in early times only by means of narratives, but in later times there were words expressing the abstract ideas, so that in the New Testament truths are expressed literally to a much greater extent. It must also be remembered that the truths of Scripture are of such a nature that a writer could not express them without at the same time presenting a large proportion of his own thoughts. Consequently, if in some cases those thoughts were ignorant thoughts, the ignorance would necessarily appear in conjunction with the divine truth, just as the writer's Orientalisms would. The one is not essentially more derogatory to Scripture than the other is. This applies more to the Old Testament; because, as just remarked, thoughts were much more matured when the New Testament was written, and there was language suitable to express these truths literally. It is a complete mistake to look down on the inferior knowledge of early writers and call them ignorant. We are in like manner ignorant considered in the light of future superior knowledge.

Again, it may seem that if the early parts of the Bible are devoted to the rudiments of the knowledge of God, and were specially adjusted to the early Hebrew, they must be of little use in the present day. But this is a mistake. Not only are they most useful to the missionary in heathen lands, but they are equally useful in the Christian education of children amongst ourselves. By their means the very foundations of our own knowledge were laid.

Herein we see the admirable structure of the Bible, its early parts being so well adjusted to beginners, its successive books becoming richer and richer in spiritual truths, its ending deep beyond all human depth.

Moreover, even those early Scriptures are rich in spiritual truths, some conspicuous, others hidden. He who reads them, searching for the *Mind of God*, will not find them soon exhausted. Notwithstanding the crudeness of the language, sometimes so manifest, he will thus be richly rewarded. Their divine truths do not lie in the letter so much as clustered about the letter. The narratives are like trees richly laden with celestial fruit. It is ungrateful and unwise to complain that the shape of the trees and branches does not suit our taste. Much better to pluck the fruit.

As Scripture was not intended to teach Science, it is a mistake to look for such teaching in it. The true standard of its excellence is its capacity for imparting spiritual truth. As our learned men write books in language suited for children, so has God been careful to make His truths intelligible to all. Whilst there is abundant evidence of superior scientific knowledge manifested in the Account of the Creation and elsewhere, this principle—the principle on which all books are written—cannot be too strongly insisted on. In this, the only true light, the Bible is a perfect instrument—perfect with a divine perfection.

Bearing well in mind the two conclusions, (1) that God works by natural means everywhere, (2) that, accordingly, the writers of Scripture wrote naturally, and were not automata miraculously inspired; we have to consider how the writers of the opening chapters of the Bible could most naturally and most effectually have acquired and diffused their information. Obviously, the first essential to the diffusion of such truth would be *some* congruent beliefs already existing amongst the people, and the writer who embodied and presented in an improved form such beliefs, would be the most effectual agent. In other words the one thing needful in the beginning was a slow and general growth of such ideas and beliefs amongst the people—ideas and beliefs *divinely* guided, fostered, and purified. And, after comparing the traditions about the Creation, etc., which were current among the early Eastern nations, we are brought to the conclusion that there was such a divine leading of traditional beliefs; beginning in the very earliest times, probably before the separation of races, limited first to the Semites and then to the Hebrews, amongst whom these beliefs eventually gave place to Revelation, for which they had prepared the way. The first eleven chapters of Genesis consist almost entirely of such divinely-led traditionary beliefs. We have seen that whilst those chapters are replete with spiritual truths, these do not lie in the literal meaning of the words so much as clustered about it, so as to enter the mind of the simple reader. Certain references in the New Testament, which appear to insist on the strictly historical character of those passages, present at first sight some difficulty, but this disappears when the question is fully examined.

By means of this divine guidance of Hebrew traditionary beliefs, and of other special control over the selection of subjects, expressions used, etc., a great efficiency has been secured for these important opening chapters of the Bible. Thus, though the language of Gen. i. corresponds to the ideas of a crude and unscientific age, there is yet manifested a marvellous general agreement with the revelations of Science, such as can be accounted for only by a divine origin. Where there is not complete agreement, this is partly due to the crudeness of the ideas of the age when the account was composed, which were not suited to express the facts very accurately; and partly due to the fact that Gen. i. presents *God's* view of the Creation, the main object being to teach spiritual truth; whereas Science reveals the physical aspect and the process of Creation. Physical Science is a knowledge of the outside appearance of things, and is therefore of the same essential nature as the early ideas which it has replaced.[6] But Genesis deals rather with the effects produced on the human mind, which psychology shows to be the ultimate elements of all knowledge—whatever other realities there be, Mind is the greatest knowable reality. Perhaps, therefore, not only on religious but also on other grounds, the aspect of Creation which Scripture presents is more important than that of which Science takes account.

A critical examination of Gen. i. reveals also the prin-

---

[6] The study of appearances has, however, revealed *principles* to which this statement does not apply.

ciples on which the account was drawn up, and a marvellous economy appears in the way in which the crude ideas of an early age were built together by God, so as to express a maximum of spiritual truths suitably for readers of all ages.

Man was not created by a miraculous process, but by a divinely-controlled process of evolution. But from the fact that there was an intermediate animal-stage we must not infer that man is a developed animal, or that there is *any closer connection* between man and the animal than that to which observation testifies. Science fails to give any real account of the genesis of the human soul. Several New Testament Scriptures teach that that genesis is not identical with the physical process of reproduction. The human Consciousness, more reliable than Reason, testifies against any relationship with the animal. Gen. ii. 7 and other Scriptures clearly teach that man received his being from God Himself.

The difficulty of accounting for the truly human qualities of man is acknowledged by evolutionists, so that some of them believe that these were produced by means of a special spiritual influx. This undoubtedly embodies the real facts of the case; but, without knowing the relation of God to Nature—doubtless a close one—we cannot say precisely in what manner man at first received, or how every individual now receives, his being from God.

The narrative in Gen. ii., iii. has long been regarded as partly allegorical. Considering the date of its composition, and the spiritual nature of the truths which it is obviously intended to inculcate, it is more rational—as it is more consistent—to conclude that it is *wholly* allegorical. We are forced to some such conclusion by what Science has revealed of the upward progress of man. And when we compare the narrative with the history and conditions of life of primeval man, we find an agreement in certain particulars. The narrative in Gen. i. represents Elohim as calling things into existence one after another during a period of six days; it has been called a carpenter-like account of the Creation. But though *on the surface* it appears unscientific, a closer examination reveals a marvellous general agreement with the conclusions of Science, and the principle of evolution is clearly discerned. It is much the same with Gen. ii., iii. There is a fall from better conditions and privileges in consequence of sin, implying the loss of eternal life and other blessings which were intended for man. But, though the language used was necessary in that age for conveying this important truth, as nearly as it could be apprehended, Genesis does not give glowing descriptions of Paradise, such as we find in the other Eastern traditions. The first of the human race are in fact presented as children of nature, naked, living in a garden, upon the fruits of the trees; and when we compare this with the conclusions of Science as to the very earliest conditions of the human race—remembering how primeval man's constitution was adjusted to his own environment—we find an agreement in some respects at least. Parts of Gen. ii., iii.—such as some of the judgments passed on the man and woman—have long been regarded as applying to man and woman generally, not merely to the first pair. The whole passage applies to the race, the history of 'the man' representing that of the race. But the parallel is not intended to be complete, the chief object being to impart, in the most effectual manner, the *spiritual history* of man. Thus many spiritual and other truths are expressed or implied :—the first natural out-of-door life, the beginnings of speech and of clothing, followed in Gen. iv. by the progress of civilization; the beginning of sin, and its increase (in Gen. iv.–vi.) ; the (gradual) process of the formation of the soul of man, and thereout of the soul of woman, with the mutual relation of the sexes, implied in the story of the rib ; the sacred character of the marriage-tie ; the (unseen) presence of God amongst, and His interest in, His creatures, till sin caused alienation ; the temptation presented (inwardly) to the human heart by the devil, and the yielding thereto ; the opening of the eyes to the knowledge of right and wrong ; the change in man's mode of life to a life of labour, eating bread instead of natural fruits ; the forfeiture of the life and spiritual blessings which God intended for man—these and other truths, so difficult to impart to the human mind, at least in that age, are conveyed by means of familiar language and concrete pictures, in this short narrative and following ones.

The 4th chapter of Genesis continues both the spiritual history and the upward progress, begun in Gen. ii., iii.

The Story of the Flood presents many difficulties. No one who is acquainted with these, believes that the earth was entirely covered with water. Most theologians hold that the deluge was a partial one. Without necessarily abandoning that view of the matter, we find two important applications of different parts and aspects of the narrative, and also strong reason for attributing an eschatological signification to the passage.

CONCLUDING REMARKS.

If the reader objects that in the foregoing commentary on Gen. i.-xi., important departures from the apparent substance of the text have sometimes been taken, he will on reconsideration find that these are changes of form only, and not of substance—departures from the letter, whilst the spirit is maintained. Obviously, since, in some instances at least, the letter is quite untenable, it is not of vital importance that the explanations offered should be everywhere entirely correct in their *form*. The all-important thing is that the spirit of each Scripture, which is its vital part, its real meaning, which alone is *the Word of God*, should be duly maintained. This never has clashed with the revelations of Science; it never will, and never can.

The more one pursues this subject, the more one is convinced, that wherever there is a passage of historical character in the Bible, the reader who has read it as historical fact has, in the act of doing so, read the *Word of God;* and that if Science shows the letter of that passage to be untenable, its Divine meaning is a truth of the same order as what the simple reader gathers—so much like it that, wherever the difficulty seems inexplicable, one may safely be satisfied with that conclusion. Science, as elsewhere remarked, will never, if rightly taken, lead away from the truths of Scripture; but will afford the means of arriving more closely at their nature, and at the true essence of those words which God has spoken to us, and which "*are spirit.*"

Much that has been said in this work will, perhaps, give offence to some readers. Such readers will be of the class for whom, as stated in the Preface, the work was never intended. For it will be those readers who best know the divine origin of the Bible, who have read most of the *Word of God*, who have received most of its spirit—which is unconsciously reflected by their minds, so that the letter is credited with what is not its own—and who therefore love their Bible most, who will oppose any such departures from the letter as are here maintained. They will be the readers who will not accept, and perhaps are strangers to, such of the teachings of modern science as are well known by others to be established truth; whilst they will, perhaps, be slow to admit that these departures are, after all, changes in form only, and not in substance. But they will be the best of men; and, as such, it is matter of regret that the contents of this work should have their censure. But there are others, many others, who do not know what these do know, and who do know what these do not know; and if this work yields light to them, the censure of the former class will be outweighed thereby.

There are others, Christian readers, who, knowing both the truths of modern science and the Divine origin of the Bible, have arrived at many of the conclusions brought forward in this work. But with regard to others of these conclusions, it may appear to them that the author has erred, in attributing a present-day meaning to many Scriptures which served their purpose only in teaching the Hebrew long ago. The author would be slow to say that he has altogether escaped such mistakes.

Still it is his belief that, whilst the older views on Inspiration attributed to the Bible a *verbal* integrity and perfection which it does not possess, the modern views fail to credit it with a *spiritual* integrity and perfection which it does possess.

Moreover, the author's own endeavours to express many of the thoughts which he has wished to submit to the reader, have impressed him with the profoundest admiration for the language of these early chapters of Genesis. He has often feared that, in cases where he has endeavoured to express his thoughts literally, the desired idea will not be called up in the reader's mind; or that in other cases he has failed to avoid giving erroneous impressions. His reflexion naturally has been: Oh that I could express myself nearly as well as the Author of Genesis has done—a sentiment which the reader has perhaps echoed. In cases that model has been copied.

Of these passages in Genesis which have thus excited the author's admiration, the Account of the Creation has impressed him much ; but not *so* much as the Old Story which has too long been supposed to stand in opposition to the Evolution Theory—*the Story of the Garden and the Fall.*

Finally, the author is not very anxious that the reader should accept all the minor conclusions brought forward in this work. But with its leading principles the case is otherwise. These, at least, will not be overthrown. They rest on two strong foundations. The First is Science, or human knowledge, which will doubtless last as long as the world endures. The Second has no such limited duration. For concerning this foundation it is written :—

> "*Heaven and earth shall pass away,*
> *but My words shall not pass away.*"

THE END.

www.ingramcontent.com/pod-product-compliance
Lightning Source LLC
Chambersburg PA
CBHW030325240426
43673CB00040B/1281